Shared Visions,
Shared Lives

Shared Visions, Shared Lives

Communal Living around the Globe

Dr Bill Metcalf

FINDHORN
Press

307.7

British Library Cataloguing-in-Publication Data.
A catalogue record for this book is available from the British Library.

Cover design by Posthouse Printing & Publishing, Findhorn, UK

Layout and setting in Times by Findhorn Press.

Printed and bound by Interprint Ltd., Malta

Published by

Findhorn Press

The Press Building
The Park, Findhorn
Forres IV36 0TZ
Scotland
tel +44 (0)1309 690582 / fax 690036
e-mail thierry@findhorn.org
http://www.mcn.org/findhorn/press/ or
http://www.gaia.org/findhornpress/

CONTENTS

Acknowledgements

At an intentional communities festival held at Moora Moora Community, Australia, in 1993, two of Australia's communal elders, Bill Smale and Peter Cock, and I, over a bottle (or was it two?) of Cabernet Sauvignon, shared our vision of a book about communal living which would allow communards to present their own stories. Through their encouragement, I took on the project, and that idea became *From Utopian Dreaming to Communal Reality*, published in Sydney by UNSWP in 1995. That excellent and now popular book tells the stories of ten Australian communards. I acknowledge their role in clarifying the concept of this project.

I showed that manuscript to Thierry and Karin Bogliolo of Findhorn Press in late 1994, and they were so impressed that they offered me a publishing contract to do a similar book but with international coverage. I acknowledge their faith in this project and their consistent support and encouragement. Ah — if only all publishers in the world were as easy and enjoyable to work with as are Thierry and Karin! Thanks also to Lynn Barton for her editorial assistance.

I want to acknowledge Yaacov Oved, Andy Woods, Martin Johnson, Helen Martin, Eric Franciscus and Rosie Turnbull who helped me track down appropriate communities and communards from around the globe.

Isabell Blömer, of Findhorn Foundation, helped immensely during my residency and work there during the latter half of 1995. She read and offered opinions on all the drafts, helped with innumerable communication problems and generally supported my efforts. She was of particular help with UFA-Fabrik of Berlin. Her enthusiastic and tireless support has been critical to this book's successful conclusion.

Helen Best, of Brisbane, helped by proofreading all the chapters, not only by correcting innumerable grammatical, punctuation and syntactical errors, but also by offering many constructive, substantive criticisms. Her enthusiasm and her deep understanding and appreciation of communal issues have improved this work immensely.

Finally I must acknowledge and appreciate the work, enthusiasm and patience of the contributors to this book. Each chapter had to go through many rewrites as we polished the style and modified the content to meet my high expectations for this book. We had many arguments over titles, content, order and even punctuation - but we have managed to finish the project still on speaking terms! These contributors are all very busy people so I appreciate their time. Each one's minuscule share (one-seventeenth) of the royalties means that their work has really been a labour of love.

CHAPTER 1

Introduction

by Bill Metcalf

This book is about utopian communal living around the world in the 1990s. It is about real people who have been involved in true communal living for many years.

Books about communal living usually attempt to either tell in great detail the story of one specific communal group (what is known as an ethnographic account), or try to provide a quick overview of many groups (a survey) — but almost always by presenting the story of communal living from the objective, analytical perspective of the author, generally either a real or pseudo social scientist.

In this book, communal living is described in colourful detail by 15 communards from 11 countries who have been living communally for an average of well over 30 years. The reader is offered 15 very personal, frank and informative accounts of what it is like to live communally today, to be born and reared, to have children, and to face death within a communal group. These stories are clarified and made more interesting and immediate through the generous use of photos.

The communal groups represented in this book are *Riverside* in New Zealand, *Yamagishi Toyosato* in Japan, *Auroville* and *Christavashram* in India, *Kibbutz Einat* in Israel, *l'Arche* in France, *UFA-Fabrik* in Germany, *Findhorn Foundation* in Britain, *Community Alternatives* and *The Emissaries* in Canada, *The Farm*, *Padanaram* and *New Meadow Run Bruderhof* in USA, *Los Horcones* in Mexico and *Lothlorien* in Brazil.

While I readily admit to being a real social scientist, with a PhD in sociology, I have also lived communally for much of my life. I have done my best, as editor, to keep my sociological analysis out of these personal, biographical accounts. The final chapter is where I look at these contributed chapters from a more dispassionate perspective, and where I distil some common themes and conclusions. Only there will the reader find the passion, frustration, joy and pain of communal living filtered through my sociological analysis. Through the rest of the chapters, the communards tell their own stories, in their own words, sharing with the readers the reality of living one's full life and life-to-the-full, communally.

I have asked the communards in this book to be open and personal, so I shall do the same. I am a 51-year-old academic and author, based at Griffith University, Brisbane, Australia. My PhD was a study of Australian intentional communities, entitled 'Dropping Out and Staying In'. I became personally involved in this movement in 1972 when I helped found an urban commune in Brisbane. In 1974 I lived for some months in Australia's most famous communal group, Tuntable Falls, Nimbin. In 1980, I joined Pleiades, a twelve-member urban secular commune in Brisbane, then in 1982 I left it to co-found Mabel's Treat, a small urban commune which lasted about six years. During over 20 years of sociological research, I have visited about 120 intentional communities and communes throughout the world. I am a Fellow of the well-known Findhorn Foundation in Scotland, and have lived there for several months each year recently. I have written and published widely in academic journals and books about the global intentional community movement. My most recent book is *From Utopian Dreaming To Communal Reality: Cooperative Lifestyles in Australia*. I am on the executive of the International Communal Studies Association, and am a widely acknowledged world expert on communalism. I do not live communally at present, but will probably do so again.

Clarification of Several Key Terms[1]

Utopian refers to the intention to achieve an ideal society, *not* the outcome. While utopian is a perfectly legitimate analytical term, it is often misunderstood as 'naively idealistic'.

Communal living refers to a way of living everyday life where more rather than less is shared. What is shared usually includes ownership of resources, eating together, child rearing, social life, living space, ideology and world view, as well as interactions with the social and biophysical environment. In most cases, this sharing is freely chosen and is seen by the participants to have some worthwhile purpose beyond mere practicalities and convenience. Social life in hospitals, prisons and military barracks is certainly communal, but as this option is not freely chosen it is of no interest to this book. For similar reasons this book does not address communal living in tribal or kin-based societies, not because these forms are not interesting but because they are beyond the scope of the present work. This book is about communal living which exists as a practical alternative for the reader — and obviously that followed in tribal and kin-based groups is not generally available.

Communal living takes place in either a *commune* or an *intentional community*, the distinction depending on the degree of intimate sharing.

Commune members place the group ahead of the nuclear family unit, generally maintain a 'common-purse' and collective household, and make intimate as well as general decisions as a group. By sharing everyday social life and facilities, a commune emulates idealised family life, being another form of 'primary' group. A commune is comprised of individuals whose emotional bonds are to the communal group, rather than to any subset within that group such as a lover or nuclear family unit. Within a commune, the group is experienced with emotions beyond that of a mere social collectivity.

In contrast, members of *intentional communities*, although seeing themselves as an identifiable group, live in individual households, and the decisions that affect household functioning are private. Intentional community is not a form of family but will normally include nuclear and/or communal families. Given their less intimate interactions, intentional communities are 'secondary' rather than 'primary' groups, thus involving less affective commitment and fewer emotional ties. The group nevertheless serves to mediate between the individual and the outside world.

Intentional communities, being secondary groups, can be very large, with hundreds or occasionally thousands of members[2]. Communes, being primary groups, are much smaller, with generally less than 20 people. Occasionally, much larger groups are able to operate as communes, but only via strong charismatic leadership, and a belief system which values group above individual, and actively rewards communality. The logistical complexities of relating intimately with a large number of people preclude large-scale communes, except in unique circumstances.

Common Misconceptions about Communal Living

Communal living is often thought of as a rare form of social life. While accurate data is hard to find, some figures might help. In USA, Oved[3] was able to study 277 communes which existed prior to 1930[4], while the 1995 *Communities Directory*[5] lists over 500 American groups, but that is probably only a fraction of those currently in existence[6]. *Diggers and Dreamers*[7] gives detailed information on 69 U.K. communal groups. One of the editors states[8], "I think that we have most of the greenish groups listed. But there are many more spiritual groups … If you drew the line at groups with more than ten adults involved in a substantial amount of sharing my guess would be that there are between 150 and 200 in the UK." In Israel, there are 282 communal Kibbutzim, the oldest starting in 1909. About 2.5% of Israelis live communally, by far the largest proportion anywhere. In Holland 8500 communes have been located, meaning that almost 1% of households are communal[9]. My own Australian research discovered that 50 communal groups existed between 1853 and 1970, while I estimate that about 150–200 groups currently exist. So while communal living has always been a minority phenomenon, it is not as rare as is often imagined.

People engaged in utopian communal living are frequently presented by the media as being part of some sort of youth movement, pictured as being full of enthusiasm and naive idealism. Considerable research[10], however, indicates that the average age of participants is now in the mid to late 40s, with as many participants over 50 as under 30 years old. Urban communards are, on average, younger than their rural counterparts. The communal movement around the world is very much a movement of and for middle-aged people. Nevertheless, the contemporary movement is frequently dismissed by its critics as a youth movement.

Many scholars and communards are fascinated with utopian history, particularly with the lessons to be gleaned from the dramatic communal experiments of nineteenth century America, Europe and Australia. However, while nineteenth century communes are certainly interesting, they existed in a radically different cultural and political milieu, so comparisons may be difficult, and their historical lessons may not automatically apply today. These misconceptions are particularly dangerous and misleading when addressing thorny issues such as communal longevity.

There are a host of popular misconceptions around patterns of sexual conduct within communal groups. All sorts of orgiastic stereotypes are routinely trotted out by the popular media. In reality, communal groups do indeed demonstrate a wide range of sexual behaviour and familial forms ranging from 'corporate' or group marriage and 'polyfidelity' to complete abstinence and avoidance. Most commonly found in communal groups, however, are heterosexual, monogamous relationships — no doubt a great disappointment to those readers with voyeuristic intent! We can learn a great deal about differing sexual behaviours, gender roles and diverse family forms through studying communal living, but we must look past naive stereotypes.

Many commentators have argued — based on an alarming lack of evidence — that only communal groups with clear religious principles are able to endure. It is further assumed that such groups, particularly when 'blessed' with charismatic leadership, tend to become 'cults'. There is no historical or contemporary evidence to support this doomsday notion. Within this book I present stories from both religious/spiritual and secular communal groups, some with charismatic leaders and others without. Communal living is far too complex to analyse through such naive, stereotypical assumptions.

Another misconception is that communal groups are always short-lived and transitory, with a high turnover of members. American data, being roughly consistent with that from other countries[11], points out that "Commune membership turnover is high but not extraordinarily high compared with that of other organizations... Hospital nurses and factory workers both turnover a bit faster than commune members. University professors, civil servants, and prison wardens... a bit more slowly." While it is true that about half of all communal groups collapse within the first two years, and that about half the remainder follow within the next two years — the same applies to small businesses! So while one must acknowledge that communal ventures are often unstable and short-lived, they are no more so than are most other, comparable social forms. The Hutterites have been living communally for four centuries, and the Israeli kibbutzim go back almost a century. The oldest communal group still in existence is Bon Homme, a Hutterite commune founded in USA in 1874–5, but as it was almost abandoned for several years at the end of the First World War, perhaps the mantle for oldest commune should go to Degania, a kibbutz founded in 1909 in what is now Israel. The communal groups in this book average well over 30 years longevity, with the oldest starting in 1934. Communal groups can and do endure.

Research and Literary Method For This Book

To overcome the common stereotypes and to present the story of communal living in the 1990s as it really exists, rather than as it is imagined to be, I have collected for this book the life stories and wisdom of 15 long-term contemporary communards from around the world. I have asked key participants, with many years of communal experience, to write their story — to share their wisdom — of why they are involved, what makes their group work (or not work) and what they have learned from the long and arduous communal process of which they are the 'elders'. I selected long-term communards who have maintained their utopian zeal and their communal enthusiasm while developing and maintaining their communal lifestyle. These are the communal elders whose wisdom I sought in this research, and whose stories follow.

For such long-term communards, communal living is a lifelong commitment — not a historical curiosity or a youthful phase of growing up.

To gather these stories and present them in a consistent and useful manner I have used a technique for which I have coined the term 'biographical discourse'. Long-term communards have been encouraged to write and rewrite their stories, and share their wisdom, under my editorial guidance[12]. I asked each communal elder a number of questions which have arisen in my sociological research into communal living, and I challenged a number of the assumptions they made. Biographical discourse avoids many of the ethical issues of social research techniques, such as participant observation and social surveys, by empowering the participants, and facilitating *their* presentation of *their* story in *their* words. It also produces readable material. It is, unfortunately, very hard work for the editor!

The first phase of this research and literary project was based on ten communal elders from across Australia. The outcome is now available in the well-illustrated book *From Utopian Dreaming to Communal Reality* published by University of New South Wales Press, Sydney, Australia (1995).

This process of biographical discourse was all the more complex for this, the second stage of this social research and literary project, because for many of the contributors English was not their first language. Working through interpreters was a real challenge for me, for the contributors and for the translators. The results, however, have made it worthwhile.

Communal Longevity and 'Success'

The history of utopian communal living is more impressive in terms of the enthusiasm of would-be communards than in their ability to realise those dreams. The utopian spirit has fared much better that any communal experiment.

In her seminal research, Dr Rosabeth Kanter[13] considered one generation to be the time for which a group must endure in order to be considered 'successful'. While the question of what 'success' means for communal groups has been widely debated[14], the indisputable fact remains that if such groups are to contribute to social improvement, they must at least endure. All communards talk about what they hope and seek to achieve through their social experimentation with communal living. Such achievements can only be greater the longer the group endures. And the communal groups presented in this book have certainly endured — an average of about 33 years!

A *Very, Very* Brief History of Utopian Communalism

The notion that people can create an ideal society, devoid of social problems, where all would share equally, where 'good' would triumph over 'bad' — this is an idea as old as humanity[15].

Social observers have always sought explanations for, and the means to alleviate, inequality, oppression and injustice. Baum[16] points out how "these sentiments for a better world of sharing and cooperation have become a permanent fixture in the history of mankind, right up to today". Arguably, visions of paradise in pre-recorded history (eg. the Garden of Eden) have helped shape Judeo-Christian thinking. The first recorded utopians are to be found in the Old Testament. Prophets such as Amos in the eighth century BC decried the social conditions of their day and argued for a new social reality based on principles of justice and non-exploitation. Ezekiel goes furthest towards describing how a new social order, a utopia, might be realised. He saw the perfected society as inevitably resulting from ensuring that all is right between people and God. This enlightened position, Ezekiel argued, would result in moral interpersonal relationships and a non-exploitative State. This simple formula is still applied by contemporary communal groups including several in this book.

Beyond a doubt, Plato is the best known of the early utopian writers. In *The Republic*, published in the fourth century BC, the first fully developed set of plans for a new, alternative society was presented. Plato sought a society not of complete equality, but of strict social classes, to be ruled by a benign dictatorship of 'philosopher kings'. This ruling class would not be allowed to own property and would be expected to live communally, sharing even their wives and children. This latter feature Plato saw as necessary for development of genetically improved people. The utopian state, he argued, must involve itself in rational breeding so that humans might attain 'first class excellence'.

The first true utopian or alternative lifestyle experiment was probably developed by the Essenes in the second century BC[17]. The Essenes lived communally, sharing equally the production from their agriculture and handicrafts. They are also reported to have shared their homes and held common meals, activities found in contemporary research to be important to developing communal commitment. Biblical scholars such as Dr Barbara Thiering[18] argue that Jesus Christ lived in this Essene commune, and that much of the subsequent development of early Christianity depends on that fact.

Following the death of Christ, His followers developed a form of commune which is a direct forerunner of the numerous Christian communes in existence today, with several being represented in this book. The early Christian communes, based on sharing and equality, were counter-cultural, being in direct opposition to the materialistic hegemony of the Roman Empire. The demise of these Christian communes was a result, paradoxically, of the spectacular political successes of the Christian Church as a hierarchical institution.[19]

The communal lifestyle of the early Christians was only retained and passed on through the monasteries which developed in the fourth century. Most of these followed communal guidelines[20] of common ownership of assets, the conscious development of a family atmosphere, common work, shared meals and rituals of prayer and singing. Just as secularisation of the early Christian church brought about the demise of the general Christian communal movement and its enclosure within monasteries, so too did the secularisation and increasing material affluence of the monasteries lead to radical changes and a reduction in communal equality.

While the implementation of utopian communal ideals was suppressed on many fronts, utopianism was rekindled during the Renaissance by writers such as Sir Thomas More (who coined the term 'utopia' in 1515) and Sir Francis Bacon. Many heretical and millenarian communes had formed, such as the Cathari in France and Italy starting in the 11th century, and the Waldenses in 12th century France. There were a few notable attempts to create secular communes such as the Brethren of the Free Spirit throughout the Middle Ages in Europe, and The Diggers in 17th century England, but most were short-lived.

The Anabaptist movement from roughly the same era led to the development of numerous spiritual communes believing in all things in common, equality for all, controlled anarchism and intentional community. These Anabaptists presented such a challenge and threat to the establishment forces of church and state because they proposed a form of realisable heaven on earth. 'Longings which up to that time had been either unattached to a specific goal or concentrated upon other worldly objectives suddenly took on a mundane complexion. They were now felt to be realisable — here and now — and infused social conduct with a singular zeal'[21]. This utopian vision of a new, alternative social reality, as posited by the Anabaptists, presented a revolutionary challenge to the existing social order. In the 1530s the German city of Münster became an Anabaptist commune with full sharing of money, housing and even spouses[22]. Although Anabaptists were violently suppressed, they continued to flourish with their utopian ideal of a realisable, communal 'heaven on earth' as their guiding beacon. The communal Anabaptists have survived and prospered, still existing as Hutterites and Bruderhof[23].

The modern, secular utopian communal movement owes more to 18th and 19th century communal philosophers and practitioners such as Charles Fourier, Robert Owen, Etienne Cabet and John Humphrey Noyes than to the Old Testament prophets. These men visualised a social order freed from the problems of industrialisation. Communalism was seen to be not just an ideal which could be implemented by groups of ascetics, but a modern option for living in a complex industrial society.

It was in America rather than anywhere else that communalism reached its zenith during the 19th century. American utopian communal groups such as New Harmony, the Shakers, Amana, the Rappites, Oneida, Brook Farm and Icaria were all very public, very famous, and helped spread worldwide[24] the nineteenth century theory of 'perfectibility', an idea that a new, perfect social reality was possible. Heaven could be realised here on earth, and now, was their seductive message. These communal groups, being frequently described by newspapers around the world, played a significant role in popularising communal ways of life as an alternative to the socially degrading conditions of industrialisation under capitalism.

This wave of communal experimentation spread even to remote Australia where, under the guidance of utopian writers and practitioners such as William Lane and Horace Tucker, numerous communes were established, many with government support. Arguably, a higher proportion of 19th century Australians were involved in communal living than could be found in any other 'western' country.

19th century utopian writers not only contributed to the numerous communal experiments which occurred, but added a significant feature to social theory — the concept of intentional community. By that, it is meant that social order was seen neither as an organic, natural 'thing', nor as a result of God's (or nature's) imposition, but rather was negotiable, resulting from the interplay of social, political and ideological forces. That meant, of course, that new ways of living were possible, albeit difficult to achieve. A belief in perfectibility and voluntarism, central to the nineteenth century utopian social theorists and practitioners, has spread worldwide in a number of forms. It has been mixed with socialism, agrarian populism and various kinds of anarchism, and often with a radical Christian, millenarian and/or libertarian flavour. In spite of many failures, utopianism persisted and spread into the social consciousness and political reality of all western cultures.

Since the end of the 17th century, communal living has been continually practised in USA[25]. Since Australia's first commune, Herrnhut, was established in 1853, communal living has been continuously practised in my own country[26]. The same story is found for the past two centuries in Britain[27] as well as the rest of western Europe, and in many other countries such as with the communal Gurukuls and the Ashram movement in India. Communal living is neither a recent nor a short-term phenomenon. It has a long and rich history in most parts of the world.

*   *   *

Geoph Kozeny, a well-known American communard and communal scholar captured the utopian intent of contemporary communal groups by observing[28] that 'In visiting hundreds of intentional communities, I've discovered that they all share one thing in common: each is based on a vision of living a better life… Each group defines for itself just what that means, and no two visions are identical.'

The next 15 chapters give insights into contemporary communal living around the globe. These chapters represent and tell the stories of communal living following both secular and spiritual ideologies, whether lived in rural or urban locales on five continents, and as both communes and intentional communities. In other words, this book represents the broad spectrum of communal living as practised around the globe in the 1990s.

The stories, you will find, are full of wit, pathos and wisdom.

Dr Bill Metcalf

PHOTO BY TED HOLLIDAY (COURTESY OF THE COURIER MAIL, BRISBANE)

(1)   Probably the most detailed treatment of these terms is in A. Butcher, *Classifications of Communalism*, self-published, 1991. They are also discussed in The Bulletin of the International Communal Studies Association, No. 14, 1993, pp. 2-5; and No. 15, 1994, pp. 6-10.

(2)   The largest such group known to me is Kibbutz Givat Brenner in Israel, with about 2000 residents.

(3)   Y. Oved, *Two Hundred Years of American Communes*, New Brunswick: Transaction, 1988, p. viii.

(4)   The first American commune was established in 1663 by Dutch Mennonites under the leadership of Pieter Plockhoy. It was violently destroyed by British troops within a year.

(5)   Anon. *Communities Directory: A Guide to Cooperative Living*, Langley: Fellowship For Intentional Communities, 1995.

(6)   This number only includes the minority of communal groups which are willing to be publicised. The confidential database from which they are drawn is said to include 1219 groups although the database manager states, "My guesstimate is that there are at least ten communities for everyone in that database; but who knows? Probably a lot more than that, even". (in T. Miller, *America's Alternative Religions*, Albamy: SUNY, 1995, p. 376.

(7)   C. Coates et. al. *Diggers and Dreamers 96/97*, Winslow: D&D Publications, 1995.

(8)   J. How, Personal Communication, 30 January 1996.

(9)   T. Weggemans, 'Modern Utopia and Modern Communes' in *Utopian Thought and Communal Experience*, eds. D. Hardy and L. Davidson, London: Middlesex Polytechnic, 1989, p. 52.

(10)   For example, T. Weggemans, op. cit.; W. Metcalf & F. Vanclay, 1987, *Social Characteristics of Alternative Lifestyle Participants in Australia* Brisbane: IAER, Griffith University; D. Questenberry & M. Morgan, 1991, *A Demographic Analysis of 186 North American Intentional Communities*, presented at the International Communal Studies Association Conference, Elizabethtown, U.S.A.; and M. Cummings & H. Bishop, 1994, 'Stereotypes Challenged', in *Communities: Journal of Cooperative Living*, No. 84, pp. 10-2.

(11)   B. Zablocki, *Alienation and Charisma*, New York: The Free Press, 1980, p. 155.

(12)   For a number of reasons this method did not work with one of the communal groups, UFA-Fabrik of Germany, which had agreed to be part of this project. For that group, I had to travel to Berlin and spend time interviewing members and then writing their story. The first draft was presented for critical comments, of which there were several which helped correct minor errors. The final draft was sent back to members seeking their comments on its style, content and tenor.

(13)   R. Kanter, *Commitment and Community*, Cambridge: Harvard University Press, 1972.

(14)   J. Wagner, 'Success in Intentional Communities', *Communal Societies*, V. 5, 1985, pp. 89-100.

(15)   Many books discuss the history of communal experimentation. Five of the best are A. Apsler, *Communes Through The Ages: The Search for Utopia*, New York: Julian Messner, 1974; W. Armytage, *Heavens Below*, London: Routledge and Kegan Paul, 1961; P. Baum, *Another Way of Life: The Story of Communal Living*, New York: Putnam's Sons, 1973; N. Cohn, *The Pursuit of the Millennium*, London: Paladin, 1970; and F. and F. Manuel, *Utopian Thought in the Western World*, Cambridge: Harvard University Press, 1979.

(16)   Baum, op. cit. p. 29.

(17)   Baum, op. cit. pp. 33-5.

(18)   B. Thiering, *Jesus The Man*, Sydney: Doubleday, 1992.

(19)   Baum, op. cit. pp. 37-8.

(20)   Most of these guidelines to communal living owe a debt to Benedict of Nursi who, in 529 drew up a set of rules for the Monte Cassino Monastery in southern Italy. These Benedictine rules of communal conduct are still valid today.

(21)   K. Mannheim *Ideology and Utopia*, London: Routledge and Kegan Paul, 1936, pp. 190-1.

(22)   Cohn, op. cit., Chapter 13; A fascinating and fairly accurate historical novel based on this is by N. Salaman, *The Garden of Earthly Delights*, London: Flamingo, 1994.

(23)   Mennonites and Amish are also part of the Anabaptist tradition, but are not so communal.

(24)   We can find news about these communal groups in small Australian and New Zealand newspapers and magazines of the 1880s and '90s.

(25)   Oved, op. cit., p. xiii.

(26)   B. Metcalf, *From Utopian Dreaming to Communal Reality*, Sydney: University of New South Wales Press, 1995, pp. 15-40.

(27)   D. Hardy, *Alternative Communities in Nineteenth Century England*, London: Longman, 1979; and A. Rigby, *Alternative Realities*, London: Routledge and Kegan Paul, 1974, pp. 17-42.

(28)   G. Kozeny, 'Constructive Criticism' in *Communities: Journal of Cooperative Living*, No. 88, 1995, p. 6.

Introduction: Padanaram and Rachel Summerton

Rachel Summerton with grand-daughter Pearl

Padanaram was established in 1966 in a remote rural part of USA. The founder was Daniel Wright, a Christian preacher who founded an intentional community in this spot, after having been led there by a mystical vision. The group who joined him had been living communally for about two years in town before moving onto this land. Some two hundred members now live together, supported by several small businesses and a very large sawmill. All income is pooled and all assets are communally owned. Padanaram's founder Daniel, although nearly 80, is still very active in communal life but is stepping back to facilitate power being transferred to younger members. They now consider themselves to be spiritual rather than Christian. Padanaram is located near Bedford, Indiana, south of Indianapolis.

Rachel Summerton came to Padanaram as a young college student, with her father, Daniel Wright, and family in 1966. She taught school for some years but now works as Padanaram's public relations/communal networking person.

I first met Rachel Summerton and Daniel Wright in 1988 in Scotland at the International Communal Studies Association Conference. I found them both to be friendly and open, with a fascinating story to tell. I met Rachel and Daniel again several times at other Communal Studies Conferences, and then in 1993 I was finally able to visit Padanaram. I was thoroughly impressed with the scale of their communal buildings and businesses, and the enthusiasm with which they undertook to create and maintain a radically new social order. They are very serious about communal living, and work diligently to make their community a success. Far from being arch-conservatives, as some critics suggest, they are very radical and creative in their approach to communalism.

Padanaram welcomes visitors provided that they make prior arrangements. Write to the Visitors' Secretary, Padanaram Settlement, Route 1, Box 478, Williams, Indiana 47470, USA (Phone: +1-812-388-5571). Each October Padanaram has an 'open house' on a Sunday afternoon to which all and sundry are invited; and each May and October they hold a weekend convention at which their life and ideology is more clearly articulated. *Millennial Chronicles*, as well as the booklet *Padanaram,* can be obtained from the above address.

CHAPTER 2

Padanaram:
The Valley of the Gods

by Rachel Wright Summerton

I was studying elementary education at Indiana University when Padanaram Settlement was established in 1966 (an hour's drive from the university). Only a handful of individuals lived on the 86-acre (35-hectare) property with others coming on the weekends. I would bring a couple of college friends down with me, and we'd join in the work, be it picking multi-colored sandstone out of the creek to make fireplaces, washing dishes, or stuffing insulation in the three story log lodge we were building.

Daniel Wright, my father, with a group of eleven others purchased this wooded land in the rolling hills of southern Indiana. He was a country parson who had become convinced that religion should be practised during the week as well as on Sundays. Through spiritual leadings and insights, he sought communal living in all its facets: one piece of land, a cooperative business, a school, eating together; 'all things in common'. He found the site for Padanaram through a spiritual experience. Our origin was not of the hippy culture that was expanding throughout the United States, but rather born of house meetings and religious persuasion.

Since 1962, we had lived semi-communally in Martinsville, Indiana, where six to eight families bought adjoining properties. We had separate homes, worked outside at jobs ranging from selling appliances to construction and cabinet-making, yet gardened, built homes and shared meals on weekends. I was still going to school. Being inner-city folk, we found great delight in looking for mushrooms, walking in the woods, and being alert to snakes. We hadn't given up bathrooms, individual homes or private enterprise, but were in the beginning steps of communal living. Our next step (to Padanaram) was far more dramatic!

Back to outhouses. Back to poverty. The only structure on the farm was a dilapidated farmhouse. On the weekends, it was wall-to-wall people on the wooden floor where we warmed ourselves via 'Old Florence', the wood stove. Religion was the 'rap' sessions that took place around the table after days of hard work as we built the lodge and planted gardens.

Why was it so appealing? I felt like a pioneer. It was exciting, daring and primitive. Washing in the creek, cooking over a wood stove and sleeping on the floor were a welcome alternative to stodgy dormitory life. The dynamics of living in this small group had such appeal! It was unpredictable. People were the 'living TV'. What would happen next? Would we survive? What would happen on the weekend when everyone arrived? By the end of summer 1967, I knew that communal life, in this pristine environment, was where I wanted to be. I commuted for the next two years between Padanaram and the university where I was preparing to be a teacher for our community. I was 23 and ready for the challenge!

*　　*　　*

After graduation in 1969, I took a teaching job 30 minutes away, since we still needed funds to support our venture. Having read of Summerhill and other alternative schools, I had asked for 'any school that was doing something experimental', and was assigned to a school that looked like an old castle. It turned out to be our local 'lab school', where team-teaching and individualized instruction was used. I was thrilled! Perhaps Deity was looking out for my needs and interests? Under the tutelage of a very skilled teacher, I learned more during six months of student teaching than I had during four years at university.

Commuting, however, was not the joyful part of my day. It was rough! We had a 3 mile (5 km) dirt road that flooded when it rained. We donned knee-high rubber boots and traipsed through the woods to get to where an old truck took us on our muddy journey to town. Assuredly, I was the only one in the school bathroom (I picked the one in the basement, with the least inhabitants) who had to change my clothes, wash the mud off my shoes and hose, do a quick underarm wash, and then walk upstairs, smiling as if I'd just stepped out of a fashion magazine.

At home, it was blue jeans and shirts. Bathing was either in the basin or the creek, and both were tough! Communal life did not fit with my role as 'Miss Wright, the prim and proper schoolteacher'. Keeping immaculate fingernails and impeccable stockings was impossible. Our wood stove and iron skillets left blackened smudges on my hands. I was as wobbly as a newborn colt in my high heels after wearing boots or 'clodhoppers' at home. I could sense the raised eyebrows, especially when they heard that I was from 'the hippie commune'.

During the first few years, the older Padanaram children travelled for an hour to reach the public school where they were taunted. Our neighbors had no idea what we were about and didn't care to find out. Words like 'free love', 'hippies', 'men with beards', 'people dressed in black' and 'Shakers' circulated. The 'Shakers' was in reference to 'Shaker Hollow', part of the land we had purchased.

Marjorie, my college friend, had moved into Padanaram in 1967 when I did. In 1972, upon completing her degree in elementary education, she started a school for our five to eight year olds. We planned our own school to reflect our ideals of cooperation. I was a consultant teacher and helped gather materials. It was difficult to find books that reflected our lifestyle. We started with donated Sunday School materials (at least the men had beards!), and many homemade items. In a small caravan-trailer, the refrigerator became a library, the bathtub an aquarium, and the kitchen a science lab. In 1973 Steven, our schoolmaster to this day, arrived so we had certified elementary and high school teachers. Our high-schoolers returned home and the school was moved to the second floor of our barn, the first floor being occupied by the mule. Steven was also an excellent carpenter who worked many hours in building and improving the school.

In 1974, I became the part-time kindergarten teacher at Padanaram. My pleasure was in teaching in our school and raising my children, ages three and five, in our beautiful communal home which came to be called 'The Valley'. In my spare time, I studied graduate education at university.

We gathered many kinds of people as a result of our open-door policy. For the first time in my life, I gained an insight into people very different from myself. I had been raised as a Christian in a very protected home, a strong family unit. But communal life brought in misfits, drones, degenerates, utopians, builders, the industriously competent, migrants, dopers, dreamers and thinkers. This mixture of individuals acted as a melting pot in which many of our basic ideals were formed. Our diversity has been one of our survival mechanisms.

*   *   *

We left society to build a better world, so we questioned every facet of our past lives. 'Who says?' was one of our favorite sayings. We threw out radios, televisions, music and books, and decided to build from scratch. Maybe we could find originality and creativity if we stopped listening to outside influences? One of the areas in question was the role of women.

It was not our intention to become 'only housewives'. We women, as well as the men, were an economic force. We were cooperative equals and would contribute to the well-being of Padanaram. We retained the nuclear family within the larger communal family, living in apartments in large communal structures. In the early years, that might mean one room, but today it is based on the size of one's family. Our style of life is 'familyism' (dad, mom, brothers and sisters) although this includes the concept of super mom and super dad caring for all our young people.

PHOTO BY LARRY SUMMERTON

The entrance Padanaram. The building (the left is the school, while the right is th(dining hall.

We wanted children, and we decided that they would be born at home — with midwives but without doctors or hospitals. We developed a 'code of rest' and gave birth amid spiritual songs, sung with gusto by our midwives. We name our children by inspiration, a dream or an impression. There are no Toms or Janes, but names of meaning: Utopian, Harmony, Rock, Joy, Charity or Hebrew.

As more people joined Padanaram, and more babies were born, we started a preschool in 1975, then a nursery in 1978. They were operated by women who really wanted to take care of children. This enabled us to work while our little ones were cared for by trusted friends. Those of us who were breastfeeding would take a break from our jobs to go to the nursery. We could look out the windows and see the children playing in the preschool yard. It was safe and secure!

Our work differentiation includes the kitchen, bakery, nursery, preschool, school, business office, farm and garden. Over the years, I have taught school, been a secretary, midwife, public relations person, and I have cooked, cleaned toilets, swept floors, and helped to care for our communal family.

We women have the highest respect for the men and they for us. We're not in competition with them for jobs or in any other way. Sawmilling, farming and construction are beyond our physical capacities. We women have chosen health care, teaching, midwifery, childcare, office work, gardening, canning and running the communal household. In no manner are we demeaned! It is a matter of 'Who can get the job done most efficiently?' The rest is trivial, intellectual garbage and a time waster.

We've lived down the 'libbers' who pointed the finger, accusing us of doing 'typical woman's work'. It takes intelligence and expertise to cook, order food and plan a menu for 200 people. It takes mathematical know-how to plan a quilt. It takes planning, energy and tender loving care to run a preschool. Now those ideas have come full circle as our critics bemoan not having children, and race to beat the 'biological clock'. I'm convinced that the only truly liberated woman is one who lives communally. She has control and input into what goes on around her. That is enlightened freedom!

However, we're not out to perpetuate the status quo of marriage. Visitors frequently have difficulty figuring out who is with whom. The divorce rate in this country is up to 50%, with 'community' vanishing as families become scattered across the globe. The family unit has become isolated, with increased burdens of higher cost of living, absence of relatives to care for children, and the requirement that both parents work to survive.

The isolated nuclear family is not a part of Padanaram. Familiarity breeds contempt! I feel that husbands and wives go crazy looking across the table at one another for 50 years. Who said I have to eat 18,250 supper meals with my husband? I know how he picks his teeth with his knife after eating meat, and he knows how I chew on the right side of my mouth. The table is longer in communal living, with more faces to talk at.

I'm with Larry, a man who has been here 20 years. We have six beautiful children and one grandchild, but there's still uncrowded space. We both work for the common good of Padanaram Settlement. I like to breathe the air, open up the windows, and expand my mind. I like to look beyond the mythological utopia of the American Dream: isolated family units and materialism. We're building a realistic utopia at Padanaram, one that works, one that gives peace and tranquillity. I need more than a mate and a full cupboard; I need a sense of community and purpose. I want a world of peace and cooperation. If communalism works here, it can be replicated.

*   *   *

After waking up in the morning, I gather my children and head for Padanaram's central dining room where several women friends have been up since 3am fixing breakfast. Here, we'll swap 'kid stories', share events of yesterday, and look ahead to the business of today.

This summer morning, the 50 or so men have already eaten and left for our businesses in town, or are doing maintenance, construction or farming work. By 6am they are

PHOTO BY LARRY SUMMERTON

Children in Padanaram Dining Room

on the road to work, or are fixing water lines or electrical problems, feeding livestock, picking apples or repairing farm equipment.

Hot coffee and a breakfast of apple and grape juice, yogurt, granola, eggs, potatoes and homemade bread await me. This is fresh bread, baked with love, without preservatives or chemicals. We bake 60 loaves daily — wholewheat, white, rye, 'veggie' and specialty breads. A hearty breakfast signifies hard work. One of our principles is 'One who won't work shall not eat'. How many visitors I've seen coyly smile at this adage! If they could but realize that this has been one of the strongest principles of our survival. How many communities have failed due to laziness and lack of commitment?

After breakfast, my six-year-old walks with her friends to the 'headstart' class where she is learning ABCs in preparation for starting 'big school'. My ten-year-old daughter is on garden detail for an hour. My fifteen-year-old is helping in our summer school and thinking of future career choices. My son is picking apples in the orchard. My two oldest children are at university, my son working on a research paper while my daughter does medical work.

My family settled, I look beyond to the survival of our communal family. In my current job, I answer correspondence and publicize events such as Open House and the conventions we hold twice a year. I also manage Padanaram Press, printing booklets, articles and Daniel's spiritual writings. I co-edit our newsletter, Millennial Chronicles. My typewriter has been replaced by a computer, and I'm getting onto e-mail. Sundry tasks come my way during the day: phone calls, a visiting college class or newspaper reporter, or a baby being born.

*   *   *

As a 30-year communal veteran, I've seen that there is always a turnover, especially in the early years. Many people came to try their communal wings but never learned to fly, so they stayed awhile then journeyed on. At times there was plenty of help; at other times we had to fill in.

I remember the initiation of one daily work schedule several years back. To keep the meals prepared, fruit and vegetable canning done, and communal buildings cleaned, extra help had to be gathered from all work areas: preschool, nursery, school teaching and the office. To bridge the gap, it was decided that we would give one extra hour per day besides our normal work.

There was instant rebellion in some who felt that others were not doing their share of work. They would now be 'carrying my load and theirs'. These months provided some of the juiciest gossip Padanaram had ever seen as many wriggled on the 'hot plate' planning ways of escape! 'Let's see. I'm already an extra miler who does hair cuts, so I'm exempt.' There was much complaining and griping but the schedule gave us more free time, made Padanaram a better place, and tied up loose ends where 'everybody's business was nobody's business'. Over time, the work schedule evolved until it is now accepted without complaint.

A similar instance was the rotation of Sunday meals. Everybody knew that Sunday was 'the day of rest'. No one works, not even God! Everyone wanted to rest — but they still wanted to eat. However, it seemed that this utopia, especially on Sundays, should be a place to sit and eat off one's own fig tree, like in the Garden of Eden; no work, no dishes but plenty of food.

The garbage, dirty dishes and unmopped floors became more and more apparent. Since it was confined to Sundays, with every other day handled on schedules, the slovenliness of the kitchen could be handled by most! For weeks, good-hearted members would clean up the mess, wash dishes and mop floors for the sake of sanitation or because they felt sorry for those who would face it Monday morning.

Finally, one Sunday it stopped: no dish washing, floor mopping or putting away food. On Monday, after the rebellion of the kitchen crew and others who could stand it no longer, a change came. On our bulletin board was placed a note: 'EVERY PERSON FROM HENCEFORTH WILL BE RESPONSIBLE WITH OTHERS FOR TWO WEEK-END MEALS EVERY TEN WEEKS'. And it worked! The beautiful, cooperative meals served from the next Sunday forward couldn't be matched in the finest restaurants.

These things affected me right where I lived. Philosophies of 'how to' didn't help. It's what I lived, what I experienced, and sometimes it was raw! It was the nitty-gritty of communal life, the daily ups and down. It is called 'working together'.

*   *   *

I had nothing materially when I came, but now I have the things that really count. If I had wanted riches, I'd have remained in outer society. It's the intangibles which one can't buy that matter: friendship, care, support, spirituality, peace and vision. I earned these things by working together with others and by trying a new, communal lifestyle — giving up the old for the new. Communal living is my sanity and my health. No one promised it would be easy! Walking a new way through the briars and thistles of communalism is much more difficult than following a well-worn path. I can, however, stop and smell the roses.

Communal living, with its tangibles of food, land, shelter, clothing and a good school, is the best place for me. I started out in one room, but today I live in a beautiful, comfortable apartment, built by ourselves. Each child has a room. It is rustic, reflecting the surrounding woods and lakes. As I look into my fireplace, built of sandstone from our creek, I feel cozy and warm. Out the window, I see the efforts of hard work — wood stacked by the young people in preparation for the snows and cold weather ahead. We'll be warm through the coldest storm!

*'Ye Ole Inn'
dining room
and kitchen
(on right),
'Parthenon'
residence
(upper left)
and
Padanaram
office
(lower left)*

PHOTO BY LARRY SUMMERTON

I feel wonderful driving around the 2400 acres (1000 hectares) to which size we have grown, realizing that I share the ownership of this land. Seeing our 100 cattle grazing, passing by our sheep and llamas, watching our kids on horses, or hay being put in the barn makes me swell with pride. Knowing that our gardens have been certified organic gives me the satisfaction that our food will be healthier, perhaps our lives lengthened. Seeing our storehouse with row upon row of home-canned food — fruit, juices, tomatoes, peppers and pickles — makes me look forward to the winter snows.

Our main income is from our renewable forest products business: sawmilling, selective timber buying, veneer sales and land improvement. We have the largest sawmill in this area and are still enlarging. We are guardians of the earth, our only home in the universe. It's all we've got! We are environmentally conscious as we utilize the entire tree, selling bark mulch, compost and garden blend. New enterprises are around the corner, even a use for sawdust. We have now started a sister community in Arizona. In our first year, Padanaram earned $4000, while last year we made $7 million, and our businesses are still expanding.

All income goes into a 'common purse' to be used for various needs: medical and dental care, gas, food and lodging. Five principles guide us: (1) 'As one would that others do, do unto them'; (2) 'Hold all things in common; count nothing one's own'; (3) 'Distribution to each according to the need'; (4) 'Of one who has much, much is required'; (5) 'One that won't work shall not eat'.

*   *   *

To me, communal living is about expansion in all its forms, both naturally and spiritually. It's about building an earthly home, but it is also about expanding the inner person. Who am I? What have I always wanted to do? What are my abilities? Over the years, it has been different things: poetry and song writing, plays, crafts, writing, and organizing social events. These things, however, come after my communal responsibilities.

One of the most beautiful aspects of communal living is that we can experiment. When society gets so large that it ceases to appreciate its members and treats them as objects, individuals lose a sense of worth and identity. In a small setting, an individual can be the star of the moment. I found that I could write plays, act and be appreciated on our 'small stage'. To us, the greatest plays are those we identify with and understand. Songs only touch our hearts if they contain ideas that we live and know. Out of this context comes our social life of plays, songs, poems and mime reflecting Padanaram's communal life. Hardships of communal life become great comedy sketches! We can laugh at ourselves. Our children know they can be creative and original. God didn't limit creativity to just a few!

To me the city is too vast. I like to touch the earth and dig in the dirt. For years I raised house plants. Both my grandfathers had gardened in their spare time, so this was probably where I got my green thumb. One of my desires was to make my own cosmetics and herbal remedies. Perhaps back in my ancestry there was a medicine woman interested in natural healing? I have always looked for alternatives, be it lifestyle, school, philosophy or religion.

We already had an established herb garden, but I made a small, organic garden near my dwelling. I love crushing and smelling herbs, watching them grow, weeding, stripping the leaves, drying them and placing them in jars. Rosemary, thyme, fennel, lavender, comfrey and marjoram became a fascinating part of my life. I learned their uniqueness — their smells and healing powers.

The next step was making teas, infusions, decoctions and tinctures. I tried all the recipes I could find. This led me to the beauty of beeswax (from our own hives) and its healing powers. I began to make facial and hand creams, lip balms, shampoos, salves and poultices. I shared my creations with friends who shared them with other friends. It was my stab at the false advertising system where cosmetics are as full of preservatives and harmful ingredients as the food we eat. I was making a change. Half a dozen of us, interested in growing plants, drying herbs for food or craft projects, and giving herb classes, now work together building an economic enterprise. Though in its infancy, it will become a viable entity and create jobs for our community.

Among 200 Padanaram members, from 0 to 97, I find people who help me to improve. Leacy, a 'young' 97-year-old, came to Padanaram at 80 to start her 'new life'. At 83, she got her ears pierced. She dresses in the brightest colors, deploring the idea of oldsters in brown, gray and black. She wears big-brimmed, multi-coloured hats that match her dresses, with jewellery on her fingers and around her neck. Stoop-shouldered though she is, there was never a more attractive lady.

Her favorite kitchen job is one which no one else wants, cutting up onions. Most ladies avoid that job; don't like the tears. Leacy says it cleans out her sinuses, so she is always wearing an apron ready to face the onions. Her shelves are lined with herbal concoctions, one for every occasion: insomnia, pregnancy or upset stomach. She is constantly busy, walking a couple of miles daily to keep her health. She has no relatives here so she adopts us all.

Lois, a prophetess, is a 30-year communal veteran who has given me strength and hope. She has visions and dreams, and hears inner voices. One time in our Sunday night meeting she was meditating about a business problem that seemed to threaten our economic survival. Later in the evening she told of the vision she had experienced. Her body was moving forward rapidly toward a stone wall made up of what looked like cement with small pebbles in it. Without fear, she contemplated what would happen as she approached the wall. Would she crash into it? Would a hole open up through which she could pass? As she approached, to her surprise the wall laid down and became a road with ingrained small pebbles and rocks.

She interpreted this vision as 'whatever loomed ahead, what seemed to be insurmountable obstacle, was only a temporary imposition. It would pass.' Such has been the spiritual course of Padanaram. There have been many voices, visions and dreams to guide us.

*   *   *

Daniel Wright had a spiritual experience in finding our valley. He heard a voice that said, 'I will show you my valley'. Daniel 'walked the talk', digging ditches, driving trucks and pounding nails. He took vows of poverty just as we did. He and his wife Lois worked hard!

It was his vision, but it became ours. It made sense to build a utopia where there was neither rich nor poor, without unemployment, where everyone had health care, and where we could live communally following the values in which we believed. We challenged the social, religious, political and economic status quo, and made a new life. So that our settlement and many more like it could be built, we pooled our meagre resources. It was to be an example to the world of what could be done through communal work. No gifts were accepted. No bank gave us loans. Padanaram started through positive effort and grew to its present dimensions.

Daniel, now 77, continues to be active in our business and community. He walks 4 miles (6 km) daily. He is our spiritual mentor and leader. His teachings and foresight of the millennial age keep us looking ahead. While he once solved all the problems, we have now delegated authority to those who have been here for many years. The mantle falls to the next generation, one which believes in spiritual guidance, hard work and a realistic vision of the future.

We use the word 'Kingdomism', a new political and religious philosophy applicable to our present world and throughout the millennial age. Kingdomism is a concept of divine politics involving twelve steps: Birth, Vision, Familyism, Equality, Love, Law, Direction, Friendship, Education, Artistry, Evolution and Leadership. I live these twelve steps in Padanaram and they work. In simple terms, Kingdomism means sharing, cooperation, a school, businesses, a common table with wholesome foods, children — important things in our daily lives. Utopian communalism is the first step of Kingdomism. We believe in peaceful revolution and communalism is that revolution. This new age philosophy will spread throughout the world via small intentional communities.

*   *   *

Dining room, kitchen and bakery at Padanaram

Have I changed since joining Padanaram? Granted, there have been physical changes. I'm now 52. My once dark, curly hair is straighter, a bit thinner, a mixture of gray and black. But inside, I feel 25. I'm still growing. My horizons continue to expand as new challenges arise.

In our dining room hangs a sign, wood-burned by our village artist Bob, which says, 'If all people here were just like me, what would this place be?' Everyone is not like me, doesn't think like I do and doesn't approach problems like I do. I have learned patience, tolerance and to appreciate the differences between people. My spiritual insight is keener, and I'm sharper on human nature.

Last year I was midwife at the birth of my first grand-daughter. When my daughter (a senior medical student who plans to be our village doctor) decided to birth at home, she was admonished by her colleagues and friends to 'safely birth in the hospital'. This fear almost rubbed off onto me. It was different for me — but this is my daughter! When I voiced my concerns, this second-generation communalist rebuked me: 'I will have my baby at home. You did.'

We adults didn't foresee what would take place with our teenagers. They blasted their music and rebelled just as we did against our parents. They followed society's norms from a distance, but it was like being in a protected womb. Their every move was not monitored but we adults were fully aware that they were around. Sometimes, with the din of their rock music, only too aware!

We have dances and plays, with our own special holidays and celebrations through-out the year. We have just held our December Passover Celebration in our new recreation center called The Barn, a rustic building of wood and stone, with homemade lights. One event during this five-day festivity is called 'The Night of the Candles'. Each child lights a candle from the seven golden candlesticks. Our 100 children then stand together with their lighted candles, illuminating the large hall. How dark it becomes when they blow them out! Where would we be without them?

Most of our young people are choosing to marry and stay within Padanaram. We chose to come here, however, while they were born here. They have ideas to which we must listen with respect. They have modern facilities that we didn't have when we started out, however they are not isolated from the earth. They know how to pick tomatoes, hammer nails, and work with others, and they know about faith in Deity. Seven of them are attending college (two of these are mine). They face a different world, a world of modern communication and global thinking. They must be true to their calling. I see a strong drive in our children to remain communal and to carry on with what we started. Our second and third generations are the 'keepers of the flame'. They are unique individuals, strong, beautiful and healthy. They are the continuity of Padanaram.

*　　*　　*

Some words from a song written by Larry, one of our musicians and my companion of many years, express my sentiments, 'In the Valley where the gods tell us what to do / it's all up to me and you'.

It's been a great trip! What's next?

PHOTO BY LARRY SUMMERTON

Rachel Summerton in front of Parthenon

Introduction: Communauté de l'Arche and Thérèse Parodi

©THÉRÈSE PARODI

*Thérèse Parodi with
her husband Pierre
(who died in 1989).*

L'Arche is a group of several small but very active communal societies in France, Spain and Italy. It was started in 1945 by Lanza Del Vasto, who had lived and worked with Mahatma Gandhi in India. L'Arche is a communal society with a strong commitment to social justice, environmentalism and equality.

As a young and idealistic woman, Thérèse Parodi joined l'Arche in 1953, and has been a member ever since. She is still actively engaged in communal affairs as well as in various protest actions for peace, equality and environmental sanity. Her second draft to this chapter was delayed when this elderly lady had to fly off to Tahiti to protest against her own French Government's insane testing of nuclear weapons on my doorstep! I could hardly complain about the delay!

Thérèse Parodi lives in l'Arche at La Borie Noble in the wild and beautiful, but sparsely settled Languedoc region of southern France. They have about 45 residents.

I want to thank Michèle Le Boeuf, a member of l'Arche who served as translator, being caught halfway between Thérèse's excellent French and my demands for a certain style of English.

L'Arche offers workshops about themselves and their work in English, German, Spanish and French. While visitors are welcome to come and stay at l'Arche, they must always write first and await a reply. Their address is Communauté de l'Arche, La Borie Noble, 34650 Roqueredonde, France (phone: +33-67 44 09 89).

CHAPTER 3

L'Arche: In Search of Non-Violence

by Thérèse Parodi

For this biographical account I want to follow a chronology along the two important factors which have helped me to find meaning and make sense of my life: my search for justice and liberty, as well as my search for God.

I was born in 1925, the sixth child in a Catholic, bourgeois family on the west coast of France. The first great tragedy of my youth was when my father suddenly died when I was only 13. Then, a year later, the madness of World War II engulfed my secure, carefree adolescent world. My mother, with no financial support, brought us six children back to my grandmother's previously happy home where we existed, rather than lived, during the German occupation. Our 'happy home' was in a region occupied by the German SS, so from my girlish innocence I quickly came to grips with invasion, loss of freedom, violence, hostage taking, executions and bombardments. I witnessed and experienced the terrible suffering resulting from this violent, sadistic madness. Thirsty for freedom and justice, I turned my eyes to search for an apparently absent God.

One day while I was alone, riding my bicycle along a quiet country road, wearing my pretty pink skirt (made from a curtain), suddenly an Allied plane, flying very low, started to fire a machine gun at me and my bicycle. Jumping into a ditch, my reaction was not so much fear as a sense of outrage and revolt. That dutiful pilot, flying so low, could clearly see that I was only a young girl and not a German soldier, but he obeyed his officer's orders to shoot anything that moved — no matter what it was. As I lay there in the ditch, frightened and angry, I promised myself that if ever I had children, I would teach them to disobey rather than to blindly follow an order which goes against their conscience.

After the German SS troops pushed my family and me into only three rooms of my grandmother's beautiful house, they occupied the rest, using it for their own accommodation and to hold Jewish prisoners. Then, after the war ended, the American army held SS prisoners in our house. During all this time we too were like prisoners in our own home. Violence and suffering were everywhere — yet where was God? These terrifying wartime experiences led me to a determined, lifelong spiritual search for God.

In 1945, when I was 20, I began to study philosophy at the University of La Sorbonne in Paris. After studying Marxism and Communism, I followed my search for God and the meaning of life through the great French thinkers of the time: Sartre, Valéry and Camus. They all had answers about the existence, or absence, of God but none of them could really answer my questions. My passionate spiritual quest was far from satisfied.

I Find My Spiritual Path

Then, in 1952, I was deeply affected while listening to a talk by Lanza Del Vasto, the founder of l'Arche community. 'Who is God?' I asked him. After a moment's silence he replied, 'I can't answer you. You must go and search for yourself'. His pithy and provocative answer provided me with a great source of hope in my search for God.

One year later, in 1953, I joined l'Arche and took my vows to join the eleven other 'companions' (the name given to l'Arche members, and literally meaning 'those who share the same bread'). These vows have been at the heart of l'Arche since its foundation. Our vows are a commitment, a concrete sign of our alliance with God, in sacred communion with the other companions. We, like the wise people in all traditional and ancient cultures and civilisations, believe in the creative strength and power of words. Our vows are an exchange between companions, and between ourselves and God. They help us to remember the sense and the direction we want to give to our lives. I had already studied the function of monastic vows, and had previously thought about entering a convent, but in l'Arche all dimensions of my thirst for justice and liberty and my quest for God were covered. At last, I had found my place, my spiritual home.

L'Arche was born in 1945 when Lanza Del Vasto started weekly meetings in Paris. He was inspired to talk about and share his wisdom and divine insights, which derived from his lengthy spiritual pilgrimage. The important question 'why is there war and violence?' had haunted him. On his quest for an answer he went to India in 1936 where he lived and worked with, and learned from, Mahatma Gandhi. There, with that exceptional, saintly man, he discovered not only the reasons for war, but also a hope — the possibility — for its resolution: ahimsa (or non-violence). Ahimsa is a form of non-violence which is not so much a political strategy as a manner of acting which derives from a way of being. Ahimsa is non-violence which has spirit at its heart.

When I joined l'Arche in 1953 we were only twelve companions, living communally at Tournier, 100 km (65 miles) from Paris. For all of us, this was our first experience with communal living — for which we were ill-prepared. We came from such individualistic lives! Over time we had to learn to find the balance between our ideals, the principles of the teachings of Shantidas (Lanza's name which was given to him by Gandhi, and which meant 'Peace Servant') and their practical application in our complex, modern lives. We had to learn the art of compromise. We were almost all intellectuals with no training for practical work. Our communal difficulties were not so much connected with matters of principle as with mundane, daily-life situations. Non-violent social interaction, we quickly discovered, was practical as well as theoretical. For example, for one companion our rubbish bin was 'full' when it was three-quarters full, and it was an emergency(!) to have it emptied — while for another companion it was 'full' only when it overflowed. Through such naive disputes and a comedy of errors, our first commune, not surprisingly, lasted only four years.

Our experience in this l'Arche commune made us realise that we are not non-violent — but rather we are searchers after non-violence. This search takes place in the balance between two realities: our ideals of how to live and the reality of how we actually do live. I am convinced that mundane, daily life, lived in common, is the more efficacious and fertile 'land' on which to grow our 'communal tree'. But it's not enough merely to grow and live in harmony — we also need to have clear principles to help guide us along the way. So, to that end, Shantidas wrote a commentary on our vows, a 'Rule' that could help us to practise them. Our vows have the sacred job of keeping our spiritual memory awake, but we don't promise to accomplish our vows in totality and plenitude. Instead they are a direction toward which we are walking. Our seven vows are a commitment to work, obedience, responsibility and co-responsibility, self-purification, simplicity, truth and non-violence. Our Rule is a commentary or explanation of these vows. These vows are not a weight placed on our shoulders but rather an inner, supporting frame that helps us to stand tall and straight. Our vows function something like a human skeleton. Now what would we be without a skeleton? — A sort of slug!

Those first years in l'Arche commune were hard but rich in experience. In spite of personal difficulties, I was confident that communal living was good for me — all the more so because of the difficulties presented, which allowed (and forced) me to grow. I always look upon communal living as a great, exciting adventure, like crossing the ocean in a sailing boat or searching for an Incan temple in the middle of a deep jungle!

In 1954 when we closed the l'Arche commune at Tournier, we twelve companions moved to Tourette-sur-Loup, a small village in the south of France. Our goal was to learn practical skills, and to support ourselves through handicrafts such as weaving, woodwork and forge (blacksmith) work.

My apprenticeship in spinning and weaving took me through a really meaningful process of personal discovery. Given my intellectual background, manual and craft work helped me to enter into an unknown world of knowledge about myself, truth, creativity, service to others and a search for social justice. Philosophy is an abstract world composed of formless words and ideas which we can't touch, a world without limit or substance. In manual work we touch, we build and we meet our own limits, on real ground. I don't mean that philosophy or any other intellectual work is useless, but only that it is quite incomplete on its own. Wholeness is important in life, so we should try to develop all the different human aspects of which we are composed: physical, emotional and intellectual. Specialisation in any one area is a handicap to spiritual growth. At that critical period of my life, manual craft-work was exactly what I needed to help me progress along my spiritual path.

A year later, in 1955, we moved from our rented property in Tourette, to settle in the countryside near the village of Bollène, in the Rhône valley, also in the south of France. We moved to the old family home of Chanterelle, Shantidas' wife. We thought that we would only be there for one summer, but instead we stayed for seven years. At this time, l'Arche consisted only of two families and twelve single people. Perhaps because we were mainly single, we were deeply inspired by a monastic daily rhythm. But this rhythm slowly changed over time with weddings and new arrivals. By 1960, we were 5 families, 13 children and 10 singles. This was a time for us companions to put down roots and to develop and implement our ideas, our practical knowledge and our ability to give of ourselves. It was for me and for all our community a time of spiritual preparation for the many non-violent political actions which lay ahead.

It was in this l'Arche commune where I met Pierre, a medical doctor and companion, whom I then married in 1959, when I was 34 years old. Soon we had two children, Marie-Trinité and Vincent. We thought a lot about the best way to raise our children, and how to integrate them into l'Arche's communal life. We thought about and discussed trying to develop along the lines of an Israeli kibbutz. Finally, however, we chose the 'communal-family' or 'tribal' social form for l'Arche. Within l'Arche, I have lived on quite different spiritual paths, as a single woman and as the mother of a family. In motherhood, I had the great advantage of finding in my children the best gurus possible.

During this period we companions started to commit ourselves to direct, non-violent actions. We undertook a ten-day fast in Sicily to press for more social justice for the urban poor. During the war between France and Algeria (for Algerian independence from French colonial rule), we undertook non-violent action against the torture and inhumanity within the French Detention Camps. These camps were not as bad as the German Concentration Camps — but they were still barbaric. In trying to raise the consciousness of French citizens, I remember distributing thousands of leaflets. One day, at the door of a church, a well-dressed, elderly 'gentleman' violently struck me on the hands with his cane because he said we were discouraging French morale! That was our first non-violent action which went directly against French public opinion as well as the dictates of the French Government and army.

During the Vatican II Council in 1963, Shantidas did a 40-day fast in Rome to ask the Catholic Church to condemn nuclear weapons. Pierre, my husband, was with Shantidas to monitor his health. Pope Paul VI received them in a private audience and warmly encouraged them in our non-violent work for peace. In 1983, Pierre and I undertook a 30-day fast to try to stop France's nuclear testing program in the South Pacific. In 1995, as I write these words, renewed French nuclear testing in the South Pacific is again an issue which troubles me deeply.

Our communal house in Bollène was far too small for all companions, even before a nuclear power station was constructed nearby (what a charming neighbourhood!), so we searched for a new home for l'Arche. In 1962 we moved to La Borie Noble, a 450-hectare (1000-acre) property, at 700 metres (2300 feet) altitude, in the Languedoc region of southern France. The climate is difficult and agricultural potential is limited, but the landscape, animals and plants are beautiful. This area is almost deserted except for a few shepherds. Our most bothersome neighbours are wild pigs! This property had been aban-

*Women spinning wool
at l'Arche.*

©THÉRÈSE PARODI

doned in the 1930s, so the buildings were in ruins and the land neglected and overgrown. We had so much work to do to make it habitable — so we had no problem of unemployment for companions!

In 1964 Shantidas proposed that Pierre become the next leader of l'Arche. As with all important decisions, we sought consensus between all companions. Pierre wanted to push all companions to reflect on the work of the 'Pilgrim' (our name given to l'Arche's leader). Pierre strongly believed that the vocation of the Pilgrim was to promote unity between companions (like Christ, who washed the feet of his disciples) rather than to be a boss with power and privilege.

For me, in my spiritual search, this period was marked by our collective reflections on non-violent authority. Shantidas helped us to understand that peculiar form of authority, while Pierre made us really experiment and work with it on a concrete level. My search for God, justice and liberation became far more subtle through that reflection. Pierre's character was quite different from mine, so we helped each other's vocation. When one of us had an intuitive insight, the other always helped to discriminate whether or not it was right: did it come from attunement to God's wisdom or merely from our own ego?

Non-Violence in Morocco

An example of how this intuitive insight operated was our eight-year stay in Morocco. An idea came to Pierre, who was very concerned about religious conflicts and the damage resulting from French colonialism in Morocco. He shared, first with me and then with the other companions, his wish to undertake a l'Arche mission in Morocco. As soon as he had this inspiration, I felt deeply attracted to it and appreciated God's calling. I was revolted by colonialism because I had suffered from it, and to me, dialogue between religions seemed crucial to any peace work.

We prepared for this project over several years, until our second child was four years old. We wanted our stay in Morocco to help restore fraternal relations between colonisers and colonised, blacks and whites, and Muslims and Christians. We had to be patient because many l'Arche companions were not happy for us to leave. But the fruit slowly ripened at its own rhythm, which was important as much for this project as for the opportunity for us to be away from Shantidas in order to allow Pierre to later succeed him. Shantidas had wanted to officially name his successor well before his death, because he thought that he could work with him on our communal problems, and help guide and develop him while together on tours and at conferences. But in reality, Shantidas had a very strong temper and it was far from easy to coordinate and work closely with such a man. So Shantidas remained the Pilgrim until his death in 1981, when Pierre at last took his place.

But before then, in 1966, Pierre and I started a small l'Arche community at Tatta in the south of Morocco. Our integration into that sadly exploited culture was difficult at the beginning, but I was convinced that we had to dive in 100% to make it positive. We were about 20 people there at our communal table, including a former slave and a 'repudiated' woman (rejected by her husband — a terrible shame and an unforgivable sin in Morocco). We adopted traditional housing (mud-built), clothing (djellabah & fokkia) and food (barley couscous with vegetables and yoghurt). This traditional food was difficult for any of our European friends who came to visit. After a few weeks of such a traditional diet they wanted to run screaming to the little store to buy sardines and other treats!

Pierre started a small hospital, serving a large area in southern Morocco. Because of Muslim tradition, I had to stay at home with the other women. My taste for freedom might have felt suppressed by this, but the silence and the beautiful desert scenery helped me to develop my inner, spiritual self. We had a simple and harmonious life. Ever since, simplicity has meant beauty to me, while complexity represents misery and ugliness. We do not suffer from simplicity, but misery and ugliness degrade our spirit.

Even as a practising Christian, I was deeply impressed by the Muslim faith. We followed the five Islamic daily prayers, as well as Ramadan fasting and other rituals. We used to read together from both the Koran and the Bible, with a deep respect for each other's religion. We were witnesses to one another's faith by respecting, observing and encouraging each other to mutually practise our diverse religious rituals.

I didn't suffer from solitude or the lack of social interaction with other Europeans because Pierre and I felt adopted by the wonderful people of the village of Tatta. We would return to visit l'Arche, at la Borie Noble, every two years. Many Moroccan friends also visited l'Arche and they felt at home there because the tribal feeling of our commune was similar to their own lifestyle.

At the same time as he was developing the hospital, Pierre started a palm-grove project, in partnership with the former slave. There were many human as well as practical problems with this project because even if the sheik who owned the land might have agreed to give land to the toubib (doctor), he definitely refused to give anything to a former slave! Finally, we had to develop this project on desert land where we had to dig a deep well amongst the sand and stones. In the Sahara Desert, life is impossible without water, so we absolutely needed that well for the palm trees. It was very hard work but we found water at 30 metres (100 feet) deep.

Our children were growing up with Muslim people, learning Arabic and Berber languages. They attended a Moroccan school while I completed their French education at home. For me it was a time of closeness with them. My son wrote a poem describing his joy at living with a desert tribe: 'Each time I'm lying down on my Berber blanket, my look falls upon you, my dear drum. Do you remember the evening festivals on the village square? This beautiful square surrounded by high, red, mud walls, pierced by windows and crowned by terraces where veiled women and black, curly-haired children appeared. Then I made you resound with the other drums and, little by little, we were irresistibly pulled in by the dance. In spite of your gray skin you were the sunlight of the feast. You are the sign of our deep accord, and your beat is coming from the heart of the earth!' I can bear witness that we can live with people of another culture and religion if we are receptive to the deep, essential spiritual and humane reality common to all people.

Home to l'Arche in France

Just when our project started to prosper, when the hospital was well organised, the palm trees bearing fruit, and our Moroccan friends starting to enter into the philosophy of non-violence, Shantidas and his wife Chanterelle came and asked us, in the name of all the companions, to return home to l'Arche in France. It had been clear from the beginning of our mission in Morocco that we wouldn't be there forever, because of

Pierre's intended succession of Shantidas as the Pilgrim. But even though we expected this, it was for Pierre and me an important test of our obedience to God's will, and detachment from our own egos. In the silence of meditation and prayer we found the strength to accept that we had to leave Morocco and resume our lives in France. We understood in our heads that it was necessary for us to return to l'Arche to start assuming the responsibilities of the Pilgrim, but our hearts suffered a sense of renunciation on leaving Morocco.

Back in l'Arche we received a warm welcome which helped us re-integrate into the community after having been away for so many years. Until his death, Pierre and I went to Morocco every two to three years to maintain contact with our Moroccan friends.

L'Arche companions had already started the 'Battle of Larzac', a famous non-violent action. For ten years, local farmers protested against selling their land for the extension of a military base. I participated in many fasts and non-violent actions, some of them very dangerous because we were confronted by angry police and soldiers. I already had white hair, and it often helped me because most policemen hesitated to beat up an elderly woman. Once, after having been pulled away from the demonstration lines, a young policeman begged me, 'Please don't go back there. They're going to hurt you!' A long and deep friendship developed between these farmers and ourselves during all those years of protest and non-violent actions, even though they had not previously been convinced of the efficiency or effectiveness of non-violence. At long last, with the change of French Government in 1981, those farmers won their campaign to retain their land.

During the 1970s we welcomed many new people to l'Arche. Communes were then à la mode, but while many people were interested in our communal lifestyle, few stayed. Nevertheless, we grew rapidly and had enough companions to open new l'Arche communes. Between 1981, when Shantidas died at 80 years of age, and 1989, when Pierre died, we opened nine l'Arche communities in France, Spain and Italy. Some, however, have now closed for various reasons.

La Borie Noble is both mother and grandmother to these other l'Arche communes. All 80 companions within the eight l'Arche communes have taken the same vows, and follow the same essential teachings of Shantidas. But there are differences between these communes, with some depending for their livelihood on agriculture, some on handicrafts, and others on providing hospitality and retreat facilities for individuals and groups. Each l'Arche commune has a companion who, during a three-year commitment, coordinates and manages that group's economic affairs, as well as its other activities and meetings.

Here at La Borie Noble we try to do a little bit of everything, but most of our livelihood is gained from agriculture. We are not self-sufficient but we produce all the basic elements of our vegetarian diet — bread, dairy products and vegetables. We also have workshops for woodcrafts, blacksmithing and pottery. Each family or individual member has an appropriately sized private apartment in which to sleep.

Our week days start with all companions coming together for a half hour of silent meditation, followed by a short group prayer. In winter, we do this inside, in a circle around three candles, while in summer we all stand outside, in line to face the sunrise. Every day we pray in communion with other religious traditions by reading from their sacred texts. Monday is for Hindus, Tuesday for Muslims, Wednesday for Searchers Without Church, Thursday for Buddhists, Friday for Christians, and Saturday for the

Two companions baking bread at l'Arche

Jews. We are ecumenical, open to different religions and spiritual quests, but we do not propose a mixture of religions. We are certainly neither a sect nor a cult.

Each companion works for four hours in the morning and three hours in the afternoon. At the end of each hour, we have two minutes of silence during which we meditate and recall our spiritual purpose for the day. All companions eat the midday meal together, but breakfast and supper are eaten within the family unit, and with all singles eating together. We finish each day with all companions meditating and praying together around an open fire.

We have three meetings each week, one for organising our work, another for making the numerous practical and trivial decisions, and the third meeting is for us companions to make those important decisions which are at the heart of our communal spiritual path.

We have a common bank account from which each companion can take money for her or his personal needs. We do not exchange money between us, within the commune, and we do not receive wages or a set allowance.

Making feasts is a very important ritual within l'Arche, a special time to reaffirm our unity and our common spiritual path. We celebrate four main feasts during the year. At the end of June, we hold a feast in honour of Saint John the Baptist, and we then renew our vows at dawn, after an all night, hill-top vigil. In autumn, we hold Saint Michael's, or Noah's Feast in thanksgiving for our bountiful harvest and for all the fruits of the earth. After Christmas we have an Epiphany Feast, representing our quest for our 'inner star', or guidance, which will help lead us to the newborn Christ. In the spring we hold an Easter Feast, during which we reflect on the mysteries of life and death. During our feasts, all companions dress in white, and we enjoy music, dancing, singing, poetry and theatre.

A more serious activity during our feasts is to decide in what non-violent actions we will become involved. One of our companions has been three times on a peace mission to ex-Yugoslavia, but now, in late 1995, we are putting more time and energy into demonstrations against our own French Government's nuclear testing in the South Pacific.

We regularly receive many visitors who are interested in l'Arche, in our spiritual path, and in our communal lifestyle. Several times each year we offer a week-long programme, during which we give formal talks and engage in discussions about our beliefs, and share our daily life with those who are interested in our special way of living at l'Arche.

While it's a great adventure to live communally it is also very demanding, and it is difficult for any commune to endure for a long time. Since 1994 we l'Arche compan-

©Thérèse Parodi

Companions at evening common prayer

ions have been reflecting on two important questions: Why are fewer people joining l'Arche and why are many companions leaving? We have worked with a wide range of people from convents and psychotherapy centres to try to help us to understand our situation. Is the communal movement dying? Is there too much 'rust' in our structures and traditions? Such questions about our communal way of life keep us searching for answers.

My Final Years

In 1989, Pierre's sudden death affected me very deeply. The position of Pilgrim was passed to Jean-Baptiste Libouban, by the unanimous consensus decision of the 80 companions.

I then entered this last phase of my life. After having been a single woman, a wife, and then a mother, I'm now in a more contemplative phase where solitude gives me renewed strength. At 70 years of age I still participate in manual tasks such as sewing for the guest rooms, peeling vegetables and other tasks which require little energy. I participate, of course, in all our meetings and the decisions of l'Arche, and for some years I have been active in trying to help transmit the teachings of Shantidas to newer members.

During the summer of 1995 I spent a month in Tahiti, with other l'Arche companions and other non-violent protesters, demonstrating against and trying to stop our French government's renewed nuclear testing in the South Pacific. Our main goal was to work with and support Polynesian people in the anti-atomic testing campaigns. We were often with the non-violent mayor of Faaa, Mr Oscar Temaru. One of our younger and more athletic companions joined the Greenpeace team on their boat. To be once again involved in non-violent political action, to protest and to face angry police as well as the international media was a challenge at my age. The other companions watched us on TV in France! It was a deep joy for me to contribute to that non-violent, peace action against the madness of my government — a government of which I am now deeply ashamed.

*   *   *

All my life has been a search to find the balance between solitude and the stresses of communal life. Shantidas, who used to give a poetic animal or plant nickname to each companion (it is like Noah's Ark!) called me 'the seagull', which is an ocean bird in love with freedom and — why not? — with justice and God.

I've never regretted for a moment my commitment to l'Arche. My roots are here, and here I feel so alive. I want to stay here until my last breath will fly away on the wings of a seagull. Returning to the purest Holy Light... returning to God.

Thérèse Parodi with other anti-nuclear, non-violent protestors in Tahiti, August 1995

Introduction: Community Alternatives and Jan Bulman

*Jan Bulman
(with husband Tom)*

Community Alternatives began in 1977 in Vancouver, Canada, although members did not occupy their present communal home until two years later. It is one of only two urban groups in this book. Although not well known, Community Alternatives serves as a wonderful example of how communal living need not imply the rustic-hippie image so common in the popular media, but how it can also suit middle-class professionals living in a modern city. In fact the logic of communalism may apply even more in an urban than a rural context! Community Alternatives is an exciting social alternative precisely because it would suit a wider range of people than would be attracted to, or able to exist happily in, most of the other communal groups found in this book.

Jan Bulman is one of the founders of Community Alternatives. She has recently retired from a long career in social work and involvement with social justice and environmental issues. She remains passionately committed to communal living.

I visited Community Alternatives twice in 1993, staying in the same 'pod' as Jan, her husband Tom, Kaz and Ewan (all to be found in her story). I was impressed by the style, graciousness and comfort of their inner-city lifestyle in their enormous, purpose-built 100-room communal home.

Readers are welcome to write to Community Alternatives at 1937 West 2nd Avenue, Vancouver, British Columbia V6J 1J2, Canada (fax: +1-604-733-2667). Because of limited space, guest accommodation is rarely available. Do not just show up on their doorstep!

CHAPTER 4

Community Alternatives: Love Puddlers and Social Activists

by Jan Bulman

I'm sitting in one of the nine living rooms in our 100-room house in Vancouver, Canada, enjoying the view of snow-capped mountains, and reflecting on my home in Community Alternatives.

Ambre, a young member, is practising the piano in the common room on the same floor, and there are kid noises from courtyard basketball practice. Nobody but myself is home right now where I live with Tom, my husband of 43 years, Kaz, a retired public health nurse, and Chieko, Kaz's 21-year-old relative from Japan, who is here learning English. I don't have to cook supper (I only cook twice a week), so I have some time.

The road that led Tom and me to Community Alternatives is a story of villages. I grew up in villages, Tom in a small town. After we graduated from university, and Tom became an ordained Protestant minister, we brought up four children in two villages, and in one suburban congregation that lived very much like a village, next to a lake.

For me, those years were very satisfying. The minister's family is in a privileged position, close to people in life's great events: births, marriages, deaths, family crises, scandalous secrets, celebrations, and spiritual awakenings. But in the 1970s our life changed. Tom got a doctorate, and his job changed to hospital chaplaincy and university accredited chaplaincy teaching.

I missed my privileged position! We no longer had a church house, so we bought an attached townhouse in a suburban development called Manoah Village. Several years later there were only 14 of the original 120 owners left, even though the developer had tried to create a village, with a huge inner courtyard and common swimming pool. These condominiums became 'starter homes', and as people acquired equity they sold out and bought a house and a yard. We were aware of many marriage breakups, and rootless, alienated kids.

Our Provincial Government was concerned about family breakdown and juvenile delinquency. They hosted, along with the churches, a two year process called The Conference on The Family which I helped chair.

Tom came home one night around that time and noticed for the first time that the family adjoining our place had vacated. I said they had been gone four days. Tom was in total dismay. How could one be so close and yet so distant!

About then a brochure which had been sitting on our piano since The Conference on The Family started to look pretty good. It said a group called Community Alternatives wanted to create an urban / rural community, non-sexist, intergenerational, cooperative, egalitarian, 'living more lightly on the land', governed by consensus, less dependent on the unpredictable economy — all those good things and more!

We went to a meeting and here we are nearly 20 years later. The original brochure was rewritten seven years ago, but it still contains the same values. We call ourselves a value-based community.

Community Alternatives recognizes me, along with three other members still living here, as founding members, but there was a two-or three-year period that paved the way before we four and the other early members joined. Two innovative educators, John McBride and John Olsen, attracted the critical mass necessary for a viable group, through writings and workshops, partying, and know-how about group development. They incorporated Community Alternatives Society, published an innovative high school text about world development, created and published a 'Start Chart' for social change activists, got as far as pledges for a kibbutz-type farm on a nearby island, made an offer on a huge warehouse that was to have cottage storefront industries as well as housing, rented an office — well, you get the picture. Lots of excitement and endless discussion.

In 1977 our group, which still only numbered about twelve, took its first real risk. By combining our resources in the form of no-interest loans for the down payment, we went into debt for a $75,000, ten-acre (four-hectare) farm. This was not as dramatic as our earlier failed proposal for a 180-acre (80-hectare) Crown Land farm, but big enough to house two members and a small child, who were ready to try a back-to-the-land dream. It satisfied the rest of us who appreciated that the land had a history of no pesticide and chemical use, an old farmhouse and eleven little outbuildings, about an hour's drive away in the Lower Fraser Valley.

We initially saw our Fraser Common Farm as a garden for those of us in the city. We worked on individual garden beds, hired an organic gardener one summer, and did a lot of both working and partying out there. However, the energy crunch happened in the late '70s, and it didn't seem appropriate to drive 60 kilometres (40 miles) each way to work on our small gardens, so activity waned. There were several winters when those living out there (and at one time there were 13) felt very much abandoned by those of us in town.

Buying this farm in 1977 consolidated and committed us as a group. Our next leap of faith was to purchase four urban lots in a pleasant part of Vancouver just five blocks from the beach. A developer had gone bankrupt, and the city had reclaimed the property. The local council decided it should be for co-op housing. We put in our bid, and were accepted. Great excitement!

The Federal Government had instituted a Co-op Housing Program to facilitate mixed income, affordable housing, a fine program but unfortunately recently cancelled. They offered start-up money for our feasibility phase, and we set about designing our communal dream home. We wanted a village under one roof, with a library, solar panels for hot water, a common room, edible landscaping, a sauna, a darkroom, workshop, recreation room and 'pods'. We created the term 'pods', because we didn't like the term apartment or unit (we said we wanted 'a-close-ment', not 'apart-ment'!)

It took four years. We nearly ended up calling it 'Pertinacity Place'. There were many hard-fought battles and compromises, including one sit-in in a Federal bureaucrat's office, but we got all the features mentioned, if not quite in the form we imagined, and we finally started building. Rule number 1 in beginning a community: Never give up!

Early in our design process three groups started living in shared houses, so that we could tell the architect with some certainty what features would be important in urban communal living. Nine of us, including Tom and me and our eleven-year-old son David, took over a big old house near the proposed site, and lived there for two years while we were negotiating and erecting the city building. We literally came together through names from the mailing list that got drawn out of a hat. Eight of us moved right from there to the Community Alternatives building on opening day, July 1st, 1979, and remained together in a big pod for several years. It took us some months to realize that our joining Community Alternatives was almost as traumatic to our three eldest children, who were already out on their own when we joined, as if we had re-married. We had to learn not to expect them to be as excited about our extended network as we were, and to find private times to be with them exclusively.

The first year in that communal house, after years of running my own home, wasn't easy. Three other adults were pretty introverted, and my boisterousness and bringing people home for coffee at ten pm was not appreciated. Tom had adjusted to me over the years, but when I was just one adult among six, life was different. I didn't realize how unilateral I was in some things. I liked singing lusty grace at meals, for example, but our regular practice soon became holding hands and a silent grace. We found weekly house meetings absolutely essential. We posted an open agenda on the wall, and any of us, kids included, could put an item up. Often, just writing them initiated discussion, so that by the meeting time the item was no longer relevant. It amazed me how easily decisions were made at these meetings. I wished we had used this process in our own family.

Deciding during the design process to use a solar heating system to heat some of our domestic hot water was quite a saga. A local systems designer said we would need 44 solar panels on the roof, pitched at different angles for the sun, plumbing installed through the building as it was being erected, and three 500-gallon (2000-litre) tanks placed in the basement, with some kind of simple heat-exchange system. The preheated water would then flow into our conventional hot water heater for distribution. Getting the solar system operational took three years, an $18,000 bank loan, novices learning every skill imaginable of scrap dealer bargaining, carpentry, welding and work-bee organizing, but we did it. This was a powerful example of our concern for renewable energy and self-sufficiency, and a great amount of socializing and bonding went on in the process.

PHOTO BY MICHAEL MARRAPESE

Community Alternatives (Note solar panels on roof)

Unfortunately, for the last few years the solar panels have sat idle. The heat exchange design is virtually irreparable. I'll throw in that liberating phrase, 'A thing worth doing is worth doing badly!', but we might still recruit an engineer/plumber who could save it. It heated about half of our domestic hot water for ten years.

So here we are, 45 people from newborn to 66 years old, living in a huge urban commune in Vancouver, with a sister farm pod up the valley.

Before more Community Alternatives history, I'll tell a bit about myself. I was born in 1930, youngest of four children, to a liberal, witty Scottish mother with a degree from Glasgow University. She had been a Latin and French teacher into her early 30s when she married my father, a Canadian padre, at the end of World War I. He was in his early 40s, a Military Cross hero for courageous conduct in the front lines. They were married in Ayr, Scotland, and in 1919, came to the north coast of British Columbia, Canada, to a small Indian village where he was a minister and ran a mission boat. My oldest brother and sister were born there. My formative years were spent in another Indian village, Port Simpson, just south of Alaska, where I was schooled in a separate white school with seven other children. My eldest brother and sister remained in Vancouver, for high school and university. When my youngest sister and I were ready for high school we moved to a nearby town that had a two-room high school with 32 students. I was the spoiled youngest, ('Wee Ginkie', to use my Mother's Scottish phrase), always felt well cared for and well loved, a bit precocious, ready for adventure.

I value my safe, unstressed, uncompetitive background. It didn't, however, prepare me for a single-minded academic career. I mostly played my way through the University of British Columbia, spending many hours in campus social life, and two summers in Eastern Canada in Student In Industry coed work camps run by the Student Christian Movement. The year before graduating, I spent a summer in Europe travelling around to university conferences, hitchhiking and generally feeling, to quote Walt Whitman, 'afoot and lighthearted'. Then I became a social worker, and married Tom. My background, degree, and 14 years at home doing community volunteering and helping raise four marvellous children, enabled me to attract four challenging and fulfilling jobs during the last 20 years.

In case our personal Christian path is seen as representative of our membership, I'll tell a story. Early on, one of our members wanted to create an altar for devotions in a grove of trees on our farm. A few other members became alarmed. You'd have thought noxious poisons were going to seep out over the farm. When in doubt, we gather. Instead of asking for discussion on the issue of the altar, we went around our circle and each person spoke about his / her own spiritual journey. Only four or five of us regularly attended Church or Synagogue, which was quite a revelation. Everyone could speak about insights they'd had, books and family rituals that had been meaningful, and where that had led them. There was variety and commonality. Familiarity with other people's paths can lead to respect. The altar became a bare altar which anyone can use and leave ready for the next person. The crisis was resolved.

I had a dream some years before joining Community Alternatives that has served me well. It happened in the '60s, those years of group development labs, or T Groups as North Americans call them. I was deeply into an eight-day group process with a dozen others, and I was busy analyzing them all. 'Why doesn't she speak up more, she's bright enough and we're being deprived of her insights? Why doesn't he see he's in knee jerk reaction to anyone who tries to lead? Why does he have to speak at length on every topic? She treats everything with such cynical irony', and so on — it was very exhausting! I went down to the beach, fell asleep, and woke up laughing in relief. I dreamed that my head was on the belly of God, and that God was chuckling and saying, 'If they do all that changing for you, how will you know them in heaven?' I still make my judgements, 'offer feedback' as they say now, if given an opening, but now they're tempered with enjoying people as they are. They don't have to change just for me — as if they would!

People often say, 'How do you give up your privacy?' Well there had been six of us in our three-bedroom townhouse. Now that's density! Here in our 100-room house, outside our living space there is a common room with a piano and fireplace, a library on the top floor, a glassed-in meeting space, a room created for several members who collectively own video production and editing equipment, a room given over to twelve people who jointly own several computers, a games room, a craft room, a woodworking room, a large decked roof, and lots of interior courtyard. Pretty expansive! My private castle is my small bedroom.

That's an extrovert speaking. Community life has been more difficult for introverted Tom. He gets up at 5.30 am just to have a quiet, meditative start to his day. During one period he found a place nearby and only came home at weekends.

Every adult and every child has his/her own room, including children who only spend part of their time here. To be intergenerational was one of our early brochure-listed

PHOTO BY MICHAEL MARRAPESE

Community Alternatives members working in their productive garden

goals, and we spent time actually trying to define an adult/child ratio that might be appropriate! We decided to keep eleven free bedrooms available for children, and built that into our financial planning and membership selection.

We have a wide range of personal incomes, from professional incomes to almost poverty level, but living as we do, buying food at the pod level, sharing appliances and house upkeep, living near public transport, and being surrounded by a safe environment and friends, we have an enviable life.

It always amazes me the way our finances work, year after year. Between the city and the farm we currently have 46 residents, 11 of whom are children. An adult member must buy three shares, totalling $2,000. This covers voting membership in both the city co-op and the farm co-op, as well as in the overall Community Alternatives Society, a non-profit organization that lets us do a variety of external social action projects, maintain our rural/urban connection, offer a dental plan for all our members, apply for grants, etc.

Very early, in deciding how to pay for both the farm and city mortgages as well as have money to do some other projects we were already envisioning, we made a consensus decision to pool one-third of our income. I felt very proud of us. I didn't even know my brothers' and sisters' financial picture, but here was a young community ready to be open about their finances with each other, and commit considerable income.

When we were finally living together, however, sharing a third of our income proved unworkable. We tried various formulae and ways of determining a sharable net income. What about aid to an aged Grandma? What about payback of student loans or money into retirement funds? What about alimony payments? Finally, we decided on full disclosure of income, assets and liabilities, and a detailed personal expense budget, ending with a pledge. Budgets for city, farm, and Society are presented each year, and each member makes a pledge. It can take several meetings, until the pledges match the budget. Members' pledges vary from $200 to $650 per month. Tom and I together currently pledge $988, about 27% of our net income. That pledge will reduce next year when we're both on retirement income. Pledging can be both an agonizing and an inspiring process, but so far it has worked.

New members, however, are often paralyzed by this process. Sometimes they've never carefully budgeted or recorded their finances, and it's arduous! Putting it out for scrutiny is terrifying! I remember one member felt another was giving too much money in child payments, money that should have come to the community. Judgements around money are as fierce as judgements around sex!

I've mentioned Religion and Money, so why not Sex? I didn't join expecting my own monogamous, married commitment to be necessarily the norm, because in the early formative time it was obvious there were some more casual relationships in the group, and some unmarried couples. Over the years, we have celebrated marriages, couples have formed and split up, four babies have been born among us, we've had gay and lesbian members, and both fathers and mothers have done single parenting. Suffice to say, we're fairly representative of the rest of society — surprise, surprise. We're fairly discreet about each other's love lives, just expect mutual, non-abusive relationships. We've also, unfortunately, experienced the dark side. An early member sexually abused one of our children. We expelled him and saw him jailed; several of us keep in touch with him since he went into serious therapy.

Our size has enabled us to fashion a marvellous way of conducting our business. We knew from the start that we didn't want top-down leadership, or entrenched management. We wanted everyone to learn the various functions of leadership and good member skills. At the beginning, we used to say, 'Who wants to chair the next meeting?' After a lot of trial and error we evolved a system of creating a list of teams half a year ahead. Four or five people on each membership team are responsible for chairing, co-chairing, recording and 'vibes watching' for all the gatherings that happen during their month. We know that the agenda will be posted well ahead, and the team will have done their homework and preparation. We always close the meeting with a meeting evaluation.

Selection of new members is always risky. As new members are accepted, they become equal to each of the rest of us, old or recent members, so we must be ready for them to change us. An early member left because he said we were 'just a bunch of love puddlers!' He wanted more seriously committed social activists. The values expressed in our brochure, however, are assessed and reaffirmed periodically, and we ask newcomers if they see themselves on the same road. They are asked to come to our weekly communal Saturday dinner, attend a few meetings, visit the farm, and then we all wait to see if there is a mutual fit when there is a vacancy.

We place a high value on commitment to work problems out amicably, not retreat from conflict but hang in and communicate until an agreement is reached. I hate it when scapegoating and a build up of often exaggerated stories occurs. Soon there seems to be a move afoot to alienate some 'offender' to the point of wanting them to leave. I'm convinced that we are no model if we can't learn to live together when we are already selective in our recruitment process. Although we don't define ourselves as a therapeutic community, we have offered financial support for therapy if it's requested. For myself, each person has such mystery and complexity to them that the more I know them the fonder I get. I find the phrase, 'They're a mixed blessing', often sums up what I'm feeling, knowing it applies equally to me!

Recently we passed a series of guidelines to deal with behaviour we consider unacceptable. These are pretty ordinary expectations of people living communally, but there was a strong-felt need to be more explicit. In many areas of our life, members now are calling for definite procedures rather than the loose policies and expectations we have relied on until now.

So we ended up with a Respect and Responsibility Code — 'Community ODE' as we call it to get away from the 'Code' word. The Ode outlines seven areas of respect including for physical and territorial boundaries, emotional and verbal differences, personal and material diversity, and our differing approaches to community. And the seven areas of responsibility include attending community meetings, open communication, attending work parties, doing chores, working on planning teams, maintaining financial responsibility, giving information regarding one's personal situation which affects the community, and dealing with serious violations of the Ode.

This document didn't just appear out of the blue. For over a year one member who was experiencing an emotional breakdown got into conflict with several other members. He came through it, agreed to go into therapy, and is still with us. But as a result, an ad hoc committee worked on the above respect and responsibility guidelines, presented them, and after several meetings we affirmed them. There is some concern that they could become 'You're not OK' weapons. We'll see.

Front entrance to Community Alternatives

Right now, Tom and I live in one of the four-bedroom pods. When we joined Community Alternatives, David, our last child still at home, was eleven. He lived with us here until his last year of university. During those years we lived in an eight-bedroom pod. There are 3 eight-bedroom, 2 four-bedroom and 4 three-bedroom pods. When we were designing, we wanted five-, six- and seven- bedroom pods, in one marvellous octagonal structure, but it was turned down by the city as too unconventional. We ended up in this present compromise structure which the mortgagors thought could be converted into conventional housing. I liked life in the large pod but after nine years Tom found the density too stressful when he was working all day in a 'people' job, so seven years ago we moved to a smaller, four-bedroom pod. We're starting to talk about moving back to a big one again.

Talking about Ewan will give some of the flavor of life in Community Alternatives. Ewan had been around from our forming years. He was our oldest member, having joined when he was in his 60s. We had lived in the same pod with Ewan for eight years, and were living with him when he learned that he had prostate cancer. He was an inventive, entrepreneurial adventurer; started Vancouver's first flight training school when he was in his teens, was bankrupt by 21, wrote flight control texts during the Second World War, and owned a large manufacturing plant. He tackled his illness like a new challenge, became a health food nut, tried wheat grass remedies, ozone therapy, the works. But he finally collapsed one night, paralyzed down one side, was operated on and had a huge tumour removed from his back. Two more operations left him with drainage bags and extreme weakness; and he wanted to come home.

Ewan hated the hospital and he was a demanding, angry patient. As a pod we talked over bringing him home, and decided to try, not making too many promises. He was home the last six weeks, and over 30 members and friends provided 24-hour care, some in 2-hour shifts, some sleeping near him at night. He was amazing! Ewan let us do his intimate care with a rare lack of selfconsciousness, hardly ever complained or grumbled, loved company and nodded off if it got too much. He thought humour was good medicine and he loved funny videos. He never really went into a coma, just died peacefully one morning with one of us beside him. My own father had died some miles away from me, in a nursing home. What a contrast! We had a huge service for Ewan in our courtyard, and told some great stories. This was a bonding experience for us as a community.

Speaking of bonds, I love entering our farm property between huge cedar trees, and walking past the indigenous hazelnut trees that line the path. The fertile, damp land is sufficiently drained to be good garden soil. We have a huge greenhouse for all-weather planting. The house sits on a gravel hill. There's a small forest of trees in the middle of the property, with an elegant sauna along a path, and beyond that the top garden, fruit trees and berry bushes. An artesian spring provides lovely water in an undisturbed grove, and provides a lush spot for our Easter sunrise gathering.

The early city residents' gardening dream out at the farm faded, but once we had finished the city solar water-heating project, we were able to turn our attention to building a large new farmhouse out on our Fraser Common Farm. One of our early commitments was for both males and females to learn as many skills as possible in anything we undertook, as we had in the solar system. We hired a contractor who promised to help us plan and build the farmhouse ourselves. Unfortunately, he left with the building only about 60% complete. This resulted in the category 'towards farmhouse completion' in our budget for over ten years. We were distracted from spending money to create distinct space on the farm for the needs of the urban members. We call the farmhouse dwellers 'Pod Ten', to correspond to the nine pods in the city, and we're just now building a retreat cabin with its own toilet and shower, so that the farm dwellers can have their own home, and urban residents can enjoy time at the farm with separate accommodation. The property and farmhouse are nearly paid for, and now we're dreaming about renovating the barn for workshops, retreats, organic food networking, and other possibilities yet unborn.

Several years ago we started to tap our farm's productive potential. Four members were very serious about organic food production, and had become involved in permaculture. They came to the rest of the community with a proposal to create a partnership that would lease some of our farm and operate a 'Glorious Garnish and Seasonal Salad Company' business. These same people had also been movers and shakers in founding an organization that had worked with our provincial government to create licensing procedures for organic farms, and ours was one of the first to be licensed. The Salad Company became very successful, and our farm is highly regarded in the British Columbia organic and permaculture network.

One marvellous spin-off from living together with creative, innovative people is that we have initiated several businesses. We recently divested ourselves of a bakery/coffee shop we started to provide employment for a member's son who had a mental handicap. The new Society to which we donated the assets will continue to offer him work. Also, several of our members were crucial in creating a family-oriented cooperative restaurant that was innovative in its day, and is still popular.

Recycling and composting have always been a priority with us. We created a large rotary composter, fondly called 'Beulah', in our basement. It served us well for many

PHOTO BY MARET CHRISTIANSEN

Easter hats for Easter Gathering at Fraser Common Farm, Community Alternatives

years. Recently, several members raised funds to create a new model, designed for medium-sized apartment buildings. It's in the testing phase, with three units out on sites, and hopefully will find a market.

I couldn't finish without mentioning one of the chief fringe benefits of life here. We have fine musicians, singers and song writers who enliven our gatherings. For ten years a 35-member gospel choir group which included several of our members had free use of our common room for practices, and filled the place with song Monday nights. We're an easy bunch to party with. My courtyard retirement party with a live, mostly in-house band was unforgettable!

If this sounds like a little bit of heaven, well it is. Not that it's all constantly heaven on earth. Anyone living with more than just her/himself knows the ups and downs, agonies and ecstasies that go along with group living, but it's lively. As Andrew Marvell said, 'The grave's a fine and private place, but none, I think, do there embrace.'

*　　　*　　　*

It's been fun reminiscing. The sun is now going down over Burrard Inlet, I've been well fed, and it's time to retire. Four people have popped in and out, sharing news, passing on the latest gossip.

I'm now 65 years old and grateful to everyone who has given hours, months, or years to keep Community Alternatives alive. I hope more people will come along ready to attempt our lifestyle. A national Canadian magazine featured an article about us recently, with a note of admiration and envy — but the author didn't ask for membership! Oh well.

I love Community Alternatives and hope one day, far hence, to die here, like Ewan.

Members of Community Alternatives in the rain by the front gate

Introduction: Riverside and Chris Palmer

Chris Palmer,
Riverside

Riverside was founded in 1941 near Nelson in the north of New Zealand's South Island. It was originally comprised of conscientious objectors and peace activists - all with a strong Christian commitment. The Christian element of Riverside has partially lapsed, but not its commitment to peace, non-violence and justice. With about 55 members it is one of the smaller groups in this book, as well as the second oldest.

Chris Palmer joined Riverside in 1952 and has lived there ever since. He certainly did not come to communalism through the 'hippie-path' mentioned by other contributors, nor through a religious calling. Imprisoned as a conscientious objector during World War II, he started communal living at a time when it was not only unfashionable, but often condemned as deviant or subversive in conservative New Zealand.

I spent several days at Riverside in 1980 while undertaking PhD research. I was put to work picking plums, and was given a small room in which to sleep. The food was excellent and the work not so hard as to stop my sociological interviewing. I was impressed with the beauty of their property and the friendliness with which they interacted with the world - a world which had not always treated them fairly. Like all communal scholars, I had read about the Israeli kibbutzim, and to me Riverside was the closest to kibbutz life I had experienced. Its scale, communal economy and efficiency impressed me greatly, although even then the 'graying' of the Riverside communards was starting to become evident.

The best book specifically about Riverside is by Lynn Rain, *Community: The Story of Riverside 1941–1991* (Lower Moutere: Riverside, 1991).

'We welcome visitors to stay in our hostel, at present [NZ]$12 a night. We use the hostel for worker accommodation during our apple harvest so it may not be available during February, March or April. Please write first and make a date.' Potential visitors should write to the Visitor Secretary, Riverside Community, R.D. 2 Upper Moutere, Nelson, New Zealand (fax +64-3-5286061; e-mail: chrisp@riverside.org.nz).

CHAPTER 5

Riverside: Escapism or Realism
by Chris Palmer

My family arrived in New Zealand from England in 1923, when I was two. We lived in a small village, having a more or less 50/50 Maori-European population, 100 miles (160 km) north of Auckland. We had a small farm where we grew strawberry plants, milked a few cows and had a base for running 200 hives of bees. What follows will (hopefully) show how I, who grew up in the Great Depression, became radicalised, and how that took the form of membership in New Zealand's oldest intentional community.

I must have been incredibly lucky in my choice of parents. They were active in the Methodist church, and we grew up very aware that their religion was not an optional extra. They took it seriously in the sense that it was for every day and it reached out to those they met in their daily lives. During the Depression, Dad became involved with the local Left Book Club and I remember he brought home *Why You Should Be a Socialist* by John Strachey. The essentially Christian message in this little book influenced me greatly, and by the time World War II came along I was not only a convinced pacifist but completely disillusioned with the capitalist system.

In 1940 I went to work in Auckland as an apprentice motor mechanic. Going to the city from a small country village ('straight off the turnips', as a friend described it) took a bit of getting used to. I was a member of the Christian Pacifist Society, many of whose members were conscripted by 1941, and who appealed as conscientious objectors. We took our opposition to the war seriously, and spent hours discussing tactics and 'what-ifs'. I felt it was not good enough just to be against the war — some alternative to capitalist society was needed which did not automatically produce a war every few years. One suggestion we discussed was communal living, where cooperation rather than competition was the basis of life.

My appeal as a conscientious objector was dismissed by the court, and in October 1942 I was sentenced to a month in prison. This was to be followed by Defaulters' Detention Camp for the duration of the war. In Strathmore Camp my general outlook broadened, as my fellow inmates were from a cross-section of society. I had my first close contact with thinking men who did not find any need for a God in their lives. I was living and working with radicals of every hue, and I had access to all sorts of literature. Time was no object and debate was endless. Again the idea of communal living as a way of life was a subject for continuous discussion.

Life in the camps could be easy or hard, according to how one reacted. I felt that it was not good enough just to sit and wait for the end of the war, but decided to be more active in my opposition to what I felt was an inherently wrong set-up. A friend and I decided to escape and go to Wellington (New Zealand's capital) to publicise the evil nature of the camps and call for a negotiated peace. We saved up some food for the journey and went 'under the wire' at night, walking more than half of the 260 miles (425 km) to Wellington. We did this over the next ten days, mostly at night, while hiding during the day. In Wellington, we distributed leaflets explaining our position and also tried to obtain interviews with the Minister of Justice. In the end, I was arrested in Parliament House,

while my friend was picked up while holding an open air meeting. As a result, I was transferred to prison where again some of us went on strike and spent some time on bread and
water. After three months in solitary confinement, with more than half of it on bread and
water, I emerged somewhat thinner and looking like a 1960s hippie.

Prison was a great place for the reading and study which, by the time I was released
in May 1946, had convinced me that I wanted to be involved in communal living. To
prepare myself further, I needed to complete my interrupted apprenticeship and I was
fortunate to find an employer who was willing to take me on. As I was finishing my
apprenticeship in 1948, I explored, with others, the idea of a community based on several trades, situated in one of the outer suburbs of Auckland, with enough land to enable
us to keep poultry and to have a large garden. I felt that several trades could use the same
workshop facilities, with a big saving in overheads. Another couple and I explored this
possibility but we could not convince others to join us. That couple moved to Riverside
in 1949.

In December 1948 I married Jean Simpkin, a Methodist deaconess, and in January
1949 we went to work on South Bougainville Island with the Methodist Church. My job
was to maintain and service their boat engines and other machinery. Jean helped with
teaching sewing and domestic skills to the young women, as well as preparing lessons for
the Sunday School. I contracted polio in 1951 and was invalided home in August. I spent
the next year as an outpatient at Auckland Hospital and ended up with no movement from
the hip down on my right side, and limited strength in my left ankle. However, with a full-
length calliper and elbow crutches, I was fairly mobile.

Communal Living — At Last

Intentional community still beckoned. The couple with whom I had been
exploring communal possibilities in Auckland were at Riverside and I knew most of the
other men there, some from detention camp days and others from pacifist conferences.
They invited us to join, so August 1952 saw us, together with our 15-month-old adopted
son, moving to Riverside, near Nelson. I was still on a sickness benefit and did not have
any clear idea of how much I would be able to contribute physically.

Riverside was founded in 1941 when Hubert and Marion Holdaway gave their
37.5-acre (15-hectare) farm to start it. Eleven acres (4 hectares) were in orchard, the rest
pasture, which would not have been an economic unit if it was not that Hubert also
managed two other apple orchards. Hubert was a veteran of World War I who had become
a pacifist. He was an active leader in the local Methodist church from which several
young men went to detention camp and prison as conscientious objectors. Most of
Hubert's assistants on the farm during the war were women, or chaps who were waiting
to go into detention or who had their appeals allowed. With several ex-COs joining, with
their wives, in 1946–7, Riverside entered a new phase in its growth. By 1949 there were
seven young couples and one or two single men as well as the Holdaway family. The soil
here, known as 'Moutere gravels', is not rich, but the climate has made the area one of
the country's best for fruit-growing.

Minutes of the early meetings reveal only a little of the debate about the basis of
membership. At that time, members had to be both active Christians and pacifists. Most
were Methodists, one couple being Quakers, and later we had some Anglicans. To begin
with, there was very little ready cash and a 'common purse' was the rule, although this

changed after the war with newcomers wanting more financial independence. From then on, there was a small weekly cash allowance for each family. Various methods have since been tried to determine how much this should be.

As well as his own small farm, Hubert was in partnership with a brother who had land nearby. Riverside community eventually bought out the brother, bringing the total area up to the 500 acres (208 hectares) which we now have. Various legal structures were discussed but at last, in May 1953, the Riverside Community Trust Board was incorporated as a charitable trust, and all our assets were transferred to it in December 1955. This is still our legal basis of operation.

When Jean and I came in 1952, only six months as a probationary member was required. It was not necessary to buy in to the community (nor is it now) but one agreed to freeze one's assets, receiving and living only on the same cash allowance as other members. On becoming a full member, one was expected to hand over any personal capital assets to the community. Jean and I had a few hundred pounds plus a third share in my family's beekeeping business.

In the early days, Riverside had only one real house. Couples with young children lived in small cottages and converted army huts spread around the farm. The first house on the site which now forms our 'village' was built of rammed-earth, in 1947–8. Many of the early houses were of rammed-earth or soil-cement. We had plenty of trees and our own sawmill and joinery. We had no qualified tradesmen, but plenty of enthusiasm goes a long way when you are young!

In those early days too, there was only one tractor and little machinery. We still had three horses in active service and one of the amusing incidents, looking back, was when the two-horse wagon was being driven across the river when it was in flood. The horses decided that it would be easier to just go down-stream rather than to fight their way across! Eventually, however, they did manage to turn the tables on the river by coming up a neighbour's ford, and slowly and bedraggled arrived home.

New Zealand's postwar churches were pretty conservative, and few church people felt challenged to join an intentional community. At the same time, we were fielding more and more inquiries from non-church people. Finally, in the early '70s, we made the traumatic decision to accept people who did not make any claim to being Christian. Sadly, this caused our longest standing member to leave. Despite that, it is a decision I have never regretted.

We were what could be loosely called 'liberal Christians', however the Church was going through changes, as was society, and I no longer felt able to draw the demarcation lines as I had once done. In some ways, our new members seemed more Christian than some of those I knew in church. I certainly had more in common with them as far as general outlook was concerned.

I was deeply influenced by Professor Lloyd Geering of Victoria University, Wellington, and later John Spong of USA, and Don Cupitt of England, and was critical of the way church leaders and theologians had not done enough to pass on the results of biblical research to their congregations who were still thinking in pre-Darwinian terms. So, while I would quite like it if there were more here with whom I could share my Christian feelings, for these are still important for me, I believe it is more important that I share my attitudes about intentional community, which grow out of my Christian background.

Riverside today with workshops in front left, orchards and fields in rear, communal dining room front centre, plus residences around sports oval

Others may come here from a different way of thinking, but together we try to show a better way for society.

Riverside Today

We have always refused to acknowledge a leader or guru, and have operated on a near unanimous basis for making decisions, especially on major matters. But in practical matters, where people have special expertise, we feel it would be foolish to ignore their advice. Our decision-making body is our weekly community meeting, where all members have equal say. A chairperson usually changes after three months and secretaries just about weekly. Our adult membership is now down to 30, of whom 6 are over 70 years old. We have 24 children. Because of our aging population and the needs of small children, only about 15 are able to attend weekly meetings in the evenings. Our big decisions are made at our annual meeting which lasts several days in early June, after the harvest is well over. Most adult members attend. Our financial position for the past year is reviewed, and plans and forecasts for the next year are considered. We make long-term decisions about planting more orchard and/or forest, milking more cows or employing another member in the joinery or building another house. Each enterprise presents a report on its activities and performance. People who would like to change work areas can see if they can arrange a swap.

At this meeting, we approve plans for the different enterprises but within each work area the people doing the work are left to get on with the job within our general plan. Sometimes this has to be modified during the year but mostly the system works. The dairy farm, with its offshoot of fattening dairy beef and store lambs, and the orchard provide our main income. As well, we have a joinery which does our own repair work as well as outside jobs. We have a small pine forest which needs periodic attention, and our homes and buildings require regular maintenance. For years I worked in our engineering workshop, maintaining our own machinery. I also packed apples during the harvest season as well as doing tractor work. I had to give this up as the post-polio syndrome affected me more, and so I took over the office work instead. We now employ three mechanics, who are not members, taking in work from the general public, plus doing our machinery and vehicle maintenance.

PHOTO BY BILL METCALF

Riverside workshops with housing behind

There have been times when members worked outside the Community. For more than ten years a member was also the local midwife, delivering babies at home. Naturally she delivered many Riverside babies too. Another member set up a rural training unit about 20 miles (30 km) away for the Intellectually Handicapped Children's Society. Another helped to set up various employment schemes at the local Maori cultural and social centre. The Rudolf Steiner Kindergarten in Motueka, about 5 miles (8 km) away, was run for over ten years by one of our members who was born and raised here. One of our members has set up PlaNet Nelson which is our local area's connection to the Internet. All income derived from outside employment goes to our common funds, and the member employed outside lives on the same economic basis as the rest of us. Special clothing allowances are available, and we provide a car where necessary.

It is not easy for those working outside to feel the same involvement as when participating in the everyday working of Riverside, so we prefer new members to work here. A new probationary member still works three days a week at the Nelson Polytechnic, about 30 miles (45 km) away. The extent to which this lack of involvement is a problem depends on the person and on their previous experience within the community.

Another aspect of work which has sometimes been a problem is when parents wish to job-share. If a man is working in the orchard it is not always possible for his wife to take over what he is supposed to be doing the next day, just because it is her turn to work and his to look after the children. Some jobs lend themselves to this better than others. We have never had a full-time creche to enable both parents to work, although for short periods we arrange child care to enable a specific project to be done. We believe that until children are at school it is a mother's right to stay home to look after them. Once all of her children are at school, the mother should contribute economically. Many children go to kindergarten during the mornings, and this allows a mother to take part in communal activities.

Over the years we have tried various social get-togethers. Before my time it was folk-dancing, later on music or card evenings. We have held biography evenings where we each shared the story of our lives. Working bees as well as communal meals, however, seem to best promote a sense of community. We started with having lunch together three times a week, then added the evening meal on Saturdays which could more easily be followed by talk, cards, Scrabble or TV. We celebrate special occasions like Founders Day, and in May we have a special meal with a colourful display of autumn leaves, flowers and produce to celebrate the harvest. The children spend the morning carving lanterns from orange pumpkins. It is dark by the time the evening meal is over and the lanterns are lit. We all march up the hill, ending up around a blazing bonfire for music and singing. We have Easter egg painting, a winter solstice party, a special Christmas dinner together, as well as a picnic at the beach on New Year's Day. When we joined, we used to go carol singing at Christmas. We would load onto one of the horse wagons, complete with Christmas tree and Santa Claus. A local retailer provided sweets for distribution, and we would set off, stopping to sing at intervals along the way, following a circular route home. These occasions give the opportunity to develop closer contacts with members with whom one does not work.

I have always felt that a basic reason for communal living was that by pooling our resources, we should be able to do together things which an individual would find outside his or her reach. Because of our particular concern for social justice, Riverside gradually came to be a place where alcoholics and ex-prisoners could come for a second start. Our contacts in welfare agencies phoned us when they needed a temporary home for someone in need of 'time-out', for whatever reason. To this end, we decided to convert

PHOTO BY JEAN PALMER

Communal dining room at Christmas

some unused buildings into two small, self-contained units which can be made available for non-members who have this need. We do not have qualified counsellors but we can provide a supportive environment and offer a little work where this will help.

I remember, years ago, being amused when Riverside received a letter from another community, suggesting that as we had been going for over 20 years, we should have good advice on solving problems of personal relations and tensions. I was not aware that we had any particular expertise! Looking back, I realise that it was very much a case of 'If it's too hot, get out of the kitchen'. I am sad about that, and I believe that the mediation techniques which we now have would have overcome some of the situations which arose previously. It is easy to be aware of poor relationships between members but very difficult to know what to do about it. I think that most of those who are attracted to communal living tend to be idealistic and strongly individualistic. This runs counter to the necessity to be prepared to lose some of that individuality for the sake of the common good. For communal living is just that: I can't get away from it while I'm here so I have to make it work. Occasionally, there is a need for mediation, and we have several members who are available to act as reconcilers. If their efforts prove inadequate, we seek more professional help.

Over the years, we have attracted many new members. They seem to come as a result of casual contact rather than from any outreach on our part. When a membership inquiry is made, we supply general information and if the inquirer wants to take it further, we ask them to come for a fortnight's visit. During that time they can work in various departments, talk with people and swap ideas. They share our communal meals and are invited to our homes for meals and to get an idea of how we live. To enable intending members to know our expectations, we have in our library a folder of our 'Agreements'.

Because of our pacifist background, we have always had a strong involvement in peace activity. This has resulted in public protest on many occasions, one of the first being over the referendum on compulsory military training. Since then, we have participated in vigils on the cathedral steps and on the wharves, whenever an American warship has visited. When the South African Springboks were to play rugby in Nelson in 1981, two of us held a protest banner opposite the main entrance to the sportsground. The police ordered us to leave, we refused and so they sent a constable to protect us from being hassled! Jean and I have also been involved in protests over Maori land, taken illegally by Governor Grey in 1853 and not returned until about three years ago.

People who are radical in one area of life tend to be radical in others. So the communal movement is attractive to vegetarians, environmentalists, home-birthers, as well as to people from alternative education and farming. Riverside has always obtained most of its income from our farm and orchard, using conventional methods. Many of us are interested in organic techniques, but commercial reality forces us to use sprays and artificial fertilisers, as well as a range of drenches to keep our stock healthy. When a member proposed that a newly planted orchard be turned over to organic production, we were unable to agree to this, so he and his family left. We have since managed a small apple orchard, together with a couple of acres of thornless blackberries, on a bio-dynamic and organic system, but economics has now forced us to return to conventional methods. We are caught in a bind. Some of us would prefer to have only organic production, but at the same time we realise that we are growing export apples and a way has not yet been found of doing this commercially *and* organically.

Our organic vegetable garden was a picture for years, when run by an enthusiast who worked many more hours than is expected of members. We are slowly getting back to a lesser though still useful production but weed control by organic methods is laborious and backbreaking.

Basic to Riverside's form of intentional community is the aim of financial equality and independence for each family unit. Each adult member receives a fixed cash allowance, and care-givers receive a fixed percentage of this for each child. When the cost of living changes, we adjust our allowances accordingly. Children over ten, who wish to, can get paid work at graduated rates, collecting eggs, milking cows or doing other farm work.

As well as sharing the burden of Riverside's debts, we also share the use of a limited number of vehicles. This is one of the more difficult things to become used to, when joining. Private use is paid for by the member at a low mileage rate, but for medical and similar purposes the cost is carried by the group. All medical costs are also the group's responsibility.

We expect members to act responsibly in decision-making. This used to be by large majority, but years ago we changed to consensus. We have recently modified this so that one person cannot prevent action. If one person objects, the matter 'lies on the table' for a fortnight. If, in that time, the objector cannot find someone else to agree with his or her point of view, that objection alone is no longer able to hold up the proposal. This rider is fairly recent and has only been used once.

One of the things that Riverside has demonstrated is that it is possible, as well as desirable, to have all age levels represented in our membership. Our older members still have a valued presence and feel wanted. Being in that group, I am able to work at what suits me. I don't feel that younger members would prefer me to keep out of things, and I know that I am welcome to offer suggestions. As I become more decrepit, I will no doubt spend more time at home and attend fewer meetings. If it is possible, without becoming a burden on other members, I plan to remain at Riverside until I die.

A community should be a good place in which to bring up children, and despite the tensions and other difficulties which any communal group generates, Riverside still is. Most ex-Riversiders like to visit us when opportunity offers. I was amazed recently at the interest shown and the obviously good memories held by a visitor from Australia. He was here for less than three years, over thirty years ago, and he wanted to show his wife the Riverside which had meant so much to him.

Because our membership system has discouraged those with capital from joining, and there was no way by which a member, on leaving, could extract funds which had previously been handed over, we needed to make some provision for departing members. Most members have not put in large amounts of money, but a few years ago, one brought enough to enable us to build a large house. Our difficulty was to make provision for people leaving, regardless of how much capital they had contributed. The first family to leave, after we came, had their expenses paid to a job in the North Island, plus the equivalent of a month's allowance. In the 1960s we made a cash grant of about ten weeks wages for each year of membership. This helped a couple of families to make a new start. Later, it was agreed that the length of membership should not be the determining factor.

Now, if a family or single person has been in permanent membership for three years or more they are entitled to 80% of a year's cash allowance, regardless of how much they contributed on joining. If less than three years, it is calculated proportionately.

We have had neighbour problems over the years, of course. During World War II, Riverside was not looked on favourably because of our war record — or rather, lack of it — and Hubert was pushed out of the Fruit Growers Association. After the war, some returned soldiers demanded his reinstatement, others left and bitterness resulted. Another of our members, a Methodist local preacher, was banned from preaching because he had the temerity to advocate a more charitable attitude to homosexuals. But, with our immediate neighbours, we have good relationships.

Within our group tensions have also arisen. In the late 1950s there was a minor revolution over our admission into full membership of a divorcee. But we survived that, and she lived here until her death. We asked one couple to leave because they had so little in common with us, and yet they expected us to carry them. Sexual stereotyping has raised problems, with some Riverside women feeling that their contribution has been devalued, and their opinions and feelings ignored. We value both women and men, and try to prevent sexual stereotyping from affecting our decisions. We are but a segment of society, however, and as such we suffer the usual social ills: our teenagers get into trouble, and we have family breakups with all the resulting trauma.

One couple has been lucky in that four of their children chose to return to Riverside and become members, after having left in their teens to gain qualifications. Three of them are still here and raising families. Children of other families have been members, including our daughter Judy. We encourage our young people to move out when they feel ready for it and we make cash grants to enable them to attend university or polytechnic, as well as offer them employment during vacations. Others, like our son Clive, have worked at Riverside after leaving school, before moving out into the world.

Conclusion

While my ideas have changed over the years, I am still as convinced as ever of the need to challenge the assumption that the free market offers the best way forward for society. I still think that the rich elite who are in control of things need to be muzzled. The accumulation of possessions is not the be-all and end-all of living, and the only way to convince others of this is by demonstrating a better way of life, based on communal living and cooperation. We can't achieve happiness and find personal fulfilment if we make those things our main aim in life. But those things will come to us, as a by-product, if we are able to develop right relationships with people and our environment.

I see a problem in how moral and ethical values are taught and passed on from one generation to the next. The church has tried various methods but has not found an answer. It does not seem to be something that can be taught in school — so what works? I believe that ultimately it is not possible to teach ethics. They are learned by following the example of others. I am convinced that if we want a more sharing and caring society, and a more cooperative way of relating to one another, then there is an important place for intentional communities. We are not able to opt out of the capitalist rat-race entirely, but I am sure that we at Riverside do have something to show the world.

Ultimately, the only influence I have is the life I lead.

Introduction: Auroville and Bill Sullivan

Bill Sullivan

Auroville was founded in 1968 during a UNESCO endorsed international gathering to which handfuls of soil were brought from around the world to southern India to help start 'the city the earth needs'. Auroville was founded on the philosophy of Sri Aurobindo (after whom it is named) and was largely brought into being by a French devotee known simply as The Mother. Auroville was on the hippie-route across Asia in the 1970s and has attracted many visitors and much publicity, both good and bad. It went through various stages and almost collapsed at one time under legal threats. Today, Auroville has over 1000 members and is one of the largest groups in this book, although it is less communal than many of the others.

Bill Sullivan joined Auroville in 1974. His story takes him from his conservative American childhood and adolescence, through training to be a Jesuit priest, to college lecturing, until finally finding himself at Auroville. Bill is the author of *The Dawning of Auroville* (Auroville: Auroville Press, 1994), the most comprehensive book I have seen about this fascinating communal group.

Guests are welcome to visit Auroville, but must always arrange in advance. Auroville has many reasonably priced guesthouses where visitors can stay for about US$7 per day. The nearest city is Pondicherry, from where there is easy access. Enquiries should be made to the Visitors Centre, Auroville 605 101, Tamil Nadu, India (phone: +91-41386-2239; or fax: +91-41386-2274). Auroville can also be found on the Internet in various websites (search: 'Auroville'). *The Dawning of Auroville* is available by sending US$11 to CSR Office c/o the above address. Cheques should be made out to 'Auroville Fund' specified *Dawning of Auroville*.

CHAPTER 6

Auroville: 'The City the Earth Needs'

by Bill Sullivan

The First Tree

My back rests against the massive Banyan Tree at the centre of a town being born. This tree marks Auroville's start on a barren, eroded plateau in South India.

An out of season rain has just fallen and broken the intense summer heat. Everyone and everything rejoices with the rain, the birds of the evening and the crickets of the coming night. The music from local village loudspeakers is faint enough to enhance the scene rather than jangle nerves. Florida Golf grass carpets the area around the Banyan, defining the Garden of Unity, part of twelve gardens to come. In front of me is the huge geodesic sphere of Matrimandir with its 'Inner Chamber' and 'Crystal' ready, while construction continues. Huge earthen 'petals', covered with grass and red sandstone, slope upward to surround this 'soul of Auroville'.

Nearby, I see the lotus urn in the amphitheatre where, in 1968, 5000 people applauded young representatives of every nation putting a symbolic handful of earth from their country in that urn.

PHOTO AUROVILLE ARCHIVES

*The Banyan Tree
at the center
of Auroville*

What began then is part of a much longer story. I adjust my back to a more comfortable position against the Banyan. About 10,000 BC, ancient Vedic seers sat here under the trees and broke through into what they called 'uninterrupted light' and 'the honey in the rock'.

Am I dreaming about paradise? Is the reality around me suggesting a future that will be overwhelming? Do I want to carry these words in my mind back to the computer, or am I more worried about telling a story of Auroville so loaded with my stuff? Hey, it's pretty personal!

Well, so what, everybody has an equally significant story, a dream within, and if our sharing can help, let's do it.

1944: World War II, California

A small boy sits with his back against a massive oak tree on a warm summer afternoon. The breeze bends the grass which is higher than his head. The boy is alone, his picnic is packed in a gray steel lunchbox. He sits in a hay field that borders his home. The breeze drops and the insects pause. The little boy experiences a timeless moment of oneness with the universe.

That little boy is me, and yet how many times during my life have I forgotten about this experience, an experience which has the power to reconnect me to life.

1959: University of San Francisco

'Wake up and piss, boy, San Francisco's on fire!' drawls the Army Captain, Professor of Military History.

Startled out of my daydreaming by this unforgettably quaint remark, I do. God, is he right! Not only is San Francisco on fire, but the whole bloody planet! Something has to be done. I will drop out of the university. That will only become fashionable years later when the flower children of the '60s begin to tune in, turn on and drop out. Even the Peace Corps has not yet been invented. What to do? For the final examination in my speech course, I denounce the university for its lack of ideals, and rip up the college catalogue in front of class, and stomp on it a few times in case the message isn't clear enough. My university career, begun so enthusiastically at 17, finishes abruptly at 19.

1959: Trinity Alps Wilderness Area, California

From the end of the road, a trail begins along a mountain stream. I climb into high valleys where deer are grazing, and continue into the upper bush where a startled bear runs from me. When I reach the timber line, I see the rare species of Weeping Spruce, a tree that grows only here. Higher are jewel-like lakes, granite boulders and scrub brush. Close to the peaks, I camp and wait. I watch the millions of stars each night and wonder what to do. I hope to save the world. How's a nice, middle-class, Irish-American Catholic going to do that at 19? University is a disappointment. Beer and parties are great but it's not enough. I stretch out on a flat boulder under star light bright enough to reflect in the lake and outline the peaks on the horizon.

A strategy comes to me. I will join the Jesuits. A couple of them at the university have impressed me with their dedication and sincerity to contribute to that ideal society which I feel has to replace the present madness. My uncle was a Jesuit, but his sudden death at 33, during my childhood, left me with a sense that he was cheated. Philosophy and religion fascinate me, and this would be my opportunity to get to the bottom of that stuff. The decision is not easy and I sense the long haul ahead, but my messianic complex carries the day.

1968: Chabanel Language Institute, Taiwan

My calculations on how long it is going to take me to learn Chinese, after already a year of difficult study, are discouraging. My plans to save the one billion Chinese with educational television goes on hold. I set off a firecracker in the teachers' room and leave for the Philippines.

In Manila, a Jesuit school needs an English teacher, and my unused MA degree will help their accreditation. I crammed in the academic ritual of graduate school to get that degree during my intense seminary years, partly, I realize later, because it was said that I couldn't do it. Those four seminary years were in the medieval monastic style beginning at 5am with an hour of meditation. A strict daily order, programmed to the minute and announced by a bell, is not as harsh as it sounds. I got caught up in the enthusiasm of the challenge, and the peace and splendor of the setting in Santa Cruz Mountains, California. This carried over to my next seminary, at Mount St Michael's in Spokane, Washington. Gradually, the inconsistencies of the Great American Dream, and the fallibility of One Holy Catholic and Apostolic Church become more evident. My response was toward reform, ecumenism and new frontiers. I chose China and mass media.

Choose again! The Philippines are in a political and economic mess, with Marcos and the American corporations in charge. There is nothing to do but fall in love with the people, and enjoy introducing kids to literature.

The school is run by a tough Basque Jesuit, and we have some good fights. I am recalled by the California Jesuits to mend my ways and study theology. Priesthood is the carrot held out in front of me.

1970: Graduate Theological Union, Berkeley, California

God is dead but there are plenty of awkward attempts to revive Her/Him. Berkeley is beautiful. I begin to chart my own course, heedless of the sleaze of academia and ecclesiastical dogmatics. It does not go down well. It does not go down at all, in the end. If you argue for birth control in a moral theology course, you fail. If you tell the Rector of the seminary that Jesus comes to an interdenominational communion just as much as to his Mass, you are not only wrong but a heretic. If you go to jail while demonstrating for social justice for farm workers, you can't be trusted to obey the Bishop who wants the support of agribusiness. My colleagues advise me, 'You know what they want to hear, you have to play the game until you get into a position to do what you want'. That makes me sick. As the tension builds, I decide to try a massage workshop. While being massaged, my tension is relaxing so much that I begin to sob uncontrollably, and to breathe with such force that I think my rib cage will crack open. Instead, I go out of my body, observing the scene from the ceiling, and comment, 'Look at that guy making a fool of himself!'. I could read the thoughts of people in the room, and some were quite concerned. The woman leading the workshop says, 'This sometimes happens, he will be all right. Let's gather round him and gently support him'. Just after that workshop, the Jesuit in charge of the California area calls me to a meeting. I feel the inner strength to be completely honest. I say that the Church, as an institution, has little contact with the spirit of Christianity, but operates on the basis of political and economic motives. He replies, 'You can't be trusted to obey, we withdraw all support from you'.

1973: Palos Verdes Peninsula, California.

A small path winds along the edge of sheer cliffs. The Pacific surf explodes on the rocks below. I stroll along this path toward sunset. An Irish cleric, at the end of his health and career, is my companion. We are employed to teach at a dying college on the hill behind us. We attempt to teach students who need no qualifications to enroll, except the fees. Even understanding English is not required! I was hired as an economy measure — one teacher for three different departments: Film, Theology and Philosophy. He and I laugh as we walk. Sometimes we walk against the wind or into the fog, and always the sea is powerfully present. I am teaching a course called Eastern Religious Disciplines. 'You're teaching that and you don't know Sri Aurobindo?' is his comment that wakes me up. Though I have never heard of Sri Aurobindo, the famous Indian Yogi who has been called the 'Guru of Gurus', I am deeply impressed when I start studying him. The philosophy of Sri Aurobindo becomes a focus for our seaside strolls. By the time we get to Savitri, the 24,000-line poetic epic that Sri Aurobindo worked on for 50 years, I am stunned. The power of his poetry speaks directly to me; 'One could drink life back in streams of honey-fire / Recover the lost habit of happiness'.

I bring to the beach a three-foot (one-metre) thick manuscript of my own epic poem and burn it with relief. That work of creatively condensing all of world thought, epics ancient and modern, known and unknown realities, has already been done in India, in English, and published in 1950. The disparity between his achievement and my attempt is such an abyss that transforming mine into ashes and smoke is the pure joy of dropping excess baggage.

In the college library, I read the Winter 1972 issue of *Cross Currents* magazine in which Robert McDermott surveys Sri Aurobindo's work. He includes some writings from The Mother (1878–1973), and describes an intentional community in South India which she has founded to live what is talked about. Started at the end of the '60s, and named after Sri Aurobindo (1872–1950), Auroville received the endorsement of the United Nations and many organizations throughout the world. Who is The Mother? What could Auroville be like?

The Mother turns me off, not because she seems to know everything, but because of the way people respond to her with a certain devotion, and because of my suspicion about cults — I'm not shaving my head or anything like that! I read more about The Mother and she is really quite amazing as child prodigy, mystic, seer and artist. I am still not convinced about my connection to her.

I walk out again along those sea cliffs of the Palos Verdes Peninsula. My former companion is now very ill. Alone, I stare out at the power of the sea. I begin to laugh because something bizarre is happening. The sea is The Mother and the words in French sound the same, 'mer' and 'Mère'. The pun is more than funny. The universal mother, mother nature, mother earth, The Mother in Pondicherry, India — yes, that's it! Why didn't I see it before? Then, The Mother tricks me by dying at the age of 95, just before I can go to meet her. I know enough to leave for Madras, India, immediately.

1974: Ami Guest House, Auroville.

I lie dying. Fever is burning me up and my body is so weak I can't move. 'Oh, you'll be all right in a couple days', says Dawn who runs the place with her brother, David.

When I arrived in Pondicherry, India, a few weeks before, I thought I had contracted a terrible tropical disease. Little red bumps broke out all over my body and itched horribly. The hospital could not help, only giving me some unlabelled tablets. Fortunately, I met an old British lady who said, 'That's just prickly heat. Take a few soapy showers and it goes away'. She was right.

But now, lying in what is called a 'guest hut', but is merely a little thatched pyramid tied together with coconut rope, my end seems sure. I keep complaining, 'My God, what a way to go!' However, Dawn is also right.

On an old bicycle, along sandy tracks, I try to discover Auroville. It's somewhat disappointing. There's nothing but very depleted rural landscape, a few villages in desperate condition, and a strange mixture of people seeking a new world that requires a new species of human being to make it work. That 'superperson' is destined to evolve from the current one. That could take a while, I estimate, but Auroville is attempting to accelerate evolution, right? It's very hot and sweaty. Flies, mosquitoes and ants are the dominant species. I know no one. Many Aurovilians tend to be unfriendly and 'preachy'. What am I doing here? My plans to do a film on Auroville for New Age Productions, USA, are abruptly cancelled when the producer decides to do fire-walking and trance states in Bali. 'Come with us first to Bali and then we can always do Auroville', she says.

It's too late. Auroville already intrigues me. I hear about another film-maker, in Canada, interested in setting up his studio and printing press in Auroville. 'You check it out', he tells me. I write that things are pretty primitive here, so he'd better come and see for himself. He comes but decides against it. He returns to Canada and loses nearly everything in a forest fire.

1975: Matrimandir Gardens' Nursery

Auroville is seeping into my blood — the red, rock-hard soil, the stark palmyra trees, and the mystic Banyan Tree at the center of everything. When I first look into the big hole next to the Banyan and see Matrimandir, a massive foundation of concrete and steel just emerging above ground level, it is a shock. My mind cannot reconcile the feeling of something like a space station with this rural desolation and stone-age conditions. Yet the sounds of grinders, vibrators and pumps are very real. At night, the feeling is like stumbling into a secret camp of extra-terrestrials building an outpost.

A Dutch Franciscan priest, who is also a sociologist, called Matrimandir the 'House of the Third Millennium', and worked daily on it until he died of a heart attack a few years ago. He published his dream of the finished complex describing its inauguration in the year 2000. We become good friends.

I join the 'concretings', those collective happenings where most of the Aurovilians turn up to pass and pour the huge quantities of concrete needed to build this 'soul of Auroville'. These work events are just about the only social life of the community.

I'm living in a falling-down, thatched bamboo house in the Matrimandir gardens' nursery, among the flowers and seedlings. I rebuild the house, experimenting with a free-form ferro-cement roof and an indoor garden, and make 61 windows in the little, one-room house. My work is mostly with tree seeds. The priority is to get as many trees growing all over the place, as fast as possible.

Everyone rejoices 20 years later that Auroville has planted more than 2 million trees to help restore this bioregion.

Raji and Bill planting trees

1975—1985: Dream Emerging Into Form

Life is basic, simple and work-oriented for most of the 300–500 of us building 'The City of Dawn' as 'the cradle of the new world'. Not everyone shares the same idealism, but some inner flame keeps us together and working. I eat in one of Auroville's community kitchens called Centre Kitchen where the food is basic, simple and oily. Each of the 80 participants in the kitchen collective is required to cook once and clean once each week.

One guy claims that because he worked on the construction of the kitchen, he is exempt from cooking and cleaning. No way! He's quickly booted out to eat on his own.

In the mixture of so many personalities and cultures, the evolution of the new world order might be described, positively, as still being in the frontier stage.

While continuing to live in the nursery, I shift to construction work at Matrimandir, where I fall in love with a beautiful Brazilian botanist. She is wonderful! Although we attempt to keep the relationship as spiritual as possible, it still is delightfully sensual. We love to go to the beach, and though the Auroville beach is not Rio, the coconuts and frangipani flowers are there, and with a little imagination a feeling of tropical paradise arises.

Auroville, on the other hand, turns into a battlefield. Since The Mother has physically departed, others rush to take her place. A Bombay businessman, turned ashramite, had been entrusted by The Mother with the legal and financial arrangements for Auroville, and now feels that he has somehow inherited everything. He and his group live mostly in Pondicherry, and attempt to manage Auroville without us residents' consent. There is a protracted struggle which compels Aurovilians to work together against forces that have all the odds on their side. Miraculously, the Indian Supreme Court eventually rules in favor of Auroville, and the Parliament enacts the 'Auroville Foundation' to legalize Auroville as belonging 'to humanity as a whole', and to ensure that the ideals of its charter are encouraged:

Charter of Auroville

1. Auroville belongs to nobody in particular. Auroville belongs to humanity as a whole. But to live in Auroville one must be a willing servitor of the Divine Consciousness.

2. Auroville will be the place of an unending education, of constant progress, and a youth that never ages.

3. Auroville wants to be the bridge between the past and the future. Taking advantage of all discoveries from without and from within, Auroville will boldly spring towards future realizations.

4. Auroville will be a site of material and spiritual research for a living embodiment of an actual Human Unity.

During this turbulent time, Auroville gradually grows and establishes services and infrastructure. Pour Tous (For All), Auroville's food distribution system, also becomes a financial service and coordinator of activities. Assets are all considered to be communal, but their creators can use them according to generally agreed guidelines, so I can still use my toothbrush and my motorcycle! Everyone can keep their own money and contribute when and where they wish, but commercial profits earned in Auroville belong to Auroville, and their use must be decided collectively. A formula to meet this ideal is still evolving. The system of no cash exchange within Auroville has only evolved to computerized credit systems on the organized level, although a great deal of direct sharing goes on through personal arrangements.

The weekly Pour Tous meeting becomes a general town meeting to deal with policies, the newest proposal and the latest crisis. The work areas of education, farms and dairies, forest, Matrimandir, business, health and the rest, all function more or less autonomously.

Auroville's many community settlements, scattered over a 25-square-kilometre (10-square-mile) area, varying in size from one person to seventy, also develop their unique styles of living. Contrasts can be extreme, ranging from back-to-the-land, green-belt communities to elegant town houses.

All kinds of people join Auroville. Some I like, some I don't. I guess they must be here to push my buttons, and 'outline the parameters' for Auroville's research in human unity. Daily, hundreds of visitors arrive to ask endless questions: 'Why don't you do more for the poor villagers?' 'Do you like India?' 'How old are you?' 'How many children do you have?'

Earths Stewards Peace Trees Program in front of Banyan Tree and Matrimandir

1996: Tomorrow Starts Today

Now, with more than 1000 community members and 3000 other people working for Auroville, our future appears ever more interesting, not to mention challenging. The big questions are not answered, the ideals are not realized, but there is definitely something here that can be experienced by almost anyone.

I always want to understand Auroville. Maybe most people who come try to figure out what they see, but the explanations are not catching the experience. I know that I see mostly what I want to see, while others want to jerk my chain toward what they think.

My Auroville is loaded with impossibilities at many levels. Yet, in a very physical way, I experience that everything is possible here. It is still hard for me to believe that we could plant so many trees, and that they grew, and that they actually have an effect on the atmosphere of this area.

During the years of Matrimandir's construction, miracles became commonplace. I'm especially in awe of the spiral entrance ramp because for two-and-a-half years I was part of its building team. We started with a pile of large, rusty steel pipes which had to be fashioned into a long, elegant, ascending, spiral curve that could support its own weight plus that of people walking on it. Our first efforts indicated that it would take about 20 years to build — and still might fall down. Yet it's there, and all the people using it don't walk up it quite as lightly or proudly as I do. At the top of this ramp is a twelve-sided room of white marble, with a white carpet, and air-conditioned comfort. A transparent, crystal glass sphere is in the center. The room is illuminated by a ray of sunlight that falls on the crystal. The room is used only as a quiet space, 'a place to try to find one's consciousness', as The Mother remarked. She saw this room in a vision, and gave its precise description more than 20 years before it happened. I still find this pretty amazing!

The Dalai Lama visiting the Auroville Banyan Tree, with Matrimandir in background (1993)

The Last Word

What to say about Auroville? Trying to write about Auroville has frustrated me for years. Suddenly, I write a book about Auroville (The Dawning of Auroville, Auroville Press, 1994). I could do it because my favorite story from childhood, heard over and over, and then forgotten for more than 40 years, is given to me again. Friendship Valley begins with the world on fire. The author was a German-American writing during World War II. In this illustrated children's story is a forest fire and all the animals have no escape except through the untravelled Black Gorge. A river runs through the gorge and they must all work together to quickly construct a raft. Quarrels break out, but a female squirrel is able to organize the necessary cooperation for the last minute escape. They rescue a couple of refugees on the way, a kitten and a frog. Their journey is full of adventure until they arrive in the new land where each one is needed to build the new society around a very large tree. The frog which they rescued saves the community because only he is able to dive deep enough to recover the key lost in the lake. This is the only key to the door of the winter food supply . The kitten who had lost her mother is raised by the community, and one Christmas the old trader rat who journeys through the mountains reunites her with her mother. A rat cares for a cat? This story that delighted me as a child now makes a little more sense because I am living in a community built around a very large tree.

The aims of Auroville are embarrassingly ideal, even outrageous for some. On top of it all, it is in India! The founder of Auroville saw India as 'the representation of all human difficulties on earth, and it is in India that there will be the cure. And it is for that, it is FOR THAT, that I had to create Auroville'.

Who Has the Last Word?

I get up from the Banyan Tree and go a few minutes down the road to the CSR (Centre for Scientific Research) which was just a memorandum in my bag in 1984. Now I can even have a choice of many computers on which to record these words, but my problem is that if someone happens to read them, besides Bill Metcalf, what sense will she/he make of them? I reflect on what I wanted to know about Auroville before I came. I needed the context of Sri Aurobindo and The Mother's evolutionary approach to creating the future for a new human species. That requires *you* to read them — not me! Our schools, development programs, eco-projects, business units, and our art and culture scene could all be described — but I'm too lazy. Anyhow, some people here say that this is not so important because it might distract you from the 'inner work' which, if you don't do it, renders all the rest useless. Make what you can of that!

Aurovilians are pretty arrogant, and like to be considered as a class by themselves, while lumping others into 'groupies', 'sectarians', 'eco-freaks', 'bourgeois liberals' or something. Auroville is supposed to be a very fundamental place, born out of a great need that burns in everyone, and which goes beyond anything we can make of it. Can you see what I mean about arrogance or extravagant inflation?

After so many years of listening to the questions of people who sit in front of me and ask who and what is Auroville, and seeing them leave, unsatisfied with my answers, I should say that there is no Auroville. It still has to be created. And you have to create it out of yourself, in concert with all the others who are also in some way part of yourself. But isn't there a system of governance in Auroville? There is not one system but many, with the final responsibility not on some authority figure but on myself. The Auroville

PHOTO BY JOHN MANDEEN

Bill Sullivan (left) demonstrating an electric bicycle to engineers attending a conference at CSR

Foundation is a formal, legal structure with an international board of 'eminent people', and a national board of 'eminent people', and a committee of not-so-eminent Aurovilians as a liaison, and a fourth group which is all the Aurovilians who are supposed to have all the power anyhow. No one here will say that this is Auroville, while the Foundation is something else. But these groups, and Auroville's work-related groups, do deal in procedures and guidelines needed for organizational functioning. They try to avoid fossilization and all the ills endemic to institutions. There is a freedom that makes some feel insecure, others feel a great opportunity to learn, while for others it is the air they need to be creative. Still others complain that Auroville is becoming as conventional as a government bureaucracy.

It's now dark outside, and everyone has gone home from CSR. Before I go, as I look around the office, I want to say more about CSR because it's such a great place. Can one prove that water tastes better when pumped from the ground by a windmill rather than with a diesel pump? Does solar-cooked food taste better than gas or electrically cooked food? What science will tell me? Seriously, scientific research at CSR is applying, in the field, certain good ideas that other people have already researched, but which don't always work until one keeps improving them. We started with biogas tanks — that led to building in ferro-cement — that led to stabilized earth blocks and helped one of our architects get the Hassan Fathy International Award for Architecture for the Poor in 1992. I boast about this place because I have known it from day one. It came about without any of us deserving the credit, or having the least idea that it could really come to this. CSR promotes renewable energy — solar, wind, biomass. That's life, isn't it?

*   *   *

I'd better go home now to Aurogreen, an organic farm started in 1975, on barren land, by Charlie who still milks the cows every morning and evening, and manages the farm. Tine, with whom I live in the cosy limestone house she designed, will be wondering why I'm so late. We have no children of our own, but two are running around Aurogreen, the daughter and son of Kumar and Sumathi. Suzie is a teacher who has lived in Aurogreen longer than the rest of us. Laxman is a music teacher who also works on the farm. Our little community usually has a guest or two. Tine has horses (Sarama and Hasina), dogs (Ram and Dharma), and a cat (Schneeball), all of which Tine considers to be more special than I do. 'I'm going to be busy today, do you mind taking in the horse buckets?' Sigh! I do like them all — a little! Tine doesn't think very highly of men, in general, but she does admit that they are sometimes useful. Today, she's going to ask me why I didn't sweep the terrace this morning.

'Well, I was in a hurry and you know I've got a lot to do to save the world.'

'Could you please go get the bread.'

After all these years in Auroville, I know that saving the rainforests, reafforesting the Himalayas, or stopping the spread of the Sahara, ending the wars around the planet, and most other things really can be done.

'Okay, I'll go get the bread.'

What else can a middle-aged boy do after a hard day of messianic work?

Introduction: The Farm and Albert Bates

©ALBERT BATES

Albert Bates

The Farm is one of the best-known intentional communities, appearing in most serious anthologies of communalism, as well as in magazines and newspapers. The story of Stephen Gaskin and the 'hippies' from San Francisco who moved to rural Tennessee in 1971 has often been presented, but often incorrectly. The Farm is near Summertown, south west of Nashville in central Tennessee, USA. The Farm has undergone many dramatic changes since its founding but remains a fascinating community whose global relevance increases with time. In this chapter The Farm's story is brought up to date.

Albert Bates, trained as a lawyer, joined The Farm in 1972. I have known Albert for many years. We both serve on the executive of the International Communal Studies Association, and have met several times at international conferences, most recently at the Ecovillages and Sustainable Communities Conference at Findhorn in 1995. Albert is a practising lawyer, a committed activist and a successful author, his best-known book being *Climate in Crisis* (Summertown: Book Publishing Company, 1990).

I stayed at The Farm for a week in 1982 while conducting my PhD research on intentional communities. It had about 1200 residents, and was by far the biggest and most complex communal group I had seen. I stayed with about 20–30 members in 'Canned–Heat' (one of the communal houses), worked in the potato fields, ate soybeans and tofu, and gathered sociological data. The Farm was a very impressive commune!

The Farm is very much into cyberspace and in fact much of the www system was developed there. To obtain more up-to-date information, try URLs:

http://www.thefarm.org   http://www.envirolink.org/gaia/farm
http://www.gaia.org/farm   http://www.well.com/user/cmty/farm
http://www.ic.org/farm

'Because the villagers at the Farm enjoy the peace and quiet of their surroundings (and don't see themselves as living in Disneyland) they ask that visitors write or call in advance, or attend one of the regularly scheduled conferences and other special events hosted by The Farm. There is a small hospitality charge for unscheduled visits, presently $5/day. To contact us, call or write: Vickie Montagne, 34 The Farm, Summertown, TN 38483, USA' (Phone: +1-615-964-3574; or e-mail: thefarm@gaia.org).

CHAPTER 7

The Farm: Tie Dyes In Cyberspace
by Albert Bates

As I write, rain pelts the walls of my cabin, and trees bend at a 45-degree angle outside my window. Here, on the highest ridge between Cincinnati and New Orleans, we are feeling the remnants of a hurricane which struck the Gulf Coast yesterday. Hurricanes like this take me back to 1972 and a hurricane named Agnes.

A few months before then, I had hiked up to the most remote place I could find, a place called Isolation Shelter, in the middle of the Desolation Wilderness. There, I holed up in a pine lean-to, doing a ritual of self-purification. I'd rise at first light, stretch and sit *zazen*. From time to time I would take some walking meditation, a dip in the river, or do tai chi chuan. Occasionally I would read, usually Buddhist Scripture like the Platform Sutra. At midday, I'd take a simple meal. At sunset I'd bed down. One morning, as the sun rose over the mountains and lit the river rock, I had what might be called a peak experience.

In the 1960s, an amazing number of us suddenly awoke from the sleep of normal consciousness and saw more clearly. I had my share of religious experiences, out-of-body excursions, flashes of revelation and dumbstruck mind-bends. And because it felt right, I encouraged the flow of that sort of thing instead of rejecting it as insanity, indigestion or Satanic possession. I kept getting deeper experiences, going further, seeing more.

This experience at sunrise in the middle of a mountain stream was life-altering for me. I finished my last year of law school and got my degree. But my career path as a lawyer in New York City seemed unrelated to my religious growth as I looked at things in an odd way. There is a Buddhist saying, 'Do not seek after enlightenment, neither linger where no enlightenment exists'. The longer I cleaved to the conventions of the city, the more my cognitive dissonance grew. Soon I found my way back to my center, which seemed to be in the mountains. I began a four-month hike south along the Appalachian Trail, with no particular destination.

The first night was my last quiet night for two weeks. The wind came up and the following day a light mist turned into a downpour. I hadn't checked the weather reports before I left, or I might have known about the enormous swirl of air building up above the Atlantic Ocean and heading my way. I spent one day in a shelter, but eager to hike and figuring the rain would end, I shoved off the next morning. For several days I climbed along a mountainous ridge-line through a storm that grew in ferocity. On a clear day I had made as much as 20 miles (30 km) on the Trail, conquering numerous Appalachian summits. A poor day, in rough terrain, I covered only 10 or 12 miles (15 km). Now, a week into my trek, I was lucky to get 3 miles (5 km) in a day. I negotiated rocky slopes that were sheets of muddy water, and when I reached a summit, I couldn't stand upright in the wind. Down in the piedmont, large branches fell around me. Up on the alpine, high winds and lightning were a constant threat. The valleys were flooded so that each time I came to a river I had to divert for several miles to find a way across. When I emerged from the wilderness at the Delaware Water Gap, my pack was soaked and my tent fly torn to shreds by the winds. I hadn't been able to start a fire for days. When I warmed myself by a wood stove in a country store, the storekeeper took pity on me and offered me a job bagging dried fruit. I stayed a few days, peeling my blisters and shaking off a cold.

When my gear was dry, I returned to the mountains. There were more ordeals along the way, but I found a kind of stasis, an ability not merely to survive adversity, but to thrive on it. During good weather, I gathered and dried wild foods, and baked bread in my campfire. I darned my socks and padded the places where my hiking gear rubbed against my body. After 103 days I found myself perched on the highest mountain in Tennessee, 1000 miles (1500 km) and 200 mountain summits from where I began. Rather than continue south into Georgia, I decided to cross Tennessee and visit a place I had read about, a place called The Farm.

*   *   *

As I'm writing this, a strong blast of wind shakes my cabin. The building is framed on scrap telephone poles and huge timbers salvaged out of a 100-year-old tobacco barn which we, The Farm building crew, tore down in 1973. The cabin is rugged and can take whatever the storm can throw at it as it sits comfortably perched on a 100-foot (30-m) cliff above the confluence of the Cox Branch and Cow Pen creeks at the headwaters of the Swan River. It's my refuge in the storm.

The Farm was one year old when I arrived in 1972. The group that had settled it was older, having begun meeting in San Francisco in 1967. Stephen Gaskin was an Assistant Professor in the English Department at San Francisco State University when he noticed that he was losing his best students to the adjoining Haight-Ashbury district. He began holding alternative classes in Greek philosophy, I Ching, magic and mysticism, yoga and different religious teachings in an attempt to lure the hippies back to school. When these classes outgrew the college venue, Gaskin moved into the Straight Theater, then Glide Memorial Church, and finally the largest place he could get, a rock hall called the Family Dog. Because Monday was the only time he could get the hall, the meetings became known as Monday Night Class. Over several years, the classes grew to as many as 2000 people, coming every week to listen to the man known simply as 'Stephen'. Stephen never claimed to be a guru or leader. He said he was simply a teacher, and that if you learned anything, so much the better — you didn't need him any longer.

As the group evolved, however, it began to take the shape of a congregation, and it reached consensus on certain principles which were called 'agreements', the central thrust of which was that great, pure effort must be directed toward harmlessness, right livelihood, right thinking, etc., while maintaining a sense of humor. In keeping with this thrust, the Class adopted certain standards of conduct, which were required of all members. These included nonviolence, vegetarianism, voluntary poverty, social equality, no unhealthy practices, and fiscal and personal responsibility.

Put all the world's religions on IBM cards, Stephen said (showing the state of technology at the time), hold the stack up to the light, and the holes where the light comes through were the genuine principles. Those principles would work for you in religion, but equally well in business and social relationships.

We are all part of the same system, a vibratory harmonic of particles and waves without borders, no separation: an attosecond-to-attosecond dance of coming into existence and annihilation. If you begin to build on this understanding, the differences between people — race, gender, age and ethnicity — all melt away and you find yourself making friends and establishing intimacy. Monday Night Class was also called by Stephen a 'school of change'. Change comes from the spiritual plane, he said, from decisions made from your highest aspirations. Anything else is just 'moving the furniture around'.

Late 1970, the American Academy of Religion held its annual meeting in San Francisco, and a few academics and clerics happened by the Dog on a Monday night. Recognizing the phenomenon as a unique and refreshing experience, several delegates approached Stephen and invited him to speak to their schools and congregations. A tour was arranged, and Stephen prepared to adjourn the Class for four months. Before he left, many in the Class asked if they could come. 'Sure', he said, 'get yourself a bus'. When they left San Francisco, they were 80 buses strong! After circumnavigating America and returning to San Francisco, the caravan group had merged tighter, becoming a community on the road. Stephen and 320 of his 'students' headed to Tennessee to find a suitable home-base where they could put their 'agreements' to a real-life test.

*   *   *

When I arrived, I was sent to a 30-foot (9-metre) army tent called Sumac Road, which had no running water, a crude latrine, a dirt-floored kitchen, and wood-plank beds for its dozen male inhabitants. Showers were in the communal bathhouse, without regard to gender. There were no gender distinctions in the community kitchen either, and we took turns watching the pots of boiling soybeans and wheat kernels.

That first winter was so lean we refer to it today as 'Wheatberry Winter'. Having got a good deal on a truckload of wheat, we boiled, fried and steamed wheat in dozens of novel recipes. To many, the austerity of The Farm was a test of faith and endurance, a shakedown cruise for our new paradigm of voluntary peasantry. To me, after four months in the rugged wilderness, living at The Farm was cushy. Kerosene light, a roof, wood stove and a bed off the ground, what more did people want? But what kept me at The Farm, beyond my curiosity, was the deep ethos and deeper relationships. It was like coming into contact with an advanced civilization, one that spoke its own dialect and had its own subtle sciences.

I was captivated by shorthand terms like 'figure-ground' (not seeing larger concepts because of attachment to detail), 'self-other' (placing too much importance on individuality), and 'into the juice' (misfocusing and squandering group attention on selfish interests). The daily crew meetings, the chance conversations in the lunch line, and evening discussions over a group pipe of marijuana, betrayed a substrata of intellectual rigor refined by years of discourse.

In what little spare time the rugged work afforded, I lit kerosene lamps and slowly read through typed transcripts, notes and narratives of Monday Night Classes, hoping to catch a glimpse into how such thinking evolved.

I met Stephen shortly after I arrived, but because of their travel schedule, it was more than three months before I met him and his wife, Ina May, again. I thought that by then I had gained some basic understanding of the group and of Stephen, but what I had was still superficial. I came up to Ina May from behind her in a dinner line and waited for her to turn around so that I could introduce myself. She did, and I did, but a very curious phenomenon occurred which left a lasting impression. It was not merely that she glowed with a rosy cheer, but that when I met her eyes, I felt a strong electrical sensation, a fin-ger-tingling of energy. It has been my good fortune to meet many individuals who have strength of character and great presence, but Ina May's tangible electricity was unex-pected and astounding — virtually paranormal — and she didn't have to say any more than 'Hello, nice to meet you'.

My job in that first year was working on the horse crew, delivering water, plowing fields and picking up kitchen wastes for composting. When I married another horse driver, Cynthia, I moved out of Sumac Road and into a slabwood lean-to on Oak Ridge.

Eventually, our turn for 'new' canvas came, and we received an eight-sided, Korean-War vintage army tent which we set up on Hickory Hill, one of the more remote parts of The Farm. Pregnant with our first child, Cynthia would walk a mile across steep ridges and valleys to the Soy Dairy, where she pressed tofu and experimented with fermented soy inoculants like tempeh.

When our daughter Gretchen was a year old, I brought home a pony to carry her along with the groceries and other supplies. Eventually the tempeh trials became a tempeh business, and Cynthia went to work full time. I left the horse crew and became a brickmason, then a flour-miller. Gretchen joined the 'kid herd', The Farm's term for day-care.

We had many interesting visitors in those early days. We were proselytized by the Baptists and Hare Krishnas, approached by pyramid-energy salesmen, 'wanabe' Indians and 'spiritual consultants' of all stripes, and entertained by gypsies on horses, bicycles and vehicles with no detectable means of propulsion. One fellow was a 'Tomatarian', meaning that he ate only tomatoes. We sent him to work on the farming crew, but it was difficult to get much work out of him because he'd take a tomato break every few minutes. He even talked with tomatoes in his mouth. I guess if you are living on toma-toes, you have to eat a heck of a lot of them.

PHOTO BY ALBERT BATES

Digging potatoes on The Farm

One visitor indicated that he was deaf and dumb, so we sent for someone who knew sign language. After they tried signing with him, he wrote that he didn't know how to sign and wasn't really deaf. After several hours of our being really friendly with him, he started talking! He had acted deaf and dumb for years because he was severely inhibited. We sent him to join the farming crew, and he was a better worker than the Tomatarian. He eventually became outgoing, having many stories to tell from the years he was deaf and dumb.

An odd phenomenon in those days was that time slowed down. Walking to Tennessee was a slow way to travel to begin with, and I was no stranger to taking time to smell the roses. Those early years of The Farm — waking by the sun's rays; eating food in season; walking from one place to another, without phones, electricity, radio, television, plumbing or money exchange; and no cares about world politics, fads or fashions — had the effect of s-l-o-w-i-n-g things down. Each day was memorable, complete and special. Laughter came quickly. Children's laughter was everywhere. Everyone smiled, and even the grimiest tasks were performed with a sense of ironic humor and resignation to enjoy them for their character-building qualities, and opportunities for camaraderie. Hard work was its own meditation, and we learned that if you got bent out of shape, you had no one to blame but yourself. It was all in how you held your mind.

Over time, school buses became pumper trucks for emptying outhouses, flatbeds for hauling lumber and, of course, houses. School buses gave way to tents which we bought cheaply at government auctions, then patched with scrap canvas and carpet cement. These tents gave way to 'touses' and 'hents' — olive drab canvas blossoming with stud walls and insulation, greenhouses, tin roofs, dormers and stone foundations. A number of the houses on The Farm today had such humble origins, their secret occasionally betrayed by scraps of canvas peeking through joints in their cladding.

In 1980, the State Police made one final attempt at shutting us down. Some nutty hitchhikers told police they had been forced to work in the marijuana fields at The Farm, so a helicopter was despatched. Spotting what they thought was an illegal crop growing in neat rows in a weedy watermelon field, the police informed the Attorney General, who saw it as his ticket to everlasting political glory. Sparing no expense, the Attorney General marshalled a strike force of state, county, and local police who descended at dusk on The Farm, in a fleet of off-road trucks and unmarked sedans, with hundreds of uniformed officers, dogs and live feeds to the TV networks, backed up by helicopter air-support. Unfortunately for the political future of the Attorney General, who spent the night sitting in his limousine at our gate, frittering away a $50,000 budget, The Farm had no drugs, alcohol, tobacco or firearms. After an all-night search, all that came out of the watermelon field was ragweed (a legal, if unwanted, crop) and squashed watermelons.

The media had a field day. A radio station had a special effects sound of a watermelon being squashed by a helicopter landing strut. One cartoonist put out a 'Dick Tracy Crimestopper Textbook' showing watermelons in one panel and marijuana in another — 'Know the difference!' We joined the fray by launching a $7-million lawsuit against the Attorney General for violating our civil rights — but telling interviewers that we might settle for a truckload of watermelons.

As the 1970s passed, we outgrew our youth. We were inundated by visitors and would-be communitarians who had no understanding of what had gone before, and often weren't interested. We lacked liturgical forms and we shunned rituals as a matter of principle, which made it more difficult to integrate newcomers. We made mistakes in organization, finance and resource management. All these factors contributed to a fall from the agreements that created The Farm.

During the early 1980s our consensus was that The Farm must be more open to larger numbers and types of people, be more easily and generally replicable, and be able to exert greater influence on social, political and environmental policies of mainstream culture. This was the excusable source of the compromises that diluted the founders' original vision. The effects of opening up the permeability between the dominant culture outside and our micro-culture of The Farm were mixed.

Certainly the cultural cross-fertilization with Native Americans — particularly our close working relationships with Guatemalan Mayans, the Lakota Sioux and Six Nations Iroquois — was salutary. Likewise much was gained by direct, personal experience with The Farm's charities in the South Bronx, Southern Africa, Bangladesh and the Caribbean Isles. Rotating people, especially teenagers, from The Farm through very poor and oppressed communities, and rotating poor and oppressed peoples through The Farm, endowed both sides with invaluable perspectives, realism, purpose and hope.

However, at a size of 1200 to 1400 members, most with less than five years experience in the counter-culture, The Farm became increasingly difficult to manage in keeping with our 'agreements'. With varying degrees of understanding and practice among newcomers and visitors, and a disproportionate ratio of 'raw recruits' to 'boot-camp instructors', the group process was too often unfair, uncompassionate and unfun. Hierarchy was resented, but in the hands of the unskilled, principles of open consensus-building were misapplied, and a few disgruntled members turned large meetings into personal podiums for intransigent complaining. Attention to vibes, fiscal responsibility, avoidance of antisocial drugs, devotion to simplicity, elevation of community over individualism, and other founding principles had been shunted aside to satisfy lower order goals of open admission; diversity of lifestyle; free legal, medical and midwifery services; and free rock and roll.

The unravelling of The Farm as an institution characterized the period 1981 to 1985. The compromises of earlier years bore fruit as distrust of the founders, the communal system and the structural integration of spiritualistic, moral standards within business and family life. There was a lack of agreement about the purpose of The Farm, the ownership of property, standards for using mind-altering substances, the relationship of earning capacity or personal wealth to voting and residency, and a host of other basic elements of community cohesion.

From 1971 to 1983, The Farm had a 'communal purse' like the Shakers or Hutterites. By 1984, problems in agriculture and other enterprises had led to a reorganization to give individual members a choice between simple membership and collectivity. Since then, voluntary simplicity, in the sense of non-monetary subsistence, has not been merely eroded but has been strongly discouraged, because failure to meet the $85–$100 per month 'rent' obligation of every adult member has become grounds for sanctions, including expulsion.

Dependence on some favorable trade relationship with the outside culture is now an unavoidable concomitant of residency. Personal income and income security became matters not merely of concern, but also of emotional debate, both within families and within the community. To outward appearances, the liberalization of The Farm provided tangible improvements in our economy and diversity of our community. Inefficient, labor-intensive community services were cut back or eliminated, a steady budget reduced community debts to manageable levels, and marginally democratic processes replaced earlier, never-ending mass meetings and default rule by pragmatic oligarchies. Our roads were improved; our water supply system was certified; houses were clad, insulated, remodelled and landscaped; and business revenues stabilised.

These structural changes came at an appropriate time for our woodland ecology. Abandoning the attempt to make profits from farming, we reduced our agricultural area and went to more intensive and Permacultural farming methods, relocated outlying neighborhoods that impinged too deeply into the hardwood forests, and zoned off more than half our land from any development other than to encourage natural biodiversity.

By 1990, the 'agreements' that characterized The Farm's cultural identity had taken a considerably different tack from the prevailing winds of earlier periods. Decision-making by small, elected councils had largely replaced facilitated group process. Rules about lifestyle had virtually disappeared, except for those against overt violence. Nuclear family households supplanted large group households and extended families. Virtually everyone had a car, telephone, flush toilet, electricity and television. Many people had access to a computer and/or a satellite dish. With paving of our main road, The Farm has become increasingly difficult to distinguish physically from a planned community enclave for fixed-income retirees.

*   *   *

When decollectivization struck The Farm, I was in the midst of juggling a half-dozen lawsuits, the most pressing of which was against the Nuclear Regulatory Commission before the U.S. Supreme Court, and which attempted to shut down the entire nuclear fuel cycle as unconstitutional. I also had a case before the Tennessee Supreme Court seeking voting rights for State prisoners. Despite this active legal practice, when I looked up from my desk, I found I had no visible means of support.

PHOTO BY CYNTHIA BATES; ©FARM NEWS SERVICE

From his law office on The Farm, Albert Bates holds a press conference to announce a lawsuit against the Sequoyah Nuclear Plant, circa 1980.

When my two children had all the tofu and carrots they could eat, for free, from The Farm Store, I had no worries. However, when our store, school and clinic started charging, life changed. I would wake up at night in a cold sweat. During the day I'd take calls from the grieving widows I represented, while at night I'd look into my children's eyes and wonder where to find grocery money. I seriously considered abandoning my environmental law project and getting a 'real' job.

I worked 70-hour weeks. Gradually my work began to be appreciated by a wider audience, and that support not only put food on my table, but also gave me the courage to push even harder. The nuclear case lost, but Tennessee prisoners got the vote. The Air Force was forced to do an environmental impact statement on nuclear winter. My climate studies led me to create my now well-known textbook on global warming, *Climate in Crisis*. My writings and public talks got noticed abroad, and I now find myself being invited to international conferences on sustainable development and intentional communities.

*   *   *

Today, a conflict of values is brewing — the pressure valve being our young people. The children born in the peak fertility years for The Farm's founding families are reaching maturity and independence. A child born in 1972, when The Farm was settled, is today 24 years old. During the 1970s, more than 2000 births occurred on The Farm. Owing to the mobility of the American population, and the changes in The Farm, most of those children did not grow up here — but at least 100 of them still call The Farm their home. That makes young adults the largest segment of the population of The Farm (which hovers around 200 people today), and their values are having a significant impact on our community.

Some of the children now living here left The Farm when their parents departed during the reorganization in the 1980s. Outside, they often found themselves out of step, not only with their mainstream peers, for whom violence, drugs and antisocial behavior had become almost banal, but also with their neo-suburbanite parents, who suddenly seemed hypocritical, cutting their hair, donning ties, heels and cologne, and arguing about money. Many marriages ended in divorce; many children had emotional problems: some went to jail, some got mixed up with the wrong drugs, and some ran away from home. But quite a few rediscovered The Farm, kept contact with their cohorts, and made pilgrimages here to find their roots.

While the teenage years are often a period of disillusionment with and disaffection from parents, the distance travelled to reach this point within The Farm is very great because the departure is from the heart of the intention underlying our intentional community. An intentional community is not necessarily dependent on its children for survival. There are many historical examples of groups which have lasted for extended periods, primarily through recruitment of new members from the outside society. But an intentional community is very dependent on the maintenance of its intention, as its raison d'être.

In the early years of The Farm, everyone was committed to a lifetime of spiritual growth. Every book on every bookshelf was a religious classic (the dire shortage of paper for kindling wood fires and stocking commodes having culled all but the most closely held tomes). With no electricity for television or radio, discussions on the seat of the horse wagon, in the rows of peppers, or in the double-holed outhouse tended toward the arcane: Was Casteneda putting us on about Don Juan? What did we think about Black Elk's astral travel? Was Milarepa a sap? To imagine such discussions occurring today is fantasy. Partly, we have talked those things to death already and aren't impressed by the new books and teachers around today. And partly, these are different times.

We may be farther from the impractical, utopian dreaming of our youth, but we are closer to realizing much of the social agenda of the '60s. In the early 1990s, one could walk into the office of the Governor of Tennessee, and the first three or four people encountered would have been on the caravan that founded The Farm. If you surf in cyberspace, many of the terms you are using and protocols you are following were devised and vetted at The Farm. We created the radiation detection system that is used today by government agencies monitoring the world's nuclear sites and smuggling points. We constructed some of the largest photovoltaic arrays in the world and founded one of the first solar car manufacturers. We developed the doppler fetoscope, and published a simple cure for shoulder dystocia, an often-fatal complication of childbirth, in the *Journal of the American Medical Association*. Our soybean recipes are coming into universal use. The Farm continues to have the influence it wished for.

The Farm is managed by a seven-member Board of Directors (elected to overlapping three-year terms) which lets contracts for road and water works, while a Membership Committee (also seven members) arbitrates disputes and adjusts rents. Our communal society operates as a Committee of the Whole, deciding questions of policy and finance by consensus minus 10%. Neighborhood groups meet informally, usually deciding by a show of hands. Businesses, be they partnerships, corporations or worker cooperatives, operate formally on the basis of quora, proxies, notices and ballots.

*   *   *

The Farm is my home and refuge, but not a hideaway. We are a sanctuary from the harsher turmoils of the world, but we are also very much a part of carrying the struggle to resolution. What keeps me here is our forests and clean brooks, the lifetime friendships of those who share my dreams, and the serenity of being at home with a community that celebrates life, love and the spiritual essence of the human journey. What keeps me going out to battle 'the beast' is the certainty that comes from examining the problems facing our future, understanding their global dimensions, and feeling a human responsibility to act.

Recently, a group of us, made up largely of second-generation members, have started 'reinventing' The Farm, trying to refashion it less as an eclectic, hippie collective and more as an ecovillage. In 1993–94, we held a series of planning meetings which brought together members of The Farm with representatives from several national and international organizations involved in sustainable development. With myself as the first Director, in late 1994 we opened The Farm Ecovillage Training Center whose mission is 'to provide a whole systems immersion experience of ecovillage living, together with classes of instruction, access to information, tools and resources, and on-site and off-site consulting and outreach efforts'. Since then, we have offered a number of short courses in gardening, alternative methods of ecological construction, midwifery and health care, and sustainable forestry. Each course, as well as the construction work at the Center, has provided paying jobs for the 15 to 20 year olds of The Farm. This Center has also come

PHOTO BY ALBERT BATES

At home with a community that celebrates life, love and the spiritual essence of the human journey

to serve as a meeting place for The Farm gatherings, women's circles, board meetings and neighborhood potluck dinners.

Recently, young Farm adults began hosting Sunday circles entitled, 'The New Farm'. Some of these open, outdoor discussions have been about values, some about social structures and individual responsibility, and others about material improvements to our community. To me, the most important aspect of these meetings is that they were initiated and kept going by young people who act like they plan to remain here, perhaps for a lifetime.

To build a sustainable community, we have to be willing to set aside land for nature. Biodiversity then flourishes. We have to save seeds, build soils and protect water. Our food supply is thereby assured. Lastly, we have to make it all come together for the next generation, which means it has to be relevant, even inspirational, and might even be fun. Actually, it had better be fun or no-one will want to do it.

*   *   *

The gale outside my window is growing in ferocity, but the quiet of my cabin is warm and energizing. It is a safe harbor in the storm, built on the knowledge of what storms are capable of doing. When the weather is good, I will repair any damage to my roof and gutters, pick up the downed limbs and windblown debris outside, and divert any newly forming gullies on the slope above. One thing hurricanes have taught me is that surviving comfortably when the wind is blowing depends on how much effort you put in when the sun is shining. The Farm had a unique role in the history of the 1970s. Given the scope and caliber of our activities in the 1990s, our best is still to come.

Albert Bates

Introduction: Yamagishi Toyosato and Atsuyoshi Niijima

Atsuyoshi Niijima
in front of
'the elders house for living'

Yamagishi Toyosato is the largest of the many Yamagishi communes in Japan and, with 1600 members, is by far the biggest in this book and one of the biggest in the world. The first Yamagishi commune was established in 1958, while Toyosato was established in 1969. There are now Yamagishi communes also in South Korea, Switzerland, Germany, Thailand, USA, Brazil and Australia. Toyosato produces and markets a wide variety of foods, and also operates several schools and numerous smaller businesses. It is located in Mie Prefecture, between Tokyo and Osaka.

Atsuyoshi Niijima was a university professor and a China scholar who became interested in Yamagishism in 1959, and became actively involved in 1971. In 1972 he and his family joined Toyosato. He is currently writing the history of Yamagishism.

I would like to acknowledge the diligent and conscientious work of Ikuo Kishi, a fellow Yamagishi Toyosato member who translated Atsuyoshi's several drafts for me, and my copious feedback for him. Ikuo's patience and hard work are appreciated.

Visitors are always welcome at Yamagishi Toyosato, provided that they make contact beforehand. Write to Kokusai Bu, Yamagishism Society Toyosato Jikkenchi, 5010 Takanoo Cho, Tsu Shi, Mie Ken, Japan (Phone: 81-592-30-8028, or fax 81-592-30-8029). From this same address information can be gained about Yamagishi communes in other countries. Several times each year special events are held to help visitors learn about Yamagishism and Toyosato commune.

CHAPTER 8

Yamagishi Toyosato: In Pursuit of an Ideal Society
by Atsuyoshi Niijima

I am the oldest of seven sons, born in a small rented house in Tokyo. My father had come to Tokyo to work for a publishing company, after he left the school where my grandfather was schoolmaster. Soon, my father set up his own successful publishing business. It is likely that he never held a hoe in his hand, or grew anything. My mother, from a silk-raising farm family, graduated from a women's high school, a rare occurrence in those days. My parents both came from Kyushu Island where they were brought together in 1927 through a traditional arranged marriage, the normal Japanese courtship for that time. The next year, I was born.

There is an old Japanese saying, 'like a dressed medicine bottle', referring to a person who is always sick — and that was certainly me! I had chronic digestive troubles, and then I contracted infant tuberculosis. I was skinny and too weak to play school sports. When forced to take part in races during sport days, I always found myself the tail-ender, being bullied by boys of my age.

Those times were very hard in Japan. When I was one, the Great Depression began. At three, the Manchurian Incident occurred, and when I was nine, Japan's war against China spread. When I was 13, Japan plunged into the Pacific War. I was horrified to hear the word 'war'. When our teacher asked us to raise our hand if we wouldn't become a soldier, only I did so. I meant that I could not become one, although the teacher probably meant who didn't want to become one. I believed that such a skinny, sick person as myself would not pass the conscription examination. The teacher kept me standing while condemning my 'disloyalty'. He pointed to me as being unwilling to become a soldier for our Emperor, while I shed tears of humiliation and mortification.

Because it was near my home, I attended a missionary-run high school, where I was able to learn farm work. It had a practical subject where students went to a small farm for half a day's work each week. I was told to work at my own pace so that I could hoe and plough in accordance with my strength, not competing with my classmates. On my way home at dusk, I felt the satisfaction of being useful to society by working on the farm, rather than by becoming a soldier.

My period of relative self-satisfaction ended in January 1944, with the mobilisation of all Japanese students for factory work. Nevertheless, I was able to remain involved in farming because of the serious food shortages. Our staple food, rice, had been rationed since April 1941. My family had moved to a suburb of Tokyo which was surrounded by abandoned fields, since most farmers were away at the war. My mother rented 10 ares (1/4 acre) of farm land where she grew wheat, potatoes, buckwheat, pumpkins and spinach. She was experienced in farming, so we reaped a good harvest of wheat but our potatoes were destroyed by bad weather.

Our house, as well as my father's business, was destroyed by Allied bombing on July 25, 1945, just as hostilities were about to cease. In August, the Pacific War finally ended, but a severe food crisis followed. Rice-rationing extended to grains and potatoes, with allocated amounts so small that to feed oneself only by rationed food meant to starve.

One of my schoolmates told me that he would be temporarily absent from school to help on his family's farm, and he suggested that I join him because they were short of workers. Instantly I agreed, since plenty of food would be available, and I could thereby help to feed my family. With the help of my friend's mother, each month I would buy 36 kilograms (75 pounds) of wheat from a nearby farmer who would never sell grain to a stranger. I carried the wheat home on my shoulder, having to walk five kilometres (three miles) to the nearest station.

Farming was hard work and I often felt utterly exhausted, especially after having to push a heavy cart, like a mule. But farm life was not always so hard. I enjoyed delicious, rich meals, sometimes including eels which we caught in a trap. Every night my friend and I read philosophy books and talked for hours, dreaming of an ideal society. Our farm life was like a commune where I could use anything in my friend's house. There, under one roof and eating at one table, lived eleven people; my friend's grandpa, parents, six sisters and brothers plus two hangers-on like me.

My friend and I went back to Tokyo early in 1946, to find political turmoil. Like most young people, I drifted to the political left as a reaction against militarism. In 1947, while still a freshman at Tokyo University, I joined the Japanese communist movement. I saw communism as offering utopia, an ideal society, just like the farm life I had enjoyed in my friend's house. Wartime life had given me the frightening experience of the impossibility of buying food. It proved to me that the survival of my family and myself depended on our friendly relationships with other community members, particularly with those growing food. I entered into communism believing that through that political ideology I could develop a more humane and just relationship between people.

In 1948, however, my tuberculosis reocurred and I took five years to recover. During this time, I intensively studied Chinese language and culture. When well enough, I started to work as a China scholar at a Japanese research centre from where I published numerous scholarly articles and books on contemporary China and Chinese history, and lectured at several Japanese universities. In 1958, when China launched the political process of combining education with agricultural work, I advocated the same movement in Japan. My farming experiences in my friend's home haunted my memory and shaped my perhaps naive political analysis.

In 1955, after she caught my attention by giving me a book of her poems, I married Satoko, a fellow communist. We soon had a daughter and a son. We wanted our children to be educated in an atmosphere of liberty, and encouraged them in creative, independent thought.

I became Assistant Professor at Waseda University in 1961, and full Professor in 1966, the same year the Cultural Revolution started in China. I published an article in *The Economist*, praising the Cultural Revolution as representing what I believed to be the full 'communalisation' of China. My fact-finding visits to China had convinced me that this was the largest ever class-struggle, a movement to spread people's communes into cities, schools and the army. Some of my academic opponents, however, criticised the Cultural Revolution as merely a 'struggle for power', only a 'pseudo-revolution' because it derived from government rather than from the common people. I now admit that their view of the Cultural Revolution was correct.

Yamagishi Kai [Association]

When Typhoon Jane hit the Kyoto area in 1950, almost all rice plants were damaged except those of a chicken farmer, Miyozoh Yamagishi. Neighbours wanted to learn about his farming methods, so in 1953 they formed the Yamagishi Kai to encourage Mr Yamagishi to teach his techniques. He concealed his ideas of a radically new, ideal or utopian society for fear of government oppression until 1956, when the Yamagishism Special Kensan Course (hereafter called Tokkoh) started. Within that course, Mr Yamagishi didn't provide answers, but had the participants reflect and discuss how chicken-raising should be conducted, as well as how they themselves should live. Through meditation, introspection and discussion, he helped participants to realise that even the cause of war was in their own minds — and therefore open to rational change.

In 1922, when he was only 19, Mr Yamagishi started his search for answers to how society should operate. While being chased by Japanese political police, he hid at a poultry farm where he had the dramatic insight that a utopian society could develop by learning from social animals such as chickens. He saw that an ideal society must be based on the *Ittai* (oneness) of all humans with nature.

In the spring of 1958, the first Yamagishism commune was started, following Mr Yamagishi's proposal to construct One Million Chicken Yamagishi-Styled Scientific Industry Chicken Farming Ltd. He envisaged an intentional community of 5000 people, with a capital of 100 million yen, and 1000 employees. All Yamagishi members were called to join this project in which all personal property would be contributed to a common fund, never to be reclaimed. Work would be unpaid in exchange for the lifelong security of being provided with everything: food, clothes, housing, education and health care. At the inaugural meeting 200 members pooled all their money to buy land at Kasuga, Mie Prefecture, for building chicken houses and their own communal housing. They started a commune with 'one purse' and with no private ownership.

Late in 1958, many other people who had taken Tokkoh also tried to establish Yamagishi communes similar to Kasuga. By 1968, there were 20 such communes throughout Japan. In June 1969, Toyosato Jikkenchi, where I now live, started with four families buying five hectares (twelve acres) of farm land on which they built communal housing as well as ten chicken sheds, each 100 metres (330 feet) long. *Toyosato* means 'rich land', while *Jikkenchi* means 'demonstration site', reflecting the aspirations of the commune's founders to create 'a society of both affluence and affection'. While Toyosato rapidly grew bigger and bigger, almost all the other, pseudo-Yamagishi communes faded away.

But news of the start of these Yamagishi communes never appeared in the major Japanese newspapers or magazines. In the summer of 1959 I learned about Yamagishi communes from the sensational news reports of the 'Yamagishi Association Incident'. Japanese newspapers reported that 200 police had raided the Yamagishi Commune in Kasuga, on suspicion of a conspiracy of an armed uprising. In the midst of these investigations, with reporters watching, a Yamagishi member who was opposed to communalisation was killed while attempting to hurt Mr Yamagishi. Several Yamagishi members were arrested and charged with conspiracy and murder, but police could not find any proof — not even one rifle! On the charge of conspiracy, all were set free. Two murder suspects were, however, sentenced for 'accidental homicide', and served several months in prison. Mr Yamagishi was not indicted. Many parts of this incident remain unexplained, although, at the time, there was a great fuss in our mass media. I guess that Mr

Yamagishi took advantage of this police raid in order to publicise the Yamagishi Commune, but the death was accidental.

Through this 'infamy', the name of Yamagishi reached my ears, so perhaps it was a success in the long run? After this incident, Yamagishi communards were ostracised by nearby villagers who wouldn't even sell them rice. This persecution, however, helped the movement by giving members the strength to endure.

Two years later, after Mr Yamagishi had died in 1961, his ideals and dreams started to be realised. Many journalists came to take, and then to write favourably about, the Tokkoh course, and even my respected Professor said to me, 'If our country could become such a society in future, I would like to join Yamagishi'. One of the Yamagishism Tokyo Information Centre members came to my university office to recommend that I take the Tokkoh course.

In May 1971, I was among 60 Tokkoh participants. I brought work clothes, expecting to do some farming, since Yamagishism was known to be agricultural. But there was no work other than cleaning our meeting place, and all we had to do was sit in a circle, think deeply about set themes and speak openly about our thoughts. Without debate or refutation, eight days passed in a friendly atmosphere with all of us searching for the fundamental truths within ourselves. Contrary to my media-inspired expectations, there was not the slightest hint of revolution! In retrospect, Tokkoh was the training-ground for me to become cognizant of my standards of judgement, and to encourage me to be introspective and find that inner truth, without attachment to my logical, highly structured, analytical mind. This way of thinking is called 'Kensan', a key word within Yamagishism.

I Create An Ideal School Within Yamagishi Kai

Early in 1972, my twelve-year-old daughter, Sayaka, told me that she wouldn't attend our normal junior high school, but wanted to go to England to attend Summerhill, a school founded by A.S. Neill, where pupils select their own curriculum. I questioned her, to make sure that she understood that she wouldn't get a graduation certificate. I was surprised at the mysterious coincidence between her new ideas and my old ones, and wondered if Summerhill was what I had imagined to be the ideal school during my own school days. I was thinking of resigning my professorship, so feared that I wouldn't have money to support her. Sayaka replied that I shouldn't remain unhappily as Professor for her sake, but must make decisions for myself. She helped me to see my addiction to work and responsibility. We taught Sayaka to be independent — but oh!, how independent she was! I gave her my consent to study abroad, so she bravely flew to England.

In the summer of 1972, I published in the Yamagishi Kai newsletter, *Kensan*, my idea to found a school like Summerhill in Japan. Many members responded, saying that their movement had plenty of land, and suggesting that I should start such a school in conjunction with Yamagishi Kai. In September, I undertook the arduous two weeks of Kensan School, during which I had the clear objective of examining whether I was qualified to found such a school within Yamagishism, and whether Yamagishi Kai could make it work. I succeeded in the course, and was promptly accepted to become a member of Yamagishi Kasuga commune, then with about 500 members. Immediately after I decided to join, I resigned my professorship at Waseda University.

When I joined in 1972, the commune was quite poor. I agreed that the organisation and financial management of this Yamagishism School would be under the control of Yamagishi Kai, but that all building expenses would be paid from a fund of about 20 million yen which I created from my book royalties and by selling all my accumulated property, as well as from contributions received from other members. Yamagishi Kai provided caretakers for the School.

Because of my esteemed position as University Professor, my joining of the Yamagishi commune was widely reported in the media, thereby attracting public attention which helped promote our Yamagishism School. My wife and I travelled all over Japan for one year, talking about this new Yamagishism School. Japan Broadcasting Company televised a 30-minute programme about our new school. A couple of sites were offered for the school, but I bought land at Ayama, near Yamagishi Kasuga commune, and rented two thatched farm houses to start with. 'Yamagishism Happiness School' started in January 1973. The cost of starting this school left me penniless, but fortunately the school's management then shifted to the Yamagishi Commune. My family and I then moved to Yamagishi Toyosato commune.

PHOTO BY SHIGEKI GOTO

Atsuyoshi Niijima binding books at Yamagishism Publishing Company

Sayaka, my daughter who had been the inspiration for this school, returned from England late in 1974, and took the Tokkoh and Kensan courses. She then joined Yamagishi Toyosato commune, where she remains happily to this day.

My ideas for Yamagishism School were in accord with Yamagishi Kai, and quite similar to Summerhill. Both Yamagishism School and Summerhill started off free from compulsory public education, and both are boarding schools. But for the past nine years our pupils have also attended a local public school.

The big difference between Summerhill and our Yamagishism School is that our curriculum is still based on farm work. A.S. Neill thought that manual work would depress pupils, while Yamagishism holds that nothing has more educational potential than agricultural work. It is beneficial to human development for a child to experience agriculture, living with nature and feeling the soil, wind and rain, with the sense of seasonal change. Farm work is endlessly instructive in developing one's knowledge of natural phenomena such as biology, meteorology, mathematics and physics as well as human psychology and sociology.

The training of teachers for our new school included fitting them into Yamagishism. Staff were expected not to teach by their own ideas but to understand and empathise with children's needs. For this reason, staff were required to experience at least two months of Yamagishism life in Toyosato, and then to look within and benefit from that experience by undertaking the Kensan School. Some saw this as a sort of 'mind control', and resigned but I was adamant that Yamagishism must be the underlying philosophy for our new, radical school.

The Operation of Yamagishi Toyosato

I now live a fully communal life in Yamagishi Toyosato, together with my wife, daughter and son-in-law, and two grandchildren. I have irrevocably given all my money and property to this Yamagishi commune. When I die, I shall be buried in our Yamagishi mausoleum.

PHOTO BY SHIGEKI GOTO

The entrance to Yamagishi Society, Toyosato Jikkenchi

Here in Toyosato each member has a private room in a large building with shared kitchen and toilets. We eat in our large dining hall, which has 280 seats, bathe in our communal bathhouse and have our clothes washed in our laundry. Without using money, we collect clothes, books and toiletries from our storehouse. All income is pooled. Each day, all members gather for a one-hour Kensan Meeting, where we make decisions and allocate new tasks for the day.

Toyosato is an ideal society because Yamagishism meets the following five requirements:

(1) Yamagishism society is organised around a love of nature, with members engaged in farming, animal husbandry and forestry, and with all members deeply concerned with environmental problems. Members do not work for money, but each works enthusiastically, not loathing to work hard for the common good.

(2) Yamagishism accepts sick people, like me, treating the old and the disabled the same as normal, healthy people, thereby providing security to each member's life. We have special homes for our elderly, as well as special classes for handicapped children. Yamagishism also contributes to Japanese society by fostering the next generation of farmers and foresters, through teaching children to live in harmony with nature.

(3) Yamagishism has a Kensan system to make decisions and solve problems, by which it dispenses with dictatorship and majority decisions. In a Kensan Meeting, through introspection, meditation and discussion, we examine matters rationally and reach optimal decisions.

(4) We regard all work as being of equal value, with each member engaged in his or her own speciality. The choice of work for members is affected not by adjusting people to jobs, but by adjusting jobs to people. For example, when an artist joined us, we started an Art Department.

(5) The principles of Yamagishi communes are universal, and have been demonstrated to fit into other countries around the world.

Requirement (1) concerns solving our serious environmental problems. Not only in Japan, agricultural success diminishes as environmental damage increases, affecting not only the countryside but also our global ecology. Almost all graduates of Yamagishism School have chosen to live in a Yamagishism commune where they engage in agriculture, cattle farming and forestry. As well, a forestry expert has joined Yamagishi and is now managing our forests, while a rice-farmer, who won the first annual award for Japanese rice-farmers, has joined Yamagishi and now gives us guidance in environmentally sustainable rice-farming.

Requirement (2) concerns welfare and security, especially for the elders who have devoted their life to Yamagishism. As well, there are many old parents, living in their own homes, whose sons and daughters are committed to Yamagishism. In Japan, elderly parents are always cared for by their children, never left as wards of the state. Commune members who are active today will naturally get old, sometimes sick and infirm. Toyosato is the best place for such people. We have a clinic, with our own doctors working in cooperation with a nearby hospital. Each of the elders has his or her own room. There is a large living room and a common dining room, or they can cook their own meals if they prefer. Their rooms are connected to the clinic. They are all treated equally, without regard to their previous wealth, pension or ability to work. Light work is available to those who want it, but it doesn't follow that they will be treated any better. Anyhow, our nurses will take care of them till their last breath.

Requirement (3) concerns communal decision-making or governance. Within Yamagishi communes, decisions on individual, business and communal matters are reached through Kensan. *Kensan* means to grind and polish rough material, such as a raw jewel. But the 'material' in this Kensan is our powers of judgement which we all share as common sense. So grinding material means to release our preoccupation with, or attachment to, those fixed ideas which keep us from making a correct decision. Polishing material means to look creatively at the facts, and find the principle which flows from those facts.

Visitors at Toyosato are astonished not to see portraits of Mr Yamagishi, and they can find neither directors nor leaders. Visitors wonder how such a big commune can operate and maintain order without leaders. In my opinion, Yamagishi members always think of problems and ideas as Kensan material, that is, as opportunities to grow and learn through introspection. Indeed, Mr Yamagishi did not use the word 'truth', but would use the expression 'something like truth' to show the relative nature of reality. Truth is not fixed but must be constantly pursued.

Requirement (4) is surely the logical development of Requirement (3). Different from Marxism, Yamagishism does not aim for the society to come after the class-based division of labour 'withers away', nor for what post-modernist capitalism expects as the ideal, 'robotic' society, without factory labour. In Yamagishism, each member will be aware of his or her own social role, and will become an expert social practitioner. During June and December, through Kensan techniques, each member reflects on his or her own social role for a full month. After deep reflection, she or he can propose to change her or his role, or even place of living. But almost all Toyosato members remain in the same social role and the same residence, because they are happy and fulfilled.

Requirement (5) is demonstrated by Yamagishism having now spread into Korea, Germany, Switzerland, Australia, Thailand, United States of America and Brazil. The Tokkoh has been held in English, German and Korean, making the translation of Yamagishism materials an urgent task, as Yamagishi communes spread worldwide. All communes maintain relationships of equality and fraternity with each other. Each group enjoys a variety of products sent as gifts from the other Yamagishi communes, while each produces items appropriate to its own land and climate. This system of presenting products as gifts to each other will surely be a model for future society!

By the end of 1995 there have been over 90,000 Tokkoh participants with more and more people joining Yamagishi communes, which are now located all over Japan. Becoming prosperous, Yamagishism has proliferated. This facilitated and necessitated the business of distributing products between groups. Because we have no private property, and use no money internally, all goods are freely exchanged between and within communes, providing the foundations of a totally new and unique commercial network that functions without currency or barter.

In 1976 we started the 'Yamagishism Children's Paradise', a two-week course during school holidays, for non-Yamagishi children to live together in our commune. Many of these children then want to stay here. More and more children have joined our Yamagishism School. In 1984 we started Yamagishism Kindergarten, then in 1985 we started Yamagishism Senior High School. A few years later, our original Yamagishism School split into Junior and Elementary Schools. Today, more than 2400 children and teenagers attend our Yamagishism schools.

The main Yamagishi economic projects include poultry, pig and dairy farming, plus producing animal feed. We also grow fruit, vegetables, rice and mushrooms. We

Photo by Shigeki Goto

Yamagishi Toyosato dairy herd (Atsuyoshi Niijima on right)

process our own meat and dairy products, plus confectionery, vegetables and fruit juices. We market our products through Yamagishi organisations.

We engage in environmental conservation through various forestry, organic compost-making and industrial food waste recycling activities. Our waste treatment is so effective that drinkable water is produced.

As well, we develop, operate and sell computer systems. We have our own construction firm doing steel and wood work, plus designing, making, installing and repairing machinery. We operate a transport and distribution department, plus the Yamagishism Research Institute and our own publishing company.

At Toyosato we have 3 hectares (7 acres) of rice paddies, 56 hectares (130 acres) of vegetables, 70 hectares (160 acres) of pasture, 11 hectares (25 acres) of orchards, 70 hectares (160 acres) of forests and 50 hectares (120 acres) for living space and other projects. We have 620,000 poultry for egg production and 120,000 poultry for meat, we milk 1300 cows, and raise 3400 beef cattle and 16,000 pigs for meat.

Yamagishi pork has a good flavour because our pigs live comfortably, without stress. Our pig-houses have two metres of wood-mulch in which the pigs dig and defecate, eventually forming useable, rich compost. Many Japanese pig farms are now being closed because of neighbour's complaints of bad smells, but there is no bad smell with our pigs, so we are expanding. Probably in ten years time most Japanese pork will be Yamagishi-reared.

Through the humane treatment of our animals and our efficient handling of milk, eggs and meat, our food products taste great, so they sell very well. Our 1994 turnover was 11.8 billion yen, with over one million regular customers. We supply 3% of the eggs consumed in Japan.

As of October 1994, there were 4808 members in 35 Yamagishism communes throughout Japan, of whom 2241 are adults (including 154 elders), 2330

Atsuyoshi Niijima working in the spinach fields (Toyosato greenhouses behind)

students and 237 under the age of five. 43% of our students come from outside Yamagishi. The largest commune, Toyosato, has 1613 members while the smallest, Haruna, has only 6. There are also seven Yamagishism communes abroad, one each in South Korea, Switzerland, Germany, Thailand, the USA, Brazil and Australia.

At the beginning of Yamagishism, more than 90% of members came from a farming background, but now those joining come from a wide range of professions, with newcomers having expertise and long careers in many companies. For example, a soba noodle shop manager has recently joined, bringing along his shop which will now be maintained by the commune. Another member is an airline pilot who flies overseas, while raising chickens on his days off. Several members are doctors who work in a nearby hospital. All income goes into our communal purse. Over 200 members of the public, plus Yamagishi School graduates join our commune each year. In 1995, three more Yamagishi communes were formed.

Toyosato has over 50 different types of work for members, as we will develop a new work place for yet another expert who joins us. New members range from teenagers, who take the Tokkoh and then wish to become a Yamagishi member, to elders over 70 years old. Yamagishism attracts people from a wide range of ages and professions. It is surely worthy of being called a successful, new-age society! We welcome visitors to come to Toyosato to see for themselves.

Conclusion

Looking back over 40 years of Yamagishi history, I experience a resounding wave of feeling Ittai, or 'at-one' with all that has transpired. I have found myself anew in a happy and contented state of being. Even from an economical point of view, I am prosperous and comfortable, leading a happy life without anxiety about my future. That's because I am Ittai with the world.

Atsuyochi with a group of visiting students at Yamagishi Toyosato

I am now writing a book on the history of Yamagishism. I have found my social role and expression of contentment through this and my other writing. It may be that I become an Ittai historian? I hope that I can make a complete record of Yamagishi Kai, collecting and recording all the facts while we communal elders are still alive.

As well as my writing, I work for two hours every day in our vegetable fields or with our livestock — as do all Yamagishi members. Maintaining a balance between physical and mental work is important within Yamagishism. Living here, enjoying this rich and varied communal life, with my wife, children and grandchildren — this is surely utopia.

At 68 years of age, being in daily contact with numerous long-term communards, or communal elders, makes me realise that it is only when I, as an individual, have an *Ittai* (at one) relationship with all people, all animals and with all of nature — only then can I live a full and satisfying life, without anxiety.

Yamagishi Toyosato commune has proved to be that ideal society.

Introduction: UFA–Fabrik and Sigrid Niemer

PHOTO BY BILL METCALF

*Sigrid Niemer
in front of
UFA–Fabrik Circus
poster*

UFA–Fabrik was founded in 1979, although the founding group had already been living communally for several years. It is one of only two urban communes in this book, and is arguably the most colourful. Crowded into a small, disused industrial area of Berlin, Germany, their bright psychedelic coloured facades and buildings, plus their mini-farm and green experimental technology are all in stark contrast to their drab and dreary locale. They support themselves through a range of endeavours, mostly concerned with entertainment. UFA–Fabrik Circus is well known internationally and has been the model on which many other 'alternative' circuses have been based.

Sigrid Niemer is one of the founders of UFA–Fabrik where she is now their 'coordinator and forward-planner', as well as a musician and artist.

I first visited UFA–Fabrik in 1993, although I had known about and been fascinated by their story for many years. Early in 1995 Sigrid agreed to contribute to this book on behalf of UFA–Fabrik, but in spite of many promises in response to my reminders, nothing eventuated. In December 1995, my German friend Isabell Blömer (of Findhorn) and I travelled to Berlin where we spent several days interviewing Sigrid and other members, and writing up the story. As far as possible, we maintained the style and flow in order to have this chapter be consistent with the rest in this book. The first draft was presented for critical comments, of which there were several which helped correct minor errors. The final draft was sent to Sigrid seeking her comments on its style, content and tenor.

Visitors are always welcome to come to UFA–Fabrik's café and food shop, and attend their public entertainment. It is generally not possible to stay, however, since their large Guest House was closed in 1995, but it may well be open again in the future. Their address is Viktoriastrasse 10-18, D-1042 Berlin, Germany (fax: +49-30-75503117).

CHAPTER 9

UFA-Fabrik: The Circus of Life in Berlin

by Bill Metcalf & Isabell Blömer (interviewing Sigrid Niemer)

Today, Sigrid Niemer and her fellow communards have to make the final decision on whether or not UFA-Fabrik can afford to send 24 of their members, including herself, to Brazil. UFA-Fabrik Commune members became interested in and made contact with Brazilian culture eight years ago, and they continue to become ever more involved. Many Brazilians have visited and performed at UFA–Fabrik in Berlin, and they have established deep friendships within this commune, and UFA–Fabrik has now even started its own samba band, in which Sigrid plays.

This trip would be the first opportunity for these German communards to tour Brazil with their *UFA–Fabrik Circus* and *Terra Brasilis*, their samba band. It is a very big financial decision, involving a great deal of money and risk. It is a major investment to fly so many people and so much equipment around the world! The telephone rings and faxes are sent and received as Sigrid tries to negotiate agreements with their Brazilian counterparts to ensure that UFA–Fabrik would at least not lose money if they went. This is just part of her work as the coordinator and forward-planner for UFA–Fabrik, her communal home and work-place since 1979.

Sigrid Niemer's Background

Sigrid was born in 1954 in Itzehoe, a small city in northern Germany. During the last days of the Second World War, just before the 'liberating' Russian soldiers arrived, her family, like so many other Germans, managed to escape westward from Silesia in eastern Germany. The loss of their home and social position, all their possessions, and the death of many family members was part of the tragic cultural heritage with which Sigrid grew up. She wonders if perhaps that is why the security of an extended, or communal, family has always been so important to her?

In 1973 Sigrid moved to West Berlin, the cold-war 'island' of democratic and capitalistic West Germany, within the communist state of East Germany. She attended the University of Berlin where she studied for a degree in art. West Berlin, in the mid 1970s, was exciting and alive with political and social change, with an active subculture of social experimentation and competing radical philosophies.

In 1976 Sigrid met and made friends with seven people who had already formed a small urban commune in 1972, in West Berlin's Kreuzberg District. Their intention was to share their life, work and culture. Besides living together, they worked together as a collective, mainly doing building renovation work, through which activities they met many other young people who then became inspired by what these communards were doing, and by how they were doing it. Out of this interchange came the idea to rent an old factory building in West Berlin's Schöneberg District, and to establish what they called Fabrik für Kultur, Sport und Handwerk (Factory for Culture, Sport and Handicrafts). This was the first initiative in Berlin for a place where anyone who felt inspired to do so could share his or her skills and new ideas by offering a workshop or making personal contacts within a friendly and enjoyable social environment. This communal group also started Berlin's first food cooperative to provide a market for organic produce. Through their networking, they instigated, as well as offered a venue for, workshops offering holistic heath care and guidance on living more naturally.

Their innovative and fun approach to life appealed greatly to Sigrid, so she joined them, and soon she took an active role in their attempts to combine cultural activities with living in a sane, socially positive and environmentally sensible manner. The intense and active social life of this communal group was a far cry from her small-town youth, and yet it offered her some sense of the 'extended-family' which she had long sought. Twenty years later, she is still living communally with these same people.

The Formation of UFA–Fabrik Commune

During the First World War, the German Government established, on the side of Berlin's large Teltow Canal, the Universal Film AG (company), known simply as 'UFA', a studio to produce silent films. During the 1920s, this studio was used to produce such film masterpieces as Fritz Lang's *Metropolis* and Murnau's *The Cabinet of Dr. Caligari*. During the late 1930s and the Second World War, the studio was used to produce Nazi war propaganda films. The site was heavily bombed toward the end of the war, but it reopened in 1950, again as a film studio or 'film factory'. In the early 1970s, UFA closed this studio and moved to a larger site. Because of the former Nazi connections of this UFA site, there was pressure from many Berliners to just demolish all the buildings and to forget the past. The old UFA site of two hectares (five acres), with its many buildings and facilities, and its chequered history, lay abandoned and condemned, awaiting demolition.

In 1978, following their successful participation in an environmental festival, where *Fabrik für Kultur, Sport und Handwerk* activities were enthusiastically received, Sigrid and her communal group attracted many new members. They started to seriously search for a new and much larger communal home. They dreamed of a place where they could combine their daily life with their work and with their various cultural activities. They applied to the West Berlin City Council to rent and occupy an old, abandoned brewery building, but they were flatly refused, and the building was then quickly destroyed. When they learned that the old UFA studio was about to be demolished, they developed an elaborate occupation plan. They let it be known publicly that they would be holding a protest demonstration at the old Brewery site on 9 June1979, and while police waited for them there, about 100 of these communards and their supporters peacefully occupied the UFA site. That same night, the local television news showed a film, which the group had already made, showing them at the UFA site, already doing what they, in reality, only planned to do.

'Squatting' was the only possibility for this communal group to obtain such a large block of land, with buildings, within the crowded and politically circumscribed city of West Berlin. In 1979, squatting was not the common and popular activity which it would later become in Germany, but it already had a very bad public image. Sigrid and her fellow communards realised that they must undertake their squatting of UFA in such a way as not to create a bad public image for themselves. They did not barricade the UFA site, as other squatters would do, but instead they at once created more of a public, festival atmosphere. They opened the UFA grounds and welcomed in their neighbours, visitors and the media. Through a range of creative arts, they demonstrated their utopian visions for the future. Out of this spontaneously creative activity, at this frantic time, they developed the now famous UFA–Fabrik Circus. They opened a café, and within days had organised open-air musical shows and concerts. Because of their openness and the fun atmosphere which they generated and communicated to visitors, they were surprisingly well received by their neighbours, as well as by the conservative German media.

UFA–Fabrik members distributed thousands of leaflets, explaining that they were not an alternative or a terrorist group, but stating clearly that they had the courage to preserve and give a second life to old buildings such as UFA, and that good social ideas can result from people taking responsibility for their own lives, rather than waiting for action from politicians or from those 'above'. These communards pointed out that culture does not happen just in the Opera House, Concert Hall or Museum, but is created by each and every one of us. They wanted nothing from politicians or political parties, just wanting to live peacefully and creatively, and to demonstrate how people can change their own social reality. Because of their extensive and positive public image, and the good work they were doing in the cultural desert of Berlin's Tempelhof District, local politicians could neither ignore nor dispose of this communal group who had taken on the new name of UFA–Fabrik.

They opened the *Treffpunkt Café* as one of their first activities because of the importance they saw in establishing an informal venue where squatters and other local residents could interact amicably. As well, their café, whose name means 'meeting place', provided them with a small income. They had the motto, 'We do not just talk about our problems, we solve them, even if it takes a bit longer'.

The UFA buildings were cold, neglected and semi-derelict, but Sigrid and her friends coped as best they could, living there at first without heat or electricity. Most of these more culturally-oriented communards had little experience with carpentry, electrical and plumbing work, but they modified the old buildings, creating simple living spaces. Five to seven members slept in sleeping bags in each room. They were afraid that the police and council officials would try to reclaim the UFA, so members patrolled the site for 24 hours a day. None of them, however, had had any previous experience with this sort of fearful situation, and many of them were reminded of similar stories of fear from the war, which they had been told by their parents. This shared experience of fear and persecution, of having to patrol their isolated perimeter fence and alongside the deep, dark canal in the pre-dawn quiet, helped to bring this communal group together, and established strong bonds of interdependence which have withstood the test of time.

During this intense and dynamic period, members endlessly discussed the structure, rules, guidelines and visions for their commune. While Sigrid and 16 others had already been living communally for several years at the previous site, they now had to create a different communal structure to include the many new members. In some ways, this was like a new beginning for this commune. They knew of older, rural communes, but they knew of no large communes within a very big city such as West Berlin. This was an exciting and challenging time for them, as they had no models on which to base the new urban commune they wanted to create.

After about six weeks of such discussions, it became clear to the UFA–Fabrik squatters that they wanted to stay together as a commune, so they sought some form of legal permanency of occupancy so that they could more efficiently plan and implement the necessary renovations to provide themselves with both a communal home and a workplace. They applied for a lease from the West Berlin City Council, and when the matter eventually came up for debate, UFA–Fabrik members bravely agreed to withdraw from the UFA site in order to facilitate the council's decision-making. Fortunately, because of the good public image they had managed to create, UFA–Fabrik was granted the legal use of this site for a small rental, but only under a three month, renewable lease arrangement.

Although this did not provide the long term, guaranteed tenure which UFA–Fabrik Commune had sought, members nevertheless proceeded to renovate and make the old buildings safer and more useful. They continued for many years to negotiate with the city council, and members campaigned publicly, until they were recently granted a 33-year lease, albeit at a higher rental. This security of tenure enables UFA–Fabrik to now undertake the much needed, longer-term building renovations and maintenance work, as well as more environmentally sensitive, long range planning for water and power provision and waste treatment. Today, UFA–Fabrik members feel quite secure.

UFA–Fabrik Today

Today, 34 adults and 16 children and young people live as a commune on the UFA–Fabrik site. As well, about 100 people work there, either full or part time, but live elsewhere. Commune members, as well as those who only work there, eat all of their main meals together, although breakfast is usually taken in smaller groups of six to eight people, but this is mainly just for convenience.

UFA–Fabrik as a communal group, according to Sigrid, does not follow any particular religious or political philosophy, agreeing only to work and live together amicably, productively and joyfully. In that sense, they regard themselves as a 'free'

Communal housing at UFA–Fabrik

UFA–Fabrik Commune from the street

commune. There is, nevertheless, a shared belief in the feasibility of and potential for joyful communal living within a large city, as well as a shared vision of a healthy, creative and fun lifestyle, available to all. Culture, at UFA–Fabrik, means not only theatre and performing and fine arts, but also good education, healthy food, natural health care and social security.

Their guidelines for communal living are changing, just as the members also change. Originally, members enjoyed living very closely together with little private space, but as they age and change their priorities, they now make use of more private living space and greater personal discretion in their lifestyle. All UFA–Fabrik members work on the site and work for one of their communal businesses. They still maintain a 'common purse', while sharing their cars and televisions, etc. Without any overriding, shared dogma, the most important thing that connects these members from day to day is their shared activities and work projects.

Decisions within each specialised area of communal operations are made by those who work in that area, while the overall important communal decisions are made by general consensus of all members, meeting in a plenary session. Members do not vote in these meetings, since they are not democratic, but instead they depend on their intimate, long-term knowledge of each other to facilitate their decision making. UFA–Fabrik members use the term *Gleichberechtigung* (equality) to indicate that while commune members are certainly not identical, but are quite unique, each member should be a creative and critical thinker and a leader within her or his own area of work and life.

UFA–Fabrik has a guest house with sleeping space for up to 40 guests. In the past, this has been an important way in which they have related to visitors from around the world who have come to share their communal life and to learn from their dance, drama, music and circus activities. Lately, however, none of these communards has been willing to put in the time and energy needed to operate and maintain this UFA–Fabrik Guest House, so it is currently little used. Communal members are not expected to undertake work which does not appeal to them. Should a member, in the future, feel inspired to operate this guest-house business, then it will once again become an important part of UFA–Fabrik's way of relating to the outside world, as well as a source of income. This may have happened by the time this book comes out — or never.

UFA–Fabrik commune is not seeking more members but they are open to new people joining them. Those who do join UFA–Fabrik, however, seem to come mainly from their extensive network of friends and supporters, rather than from those who just read or hear about them. Any new member must be unanimously accepted by all current members, meeting in a plenary session. To join, one need not contribute any money, but must promise to work for the collective good, and to contribute to and to share their common purse.

When UFA–Fabrik started to employ and pay wages to outsiders, their relatively simple way of economic life was challenged and had to change. They had to separate the 'common-purse' finances of their commune from the finances of their various businesses. They have legally registered UFA–Fabrik as a *Verein* (Charitable Trust) to facilitate their economic, taxation and legal interactions with the outside world. Today, members treat their commune economically the same as one of their several businesses, so they pay rent to the trust which legally owns all their property and which is, in reality, owned in turn by themselves.

About a third of their income derives from organising cultural activities, the second third from their own cultural productions, and the final third from their bakery, foodshop and cafe.

UFA–Fabrik's organising of cultural productions takes place through their International Cultural Centre, as well as through their summertime, open-air cinema, and a range of workshops, plays and diverse social activities, for which they provide the venue.

UFA–Fabrik has two theatres. One of these, now known as the *Variété Salon*, is an important historical site, since it is the theatre where the high ranking, infamous Nazi officials would preview the propaganda films and weekly *Wochenschau* (Newsreels) which were produced at UFA, before releasing them for general viewing. This 200 seat cinema, so rich in tragic history, also has wonderful acoustics. Today, it is no longer used to screen films for the general public, but it is used for recording music, for cabarets and musical concerts, and for various other public gatherings, lectures and performances. Their second theatre, with seating for about 400 in a theatre-in-the-round format, is for live performances of UFA–Fabrik Circus, their samba band, *Terra Brasilis*, for dancing and for other social and cultural activities. In the summertime, UFA–Fabrik also operates an open-air cinema showing a wide range of films to paying members of the general public.

The *International Cultural Centre* of UFA–Fabrik, along with groups from places such as Dublin in Ireland, Bergen in Norway and Mezzago in Italy, is part of a Europe-wide network of independent, community theatres and cultural venues known as *Trans Europe Halles*. Every second year, UFA–Fabrik hosts the large and very popular International Theatre Festival, in which thousands of people take part.

The second third of their income derives from their own samba band, Terra Brasilis, their world famous and much copied UFA–Fabrik Circus, and from the Children's Circus School which they operate. The UFA–Fabrik Circus depends on human talent rather than on exploiting animals, as in a normal circus. It also endeavours to involve the audience in their own entertainment, rather than having them remain as 'cultural consumers'. Each year about 200,000 people are entertained by UFA–Fabrik's circus, samba band, festivals and cultural events. As one observer recently noted, 'UFA–Fabrik is Berlin's premier multi-cultural experiment in living, working and laughing together'.

The final third of UFA–Fabrik's income derives from their more prosaic businesses. Their wholefood bakery, *Vollkorn Bäckerei*, produces over 3000 loaves of bread weekly, as well as various cakes and desserts. These are then distributed through retail shops throughout Berlin. Their organic produce retail shop, *Naturkostladen,* sells everything from the bread and pastry produced on site to organic fruit and vegetables, candles, teas and the usual range of health foods. *Café Olé*, with seating for about 100, is popular with local office workers, tourists and with those who come to UFA–Fabrik to take part in some cultural event.

The *Berlin Free School* operates on UFA–Fabrik's premises, and is attended by about 30 children, including all the commune's children plus others from the neighbourhood. This school only covers the first six years of education, by which time the children are apparently anxious to join the mainstream schools. After twelve years of battling with officialdom, The Berlin Free School has now been recognised and certified by education officials. At UFA–Fabrik, school and social lives are interwoven, with children and adults interacting in work and play. Sigrid Niemer's own son, Hannes, who is now twelve years old, is about to leave this 'free' school to attend a normal secondary school, a move he anxiously anticipates.

For their commune's children, UFA–Fabrik also provides a small animal farm where the children themselves look after the pigs, ponies, ducks and other farm animals with which most city children would normally have no contact.

When UFA–Fabrik first occupied this old industrial site, it was dusty and unappealing, with concrete covering most of the areas between the uninspiring, rather dreary factory buildings. Since then, they have 'greened' much of the site, planting gardens, trees and lawns wherever space permits. They have planted grass on the flat roofs of many of their buildings, so far covering about one-third of their extensive roof area. This sod roof helps with insulation, reduces dust, and gives the site more of an attractive, rural, green, albeit rather 'funky', character.

They also have a small wind generator, special composting drums, and other innovative but experimental environmental technology. Cars are not allowed onto the site, so their streets are very user-friendly, and in the summer offer a popular place for people to just 'hang-out'. Future plans call for solar hot water panels and perhaps a small bio-gas system.

UFA–Fabrik receives no general financial support from any government or agency, but they have recently received government and EEC (European Economic Community) financial assistance for developing a new experimental biological water purification system. In Berlin, water is in short supply and very expensive, so it is environmentally, as well as economically, important to conserve and recycle. Rain water, collected as best they can from the streets, is purified by reticulating it through reed beds on site. This

Psychedelic murals cover the walls of work and living area

water is then used for flushing toilets and for irrigating their sod roofs. They have plans to renovate Café Olé, and part of this project is to direct all the washing-up and toilet wastes back into their biological waste-water treatment system, and then to re-use that water, once cleaned, as described above. Such ecological projects are becoming ever more important in UFA–Fabrik, since the members feel that it is important to show how even living in a large city can be more environmentally sensitive, as well as more comfortable and attractive.

UFA–Fabrik has long experimented with alternative, environmentally-friendly energy production and conservation technology. Two modern, high efficiency gas-fired plants, using 'co-generation' technology, now satisfy all of their water and space-heating requirements, and about 80% of their electrical needs, thereby making them more energy efficient and independent, while also reducing CO_2 and other emissions.

In 1987 UFA–Fabrik established *Nachbarschafts Und Selbsthilfe Zentrum*, known as NUSZ, a neighbourhood self-help centre. Here, courses are offered on health care, pregnancy, meditation, martial arts and many other self-help and personal development, as well as community, issues. NUSZ is based on their notion of healthy personal and social change being fostered through personal initiatives rather than from imposed programs. Because of UFA–Fabrik's widely acknowledged record of good social and cultural work with local residents, NUSZ now receives a small amount of financial support from the Berlin City Council.

Prior to the reunification of Germany in 1989, UFA–Fabrik was a very well-known and important part of the cultural life within the isolated political 'island' of West Berlin. It was then relatively easy for them to obtain financial support for their diverse cultural activities. Perhaps they symbolised free thought and creative life in the nervous minds of their fellow West-Berliners? But since reunification, UFA–Fabrik has become a much less important part of a much bigger city and country. With the reunification of East and

West Berlin, the city now has two opera houses, two concert halls and two symphonies, etc. The main part of the government's cultural support money goes to these duplicated, big projects, with little left for local and communal cultural groups. UFA–Fabrik is having to re-forge its identity and purpose in the light of this new political reality.

Conclusion

Sigrid Niemer believes that UFA–Fabrik today has a worldwide reputation as a multi-cultural site for innovative social, cultural and ecological lifestyles. It is important to remember, she asserts, that they occupied and squatted on this site, and developed their commune, more for practical than for abstract theoretical and political reasons. They needed a home, a place to live, to work and to raise children, within a safe and stimulating social and cultural environment. Observers often wish to classify UFA–Fabrik commune as 'alternative', 'new age', 'hippie' or even 'anarchist', but Sigrid adamantly rejects these terms, claiming that they live communally, as they do, mainly for practical reasons. Communal living allows them to enjoy a rich, diverse environment, with plenty of space, cultural activity and worthwhile employment, within the large, very crowded and expensive city of Berlin. None of the members could live half as well as they do if they were not living in a commune such as UFA–Fabrik.

One observer recently wrote about UFA–Fabrik commune: 'This utopian microcosm encourages people's involvement, inspiring many to take chances in their lives. The UFA successfully blends culture with politics, and gives everyone a good time in the process.' Their informal motto has long been, 'In one hour of action there is more reality than in a year of talking'. Sigrid believes that UFA–Fabrik can continue to live up to these high ideals and, most importantly, that they can continue to have fun.

Comfortable housing and workspace from a converted film studio

Introduction: Christavashram
and Acharya Reverend K.K. Chandy

*Acharya
K. K. Chandy*

Christavashram is the oldest communal group in this book, having been founded in 1934. It is located at Manganam near Kottayam, Kerala State, in the extreme south of India. Christavashram, its name derived from 'Christian Ashram', has about 200 residents, including a small number of core members who have made lifelong vows to this way of life. The teachings of Mahatma Gandhi and Rabindranath Tagore were instrumental in developing Christavashram's style of communal living, including the vow of poverty. It is the most religious of all the communal groups in this book. Because it is a religious commune, its structure is quite different to what is found with many others in this book, although its problems and issues are similar.

Reverend Chandy was one of the founders of Christavashram, and has lived there since 1934. He demonstrates a strong commitment to Christian principles, most particularly as applied to non-violence, justice, equity and communalism with 'all things held in common, and distribution according to need'. Having been born in 1908, he is the oldest communard contributing to this book. He has travelled widely internationally, lecturing about his work toward communal non-violence.

It is possible to visit and take part in the work and communal life of Christavashram, but only after making prior arrangements. Write to: The Secretary, Christavashram, Manganam, Kottayam 686 018, Kerala, India (phone/fax: +91-481-578227).

CHAPTER 10

Christavashram: My Communal Adventure in Faith

by Acharya Reverend K.K. Chandy

What prompted my lifelong pursuit of justice and peace through dynamic non-violence? What motivated me to live all my adult life within a commune? As a student in Madras Christian College in 1931, I worked in that city's overcrowded, wretched, fetid slums. The images of men, women and hungry children living in filth haunted and taunted me. Words were not enough — I had to do something about the poverty and hunger which I had seen. In contemplation and prayer, the Lord's answer was, 'Set your mind on God's Kingdom and His Justice, and all things will come to you as well'.

*   *   *

Christavashram was started by K.I. Mathai, M.P. Job and myself, three school teachers, in 1934. We felt called to build a Christian ashram (commune) where the motive for all activities would be God's will and His service, not individual gain. Christavashram was to be a way of realising Christ's Gospel of a supra-national nation, that is, a Divine Commonwealth and a classless society. Because even Christian churches permit inequalities of caste, race and class to go unchallenged, I felt that only a revolution could achieve a classless society, as found in the early church of Christ which had 'all things common, and distribution was made according to need' (Acts 4:32–35).

We started Christavashram near Alleppey (its original site) in Kerala State, one of the most thickly populated areas of the world. The huge coir factories nearby were mostly owned by Europeans who cared nothing for their pollution or exploitation. Alleppey, a seaport, was crammed with pavement dwellers and fetid slums, poverty and unemployment. Among those pavement dwellers were many street boys with whom we at Christavashram worked.

In Christavashram, we sought to provide a working model of how to live in order to change attitudes to property and power politics, and to have agape–non-violence permeate all aspects of life. This required the de-classing of ourselves and our functioning as a catalyst in reconciling the bourgeois and the proletariat. We relinquished private property and sought a communal life of work and worship with 'one purse, one purpose and one meal table'.

My Background

I was born in 1908 at Kuzhuvelipuram in the Indian state of Kerala, in comparatively well to do circumstances. I vividly recall the discriminatory caste system found even in the government school which had separate seating arrangements for Harijans (untouchables), and special treatment for the Brahmans (upper caste). In caste-rigid Kerala, Harijans could not even walk near a Brahman! When walking, Brahmans would cry out, 'Hoey!' and Harijans had to move away a few yards until the Brahman had passed. In villages having only narrow paths along low-lying paddy fields, the Harijans had to jump into the water and get drenched rather than 'pollute' the high caste person. Such were the social lessons of my childhood.

I was deeply influenced by Kagawa and the Kingdom of God movement in Japan. Kagawa's bold stand against war and violence, and his readiness to sacrifice every comfort for the sake of service to the needy in the slums of Kobe, and for the Gospel of the Kingdom of God, had a profound impact on me.

The Indian Independence struggle also affected me deeply. Mahatma Gandhi's letters to the Viceroy pointing out the disparity between the incomes of Indian and English people, and that over half of India's national income was spent on armed forces, caused me great heartache. Terrorism against British domination was on the rise despite Gandhi's condemnation of violence. I had the privilege of seeing and hearing Mahatma Gandhi while I was a student at a Christian High School. I was deeply touched and changed for ever.

While studying and teaching in Madras in the early 1930s, I became involved with the Student Christian Movement of India, the Servants of India Society and the Indian National Congress. I was Joint Secretary of the International Fellowship, a movement promoting friendship and understanding between Indians and Europeans. Mahatma Gandhi was also an active member of this Fellowship.

Early Christavashram

We had neither property nor money when we formed Christavashram, but somehow managed to buy and occupy 8.5 acres (3.5 hectares) of poor, hilly land at Manganam, east of Alleppey in Kerala State. We agreed on the classical vows of poverty, chastity and obedience. We differed, however, as to whether we should be interdenominational or affiliated to a particular church, and on whether we should be a celibate order or a community of married and unmarried members.

After prayer, reflection and discussions we concluded that Christavashram should be an interdenominational fellowship, guided by the Holy Spirit, a place of spiritual retreat, a centre of training and service for young people, and a centre for justice and non-violent peace action. Christavashram should not be an end in itself but must serve the Kingdom of God. We had to live with the poor to know their problems, and then take steps to strike at the roots of poverty and injustice.

In 1935, one year after we formed Christavashram, I stayed at Sevagram, Mahatma Gandhi's ashram in Wardha. He said, 'I make no decision except after prayer', and 'to be great, a man must seek nothing for himself, neither privilege, reward, nor power; he must remember God 24 hours a day'. Through practical actions, experiments with a balanced diet, and rural economic and social development programs, Gandhi was trying to translate his gospel of truth and non-violence into practical communal social reality. I took these lessons back to Christavashram.

In 1937 I visited Shantiniketan Ashram where I met its founder, the famous Indian poet Rabindranath Tagore, and there I learned about his new educational and rural reconstruction centre. This model of practical social change also became important to our development of Christavashram.

Celibacy, Marriage and Community

Making a personal decision on celibacy or marriage was not easy for me. I believed that just as the Lord had revealed to me His plan for my vocation, so too He would reveal whether He wanted me to be a witness to Him in a celibate or a married vocation. Both my founding 'brothers' were committed to celibacy and they wanted me to remain single so that Christavashram would develop as a celibate community. In Kerala, celibates were considered to be more saintly than lay people, and a married person in an ashram would be a contradiction in terms.

I believed that some people are called by God to be celibates and others to marry, and that we should each find out God's will before deciding.

My parents wanted me to either marry and get a well-paid position, or become ordained and serve the church. My work among destitute children and other ashram concerns, however, demanded more than my full attention so I decided to not even think about marriage for about seven years. At the end of that period, I prayed for God to reveal His will.

God works in mysterious ways! I was soon attracted to a young woman who took the initiative in our love affair. She was from a wealthy family, smart, good looking, cultured, well educated and religiously inclined. She showed great interest in Christavashram and in our work among destitute children. I asked her whether she would be prepared to live in a simple hut at Christavashram, and manage with only three sets of *khadi* (hand-spun) saris. Her mother said to her, 'How could I eat a meal without remembering that you and your children would be hungry at the ashram?'. Finally my love told me, 'I wouldn't be justified in allowing my children to be crippled by the poverty of the ashram'. Her rejection hurt me deeply, but the Lord gave me the strength to bear the pain. After some time I realised that it was the Lord who had stood in our way, thereby preventing me from the disaster of being unequally yoked.

Soon afterwards, Mary, who eventually became my wife, came to Christavashram as a volunteer in 1945. I had seen the leadership which she gave to the women students, and her total surrender to Christ, seeking first God's Kingdom and His justice. Mary's simplicity, her identification with our life and work, her practical ability and insight into our needs and problems, her sense of humour and her devotion to the Lord endeared her to all members, but especially to me.

Mary left Christavashram to attend college, after which she worked as a teacher. The Lord gave us many opportunities to meet and to share our ideas. Later, I visited her home to make a marriage proposal to her parents. Mary's father then visited my home and parents, and then the ashram. Christavashram, at that time, consisted of only simple structures on a barren hill. When he observed our diet and our commitment to having no private property he told me to just forget all about marrying his daughter! He then asked Mary to agree to a 'good' marriage proposal which he had arranged for her, but she said she wanted more time to think. Meanwhile, numerous attempts were being made to dissuade me from marriage in the interest of having a celibate ashram. Mary and I continued in faith and earnest prayer, supported by other praying friends.

In October 1946, I got a letter from Mary's father, offering me her hand in marriage and saying, 'something irresistible from within makes me do this'. We were soon wed and, 40 years later, are still happily together.

Now, all Christavashram members are married and have children, some of whom have also married. Although we have not laid up treasures for our children, God has enabled us to give them good educations, all with university degrees. True to the Lord's

PHOTO BY C. JOHN

*Mary and
Reverend Chandy*

assurance, He took care of problems like providing a dowry — a matter of great anxiety to parents in India.

The Institutions and Concerns of Christavashram

Christavashram now has 200 residents including members, volunteers and children. Another 30 associate members live outside the ashram and are self-supporting. We have 30 acres (12 hectares) of land on which we have built numerous residential, educational and religious buildings. Our agriculture and dairy farms and the Ashram Press provide most of our communal income. We do not work for wages but for the common good, with all money going into our 'common purse', and all expenses being paid therefrom.

Our early work among street-children has developed into the *Kerala Balagram and School* at Manganam, to where we have shifted the ashram. We have four cottages, each with 20 to 25 children being supervised by a couple who serve as 'parents'. Mary and I served as wardens in one of these cottages while raising our own three children with these once destitute and delinquent street-children. While living on the streets, some of them had contracted contagious diseases which were later transmitted to our own children. One of our sons thereby became a victim of leprosy, but we prayed, and later thanked God for his complete healing.

Visitors often wonder at the obvious good health of our own and the Balagram children who win prizes in sports, and often become school champions. Our staff in the Balagram join the boys in agricultural, dairying and other productive work, as well as in sports. Special care is given to character development, and to cultural pursuits such as music and painting. Deserving boys are sent for polytechnic or university studies. Over 1000 Balagram 'Old Boys' are now working as engineers, teachers, doctors, agriculturalists, tailors, etc. Our work-oriented school is accredited but does not receive Government financial support.

Our Retreat Centre displays on its front Christavashram's motto, 'Thy Kingdom Come'. Here we hold retreats, community meetings and conferences for people from various religious backgrounds from India and abroad. Our communal dining area is here. Also here is our *Japalaya* (chapel), built to an indigenous, no-walls model, where we hold daily morning worship and noon Scripture study and intercessions, as well as Sunday worship with Holy Communion. Both denominational and ecumenical services are held. Ashram members share Holy Communion at least weekly. Japalaya is the centre of Christavashram's spiritual life. We believe that service and social action which do not spring from worship and meditation often run to superficial waste and can even be destructive.

Members and children in front of the ashram Japalaya (Sevaks in back row)

The *Fellowship Of Reconciliation India* (FORI) was born at Christavashram in 1950. It is affiliated to the International FOR, with over 30 branches and affiliates. As Founder Secretary and President Emeritus, I serve on FORI's Executive Committee. FORI is a justice and peace-action body whose members are committed to agape–non-violence. We work for peaceful conflict resolution and for building a culture of non-violence in India and abroad.

We established the *Gurukul Ecumenical Institute and Peace Centre* at Christavashram in 1956 as a training centre for well-educated young people. This centre recaptures the spirit and practice of the ancient Gurukuls (mystics) of India, and of the teachings of poet Rabindranath Tagore. The syllabus of our Christavashram Gurukul Centre consists of the Bible and other Scriptures, social change and justice, peace and non-violence, comparative religion, psychology in everyday life, yoga and 'inner-life' culture, as well as productive manual labour and social service. Love, truth and justice are emphasised throughout. Students live, worship, work and eat as part of our ashram family. They are helped to choose their life work with a sense of God's call for service to fellow humans rather than for material power and worldly glamour.

We started the Ashram Press in 1965. It prints the *Inter Ashram Review* as well as Christian and other cultural publications. The Ashram Press trains our Balagram boys as printers, compositors and binders. The income from the Ashram Press helps to support our work but the stresses of its business problems have hampered our inner life of communal fellowship.

We started *Arunodayam* (Dawn), a socio-religious magazine, in 1937. It seeks to communicate the personal and social implications of the gospel, and to apply the standards and values of the kingdom of God in all social, political, national and international life. For its support of India's Freedom Movement and its stand against autocracy in Kerala, it was suppressed by the state regime. Police searched Christavashram, some of my co-workers were arrested, our campus was threatened with confiscation and I was threatened with violence and imprisonment.

Christavashram's *Sarvodaya Stree Shakti Kendra* is a family reconciliation centre which helps to educate women to realise their full human potential. It strives to build up the confidence of women, and to help them combat sexism and other social evils such as the dowry system and alcoholism, with their subsequent broken families. In Christavashram, men and women have equal participation and decision-making powers. We have had a woman as our leader for three years.

Against Environmental Pollution is our programme and centre for cultivating trees, and for producing compost manure from waste products and 'night soil'. Such recycling serves to deter pollution. We have won government prizes for our production of compost manure in this district.

How Does Christavashram Function?

The *Sabha*, consisting of all committed members of Christavashram, is the supreme authority in all questions relating to our communal policy and work. Obedience is required from all members. The *Acharya* (Director) is elected by the Sabha for three years. It is the duty of the Acharya (currently myself) to intercede for all the members, and to direct the ashram and its members. He is to see that our 'Rule of Life', voluntarily accepted by members, is maintained, and to grant temporary dispensation as occasion requires. An Ecumenical Advisory Board is nominated by the Sabha. The Community's general management is vested in an Executive Committee consisting of the Acharya, the Treasurer, the Secretary and four elected members. The Acharya is responsible for disbursing communal money according to the budget agreed to by the Sabha.

The Acharya can admit anyone as *Mithran* (novitiate) for six months, and can recommend any candidate to *Apekshaken* (second stage of membership) for one year. Admission to the third stage, *Bala Sevak* (for two years), and to full membership, *Sevak*, is done by the Sabha. A unanimous vote is needed for admission as a Sevak (of which we now have ten). Our associate members have only a year's probation, a simpler Rule of Life, can own private property and are free to live outside the ashram.

Sevaks must donate all their private property to the ashram when they join. Sevaks receive no salary but their personal and family needs will, as funds permit, be supplied from Christavashram's common purse. In our budget we conform, as far as possible, to the living standards of lower-working-class Indian people. Though we strive to be self-supporting, we have yet to be fully so, and still depend on financial support from friends. We must therefore be always ready to cut our meagre expenditure if anticipated income falls short. For our witness to capitalism and communism to be credible, we have to be not only self-supporting but also to make a surplus in order to help less-fortunate people around us.

Daily worship and shared meals are an integral part of our communal life. Each day, all members meet for at least one hour of bible study, prayer and intercession. Our main meal, which is vegetarian and simple, is eaten at noon, with all members and guests dining together as a community. Married members cook breakfast and supper in their own cottages. Members in charge of Balagram cottages have their breakfast and supper with their children, at their cottages.

Once Sadhu Mathai found that the dry fish which he kept for his cat had disappeared. Three members of the Youth Christian Council of Action, then resident with us but not accustomed to our strict vegetarian diet, had found it too hard to resist the temptation to steal and fry this fish in burning charcoal, before consuming it. When discovered one retorted, 'If you have to survive in this ashram you have to be either a cat or a European!' (for whom some exception was made).

'Make All Nations My Disciples'

This was the commission which Christ gave to all who would follow Him. I joined the Fellowship Of Reconciliation (FOR) in response to this commission, the fulfilment of which is possible only through the ministry of reconciliation.

My first contact with the FOR was in 1947 when Mary and I were doing research at Woodbrooke College in England. I had been invited to be a Fellow of the College with the freedom to do research for a year on any subject of my choosing. I chose 'Christianity, Communism and Non-violence' while Mary, who came with me, chose 'The Problem of Juvenile Destitution and Delinquency'. That year at Woodbrooke College helped us to know members of FOR and many other leading peace workers from around the world. They became living links in our ministry of reconciliation during our subsequent 'peace tours'. My first lecture tour, with the theme of 'Communism, Capitalism and Community', was during 1952–53 in the USA. The theme of my round-the-world lecture tour ten years later was 'Peace Culture Amidst Power Conflicts — Caste, Class, Race and State Tensions'. These tours covered five continents, offering me great opportunities to declare the Gospel of the Kingdom of God.

During one trip to Delhi in 1947 I had the opportunity to make a representation against a dreadful clause in India's Draft Constitution which would have permitted conscription during war. The offending clause was deleted. During the Sino-Indian War, I met Prime Minister Nehru on behalf of FORI, and made a representation against the compulsory National Cadet Corps. Nehru responded favourably and the government offered a National Service Scheme as an alternative. In 1954, I convened a mass meeting, under FORI auspices, to protest against atomic weapons and warfare. The resolution from this protest meeting was sent to the nuclear powers and the United Nations. Before the World Council of Churches met in Delhi in 1961, we convinced the heads of all Indian churches to sign a resolution for the WCC to strongly urge the nuclear powers and the United Nations to ban the testing, manufacturing, stockpiling and using of atomic weapons.

Christavashram has cooperated with other groups to create public support for land justice, thereby enabling the Kerala State Assembly to pass land redistribution legislation. Christavashram was instrumental in passing the Kerala State Children's Act, by which the state is committed to take care of every destitute child.

Ministry of Healing

We have experienced some wonderful healing through prayer at Christavashram. To mention a very personal experience, I received a letter from Mary during my Paine Lecture Tour in USA in 1952. She wrote that our second child had contracted whooping cough from a Balagram child, and that she herself had serious ear, nose and throat trouble. Her doctor said that she had to go to a major city hospital for treatment, but there was no one to look after the children, so she was not going. She urged me to pray for her recovery. I went to my room and prayed. When I arose, I found that the mattress on which I had bowed was wet with tears. My friend George Paine took me to the telegraph station where I sent a reply paid cable to Christavashram, so that I could get a response before I started on the next phase of my lecture tour. I got a reply, 'Mary normal'. In the letter which followed she wrote, '... healed so soon, as a result of your prayers. The children are free from whooping cough. A couple have come to help with the work in the cottage. Thank God things are all right now.' With a sense of victory, I could carry on with my lecture programme .

Another example of God's healing concerns India's Prime Minister Nehru, when he was suffering from a stroke in 1964. Mrs Lakshmi Menon, Nehru's Foreign Affairs Minister, had asked me to pray for his healing. Knowing that I would be in Delhi on a peace tour, she had arranged for me to meet Nehru. Our meeting lasted for over half an hour, and ended with a prayer for his healing. Afterwards, I was offered a sumptuous tea by his daughter, Mrs Indira Gandhi. It was a joy to read from the newspapers a few days later a statement by Mrs Gandhi that Nehru was restored to normal health. Mrs Menon wrote to me that the speech he made in Parliament after his recovery 'really contained words of healing', and that 'there has been a great conversion in him, from being an agnostic to faith in God'.

Nevertheless, Prime Minister Nehru died later that year.

Christavashram and Myself Today

When I look back over the 88 years of my life, I can see that God's abundant provisions were always there to meet each and every need, not only for my individual and family needs, but also for Christavashram. In spite of a poor diet and the strain of hard work, the Lord has given us good health and strong physiques. For example, once our ashram had no money and we were nearly starving. During one of our evening prayers we came to realise that such hardship allowed us to see anew the Lord's wonderful care and abundant provision. The next mail brought us a cheque which was enough for a month's food! I thank God that I could witness through my life in community that 'God is on the throne and could be relied upon to meet each and every need'.

I receive great joy from giving my time, thoughts and prayers to all the concerns of Christavashram. It is this joy which enables me to persevere at the age of 88, despite the many situations here which cause me pain and suffering. But whatever real suffering we have had to undergo at Christavashram was not on account of poverty, disease or physical pain, but mainly through the lack of that unity of spirit, of not being of 'one heart and one soul' as was evident in the community of the early church. Although some of my colleagues who were chiefly responsible for this communal suffering were also committed to our basic principles, their behaviour was contrary to them. Such situations caused tensions within Christavashram, and provided opportunities for disgruntled members to 'grind their own axes'. These conflicts hampered our spiritual life and stood in the way of more people joining our ashram. Those members who had joined Christavashram seeking primarily their personal well-being rather than the Kingdom of God and the well-being of all, became the devil's instruments in shattering both themselves and our community, while the Lord brought joy to those who lost themselves for the sake of His Kingdom.

Although we have fallen short of our divine calling, God has been faithful in taking care of us and providing all our communal needs at Christavashram during the past 62 years.

PHOTO BY C. JOHN

Christavashram members celebrating 60 years of communal living (Diamond Jubilee)

Conclusion

My study of communism has convinced me that although Marxism offers profound insights into the laws governing economic and social structures, it is based on half-truths, and its method of changing the world is one which self-defeats revolution. In the conflict between totalitarian Communism and an enslaving Capitalism, both being products of self-love, the only answer is Community, the ashram way of life. A new hungering after justice in the way of the cross, ie. agape–non-violence, is the world's most urgent need. If we pursue this way, no doubt we will still have to face suffering and persecution, but we shall develop, in community, the solidarity of fellowship as the 'Twice Born in Jesus Christ — The Children of God'.

Non-violent humanity is the only human species which will survive, and only the moral leadership of the non-violent Church of Christ can create that humanity. If there be any real wisdom, it is the wisdom that comes from the way of the cross. Intentional communities, living through love in all their social and economic relationships, should take shape around the world. Each commune can become a living and working brotherhood where dynamic non-violence is practised and proclaimed as spearheads of a new society. This new agape social order will come into being only with the second coming of Christ when the environment and nature herself will be freed from pollution — the smokescreen of human greed.

The saviour of humanity and of nature is to be the intentional community of the Children of God.

Introduction: Findhorn Foundation and Mary Inglis

Findhorn Foundation is probably the best-known intentional community in the world. It was started in 1962 near Inverness in the far north of Scotland, two kilometres (one mile) from the small Scottish coastal village of Findhorn from which it takes its name. The 'Findhorn Story' has become almost synonymous with what many people understand as 'the new age', and many terms such as 'devas', 'attunement', 'holding the energy', 'focaliser' and 'manifestation' owe their current meanings to this community. The community is both growing and shrinking. With 150 members, Findhorn Foundation is the smallest it has been for over 20 years - yet there is dramatic growth in the community of several hundred non-members who live nearby and support its global work. Because Findhorn Foundation has changed dramatically over the years, it is a fascinating example of a communal society that can adapt and thrive under often adverse conditions.

Mary Inglis is Scottish, although she grew up in South Africa where she worked as a journalist. She has been a Findhorn Foundation member since 1973. She has served in many capacities at Findhorn, and is currently one of the Findhorn Trustees. Mary's account is very open and honest as she reveals her frustrations with communal life, as well as sharing its joys. I first met Mary in 1988 and we have been friends ever since. I have learned to value her wisdom, honesty and insight.

I first visited Findhorn Foundation in 1982 while doing research for my PhD. Having read so many glowing reports about it, I expected to be disappointed. Instead, I was thoroughly impressed, even though I was there at a time of financial and leadership problems. Since 1988, I have spent an average of two months each year living and working at Findhorn where I am a Findhorn Foundation Fellow (like an honorary member). Much of the work on this book was done while in residence at Findhorn Foundation's Cluny Hill College in the latter half of 1995.

Much has been written about the Findhorn Foundation, the best book being *The Findhorn Community* by Carol Riddell (Findhorn: Findhorn Press, 1990). More up to date information may be gained through http://www.mcn.org/findhorn/index.html. Many thousands of people visit Findhorn Foundation every year, some only to look about and many others staying to do Experience Week. Prospective visitors must book ahead by writing to the Accommodation Secretary, Findhorn Foundation, Cluny Hill College, Forres, IV36 ORD, Scotland (tel: +44 1309 673655; fax: +44 1309 673113; e-mail: accomms@findhorn.org).

CHAPTER 11

Findhorn Foundation: Nature Spirits and New Age Business

by Mary Inglis

In April, the gorse in Scotland starts to flower. By May, it's in full bloom, swathes of yellow splashed across the greening countryside. Between the sea and the caravan park where the Findhorn Community began in 1962, banks of blossoms hug the northern edges of our property, and the slightest touch of sun wafts their peach-and-coconut aroma along the paths between our bungalows and caravans.

I first visited Findhorn in early gorse season, and it's been a special time for me ever since. For years, the appearance of the yellow blossoms signalled the start of a personal spring ritual — an early rise and a 15-minute walk (occasionally a jog) through the gorse-studded dunes for a dip in the breath-stopping waters of the Moray Firth, or a time of contemplation, sitting on the pebbles on the beach.

Recently my ritual has been reduced to a somewhat later stroll to my office through the Findhorn Community gardens where the yellow of gorse is echoed by daffodils, crocuses and poppies. The poppies have been a creeping addition since Peter Caddy, one of our founders, left in 1979. 'One year's seeding, seven years' weeding', he would declare as he strode around with his disciplinarian's eye, pulling the poppies and other 'weeds' from our flower beds. On his return visits to the Community, he would attempt to influence the gardeners, whose ideas on 'cooperation with nature', the thing for which we were best known in our early days, by then significantly diverged from his. When they didn't listen, or didn't listen fast enough, he'd collect a couple of newer members and

Aerial view of Findhorn Foundation caravan park

embark on the pruning and weeding he felt necessary, even one time making a secret dawn raid to clear the tangled gorse and brambles of the 'wild garden' reserved for the nature spirits, which he himself had established as a no-go area for humans 30 years previously. Shock waves reverberated for weeks, but Peter was unrepentant. The 'wild garden' was not supposed to be a 'wilderness', he said. Humans should do the clearing that nature spirits could not, and then it could be left to nature again.

Peter died in a car accident in Germany in February 1994, and since then the yellow poppies have bloomed unchallenged in our gardens.

I joined Findhorn Community in 1973, eleven years after Peter and Eileen Caddy and Dorothy Maclean, acting on the guidance Eileen received from 'The God Within', towed their caravan onto a site next to a rubbish dump in a caravan park on the coastal sand dunes of northeast Scotland, and began — also on guidance — to grow vegetables to supplement their unemployment benefits. Dorothy received guidance to contact the 'devas' or spiritual formative forces within nature, and thus began our experiment in conscious cooperation with nature (both the 'outer' realms of plants, soil and compost, and the 'inner' realms of devas, angels and nature spirits) that produced remarkable results. The richness and diversity of those early gardens on then sandy soil drew interest from around the world.

When I arrived, there was a community of 140 people of several nationalities (nearly half of them were Americans) crowded into a cluster of mobile homes at the top end of the caravan park, amidst vibrant and well-kept gardens. I was put into a 'coffin' room in a caravan I shared with three others — a woman in another coffin and a couple in a slightly larger room. We shared a small kitchen and living-room. The rooms were called coffins because there wasn't room for much more than a body (alive or dead!) Each room was about 4 feet (1.2 metres) wide. One half held a tiny bed, alongside which was a small wardrobe. A shelf folded down from the wall; I could sit on the bed and write at my 'desk'.

Despite our cramped living conditions, we had a tremendous sense of expansiveness and aliveness. Perhaps this was due to being involved in a shared venture and

Mary Inglis on the verge of cutting Findhorn Foundation's birthday cake

©FINDHORN FOUNDATION VISUALS DEPARTMENT

exploring a shared vision. Everyone knew each other; everyone ate lunch and dinner together in the Community Centre; everyone worked in one or more of the work departments including the kitchen, homecare, garden, maintenance, office, building, a few craft studios, printing and publishing, audio-visuals, and a grocery, craft and book shop. 'Work is love in action' was one of our maxims, together with 'Love where you are, what you're doing and who you're with', so we did our best to practise this.

Everyone was expected to be at morning meditations in our sanctuary. These were times for both spiritual alignment and for connecting as a community, and if you didn't turn up for more than two days in a row, you were likely to find Peter at your door asking you why. If your absence persisted, you were asked to leave. Peter was definitely the authority in the community. Eileen received guidance for our community's direction, while Peter made sure it was carried out. But around the time I arrived, Eileen's guidance was to stop receiving guidance for the community. People were supposed to learn to turn within and seek their own guidance, and if they were constantly turning to her, this defeated the objective. I spent hours in sanctuary trying to hear an inner, directive voice. I had great meditations but never heard a voice. After a while I realised that whenever I asked questions of whatever spiritual presence I was addressing — be that God, the Angel of Findhorn or my Higher Self — a procession of images would move across my inner screen, and if I paid attention, they usually had relevance to what I was asking. I'd been tuning in on the wrong wavelength!

Findhorn identified itself as a working community, and we worked a seven-day week. Often, I lost track of what day it was. I worked initially in the gardens, kitchen, and homecare (cleaning communal areas). After someone discovered I could type, most of my afternoons were spent typesetting in our small Publications Department. I worked mostly on *Findhorn News*, a quarterly publication that went to people who wanted to keep in touch with what was happening here, and on books by David Spangler, an inspired and visionary philosopher who had spent three years at the Foundation. David had left shortly before I arrived, and many of his lectures and 'transmissions' (communications from non-physical beings) were being put into book form. I got a thorough grounding in the philosophical roots and explorations of the meaning of the 'new age' — and I lapped it up. Groups of us would listen to and discuss his tapes, relating the ideas to our lives and experiences, our hopes and visions.

While access to David was through his tapes and writings, Dorothy, Eileen and Peter were all here and we could talk with them at any time. R. Ogilvie Crombie, or Roc, who made the original contact with Pan and the nature spirits in the Findhorn garden experiment, visited regularly and was available for conversational explorations about what it meant to work in cooperation with spirit, nature and one another.

We saw ourselves as an educational centre which grew people as well as plants, a place of spiritual practice where life itself was the classroom and people could learn to open to the reality of spirit and give it expression in their lives. It was a rich and vibrant atmosphere. As we lived, worked, meditated and shared, we had a sense that we were part of something much larger than ourselves, that there was a spiritual presence interacting with and guiding our lives with which we could co-create, and that through changing our consciousness and our consequent activities, we were contributing to the emergence of a new age. People arrived with amazing stories of how they had come here, or had 'manifested' the means to stay. Energy follows thought, we learnt, so we watched our thoughts and marvelled at the results, which often seemed miraculous.

One day I awoke, unable to open my right eye. My contact lens had scratched it, and it was extremely painful. To recover, I knew I should sleep for several hours. But there was a special event on 'Cooperation with Nature' with Dorothy Maclean and Roc which I wanted to attend, so I put on an eye patch and went to the first lecture. But the pain was too much, so I gave up and headed for bed. On the path I met a bald woman in orange robes who was visiting from Auroville. 'I don't believe it!', she exclaimed, when she saw my eye patch. I tried to explain the what and how and why of my condition, but she continued to proclaim her disbelief. I couldn't get past her. Eventually, in desperation, I said 'Ok! I don't believe it either!' and as I spoke I felt my eye open under the patch — an instantaneous healing. It was an object lesson in the power of thought and in the power of grace operating in our lives.

*   *   *

I'm one of the few Scottish members of the Community, although I seldom identify myself as Scottish. I was born in Edinburgh in 1945 but grew up in Africa, where my father was in the British colonial service. We moved a lot; the longest we stayed in one place was five years. After some initial schooling in Lesotho, I went to boarding school in South Africa, and then to Rhodes University for a BA degree in English and Politics, before joining a South African newspaper and working as a journalist for three years.

Coming to Findhorn was my response to a spiritual calling, so I look back to see the signposts in my past. My childhood wasn't overtly religious, although I learned a lot from my parents' values and how they lived. Every night, mother said prayers with each of us four children. Church was not initially a large part of my background, with the visiting Anglican priest including our village on his rota only once a month.

At my Christian, all-girls boarding school, I became interested in God and how spiritual values could be applied in our lives. Then I went to university and became involved in student politics. In terms of racial segregation, Lesotho and South Africa started off similarly, but in South Africa apartheid was being increasingly enforced by law, while in Lesotho segregation was being broken down as the country moved towards independence. As I became more aware of what was happening in South Africa, of what was being done by people who called themselves Christians, and in the name of their God, I decided that if this was what God was directing people to do, I didn't want anything to do with Him! I doubted His existence. I went on protest marches and began working for the weekly student newspaper, convinced that the world could be changed by words, writing, speeches and radical ideas.

After university, I ran the National Student Press Association, a news service for the student press, while also working for the Institute of Race Relations, and then I joined a liberal newspaper. Two important things happened during these four years. Firstly, a group of us contacted spirit beings through an Ouija board session, and for several months we received teachings from them. They emphasised that in political action, motivation was very important. Action was necessary, but hatred or violence would diminish the possibility of positive change.

Secondly, I became involved with Christian Education and Leadership Training, which used group dynamics and encounter techniques within a spiritual framework. CELT groups were ecumenical, multi-racial and profoundly transformative. We explored the attitudes, beliefs and behaviours that were part of our collective dynamic, dealt with conflict, witnessed each other's pain, strength, despair and hope, forged deep connections with and respect for one another, and generated a hope and creativity that didn't end with the workshops. This experiential and value-rich approach to personal and collective issues connected me with a living spirituality that was deep and multi-faceted, with potential for transforming our lives, relationships and society. I became increasingly involved with this work, and left my journalist position to explore it further in Britain.

I spent the next two years engaging with a variety of approaches to individual and group work — Gestalt, Re-evaluation Co-Counselling, massage, meditation, and T-group and group dynamics. I spent a summer in Northern Ireland on a project bringing Catholic and Protestant teenagers together in work and recreational activities, and six months with the St Mungo Community in London, working with destitute men. I experienced the transformative and creative power of groups, both in terms of each individual's development, and in terms of what people, acting together, can do for their environment. I noticed that when there was an explicit spiritual component the group worked smoother and faster. But most groups focused either on personal growth or social action, rarely on both. I was interested in both, as well as in spiritual aspects, and when I encountered Findhorn, it seemed to be working with all three.

My mother had heard about Findhorn while in South Africa, and when she came to Britain in 1972 we visited the Community and came away with pamphlets about the Findhorn Garden, books of Eileen's and Dorothy's guidance, and David Spangler's *The Vision of Findhorn in World Transformation*. Something deep in me responded to their message of God or spirit being in all creation, not just in individuals but also in nature, and that we could co-create with this spirit.

In 1973 I visited Findhorn for four weeks — which stretched into two months. In many ways I loved it. People weren't just talking about ideas and principles, they were living them. But I wasn't sure about joining. Although I could see how what was happening here could provide a seedbed for changes in our planetary culture and way of life, it felt a bit insular. I felt I was called to be more socially active. Perhaps I would make regular visits, but work actively in the world 'out there'? I was also uneasy that people here weren't doing more personal and interpersonal work, in particular dealing with feelings. There was an emphasis on 'building the new' rather than 'healing the old', on creating the new age and being the changes we envisioned. This was inspiring and empowering, attracting and nourishing a lot of creative people and ventures, but it also had its drawbacks. Despite the vision of the 'new' being one of wholeness, there were subtle value judgements between the 'soul' and 'personality' aspects of people. 'That's old age', or 'You're coming from a personality level', were real putdowns, and while the statement might be true, the judgement behind it resulted in people being hesitant to share feelings. Sometimes, people would cry alone or agonise for days over some personal difficulty which, had it been shared, might well have been resolved in tears and laughter with some affection and perspective from a friend.

I went to London, but two months later, when I was offered a job I'd previously have jumped at — doing group work in youth education with the Church of England — I knew I was to live at Findhorn. I've been here ever since, just twice seriously exploring moving on, and both times clearly choosing to remain.

*   *   *

The community I live in today is very different from the one I joined in 1973. In 1972 Findhorn Foundation was legally established as a charitable trust, and for many years the Foundation *was* the Community. Today it's only part of it, albeit a large part. It is responsible for six large properties, including Cluny College, a 180-bed former hotel, and the Findhorn Bay Caravan Park. Our main activity is education, with 4000 people each year taking part in residential programmes from a week to six months long, while 10,000 day visitors are welcomed annually. Our cooperation with nature now includes not just work in the gardens, but also a variety of environmental projects. In 1990, work began on the construction of an 'ecological village' at the Park. Aging caravans are being replaced with ecological housing, a wind-generator provides almost 20% of our electricity needs, and many dwellings have solar panels. We plan to expand our renewable energy systems, and recently constructed a 'Living Machine', a sewage treatment facility using plant, bacteria and animal life to break down waste naturally, without chemicals, to a quality higher than European Community standards.

Inside the 'Living Machine'

©FINDHORN FOUNDATION VISUALS DEPARTMENT

Recently our community has expanded more outside than inside the Foundation. Some former Foundation groups or departments have become independent, such as Trees For Life, an environmental group working with reforestation, Healthworks, a holistic health care practice which serves both the Community and local residents, and Findhorn Press. Other educational organisations such as the Moray Steiner School, Minton House and the Newbold Trust have been established. Some former Foundation activities moved into New Findhorn Directions Ltd, the Foundation's wholly owned trading company. NFD, which also runs the holiday section of the Caravan Park, now has a trading turnover that exceeds the Foundation's. Many individuals run small businesses or counselling and therapeutic practices. Some are long-term residents who left membership to follow personal initiatives while still maintaining a close relationship with the Foundation. Some wanted more privacy and space, some a larger personal income and different standard of living than the Foundation provides, some to pursue an activity not possible under the charitable trust. Some have been re-employed by the Foundation in a part-time professional capacity.

As a result, Findhorn Community contains a flourishing diversity of concerns and individuals associated with but not part of the Foundation — materially independent yet sharing similar values. Of about 600 people in this wider community, only 150 are full-time Foundation 'members' — employees and students — who are housed and fed by the organisation. Students pay to be here for their first two years, while staff members receive a monthly allowance of £185. Everyone else is responsible for their own livelihood. Once you could be involved with the Community only by joining the Foundation but today there are a variety of ways.

Part of me is excited by this as an opportunity to translate our values into an enduring lifestyle, to bring them into the physical, cultural, social, economic and political arenas. It's a process of trial and error, of course, and sometimes it seems there's more failure than success. There's frustration when visions don't translate immediately into reality, or when community process slows them down or kills them off. Sometimes, everyone wants a say on everything, and little gets done. New members mean that certain ground is covered repeatedly as they integrate into our community. And with more of us, there are more good ideas and conflicting visions, not all of which can be enacted. There are also differing ideas on what is 'spiritual' or 'new age'. We need to remember that we're a social and spiritual laboratory, an experimental centre where we learn as much from failures as from successes, and to take a longer-term view of what's happening here. Our achievements in giving expression to a spirit of community — with each other, with spirit and with the natural world, although relatively small-scale — have been considerable. Given the separative and anti-community forces in the world, this is no small contribution to planetary evolution and well-being.

Part of me also hankers after the simplicity of earlier years when it was easier to experience community. Many of the elements that fostered cohesion then are now absent. No longer can we all eat or meditate together. Attendance at our twice-daily communal

©FINDHORN FOUNDATION VISUALS DEPARTMENT

Findhorn Foundation on its 25th birthday (November1987) in front of the Universal Hall

meditations is low. Although everyone is expected to have a spiritual practice, there's no way of ensuring this. With jobs more specialised and widespread, the sense of shared vision and work is not as tangible. Even to get just Foundation members together is difficult; not only does it take considerable organisation, but it's also likely to be challenged as 'exclusive' by those in the wider Community. We have guests here every week, often over 100 at a time. The days when everyone knew each other are long gone.

In some ways we are several communities, and within these groups intimate connections are fostered. The 35 people who run Cluny Hill College are very much a 'family'; the Park, with a more diverse collection of people, is less so. Foundation work departments and many of the NFD businesses and associated ventures have weekly 'attunements' which include personal sharing and support for members. Collective gatherings, including an annual 'internal conference', as well as spiritual festivals, are organised by Core Group, a spiritual 'holding' group consisting of people from both the Foundation and the wider Community. People are beginning to see themselves as members of a larger community of which the Foundation is a part.

In terms of governance, the wider Community doesn't yet have structures for organising its collective affairs, although this is being explored. Part of the difficulty is that the Foundation owns almost all the collective facilities in the Community, yet it's not appropriate either for the Foundation to coordinate Community affairs, or for the wider Community to legislate in Foundation matters. Foundation management groups listen to the needs and opinions of everyone concerned, while also drawing the boundaries they feel necessary to maintain the integrity and well-being of the Foundation.

Within the Foundation, governance is clearer. As far as possible, decisions are made by those affected by or responsible for them, while a management group coordinates and makes decisions for the whole. Certain decisions *have* to be brought to members, and we require that these be made by consensus. If we can't reach consensus, then a decision can be made by a 90% majority of those voting at the next meeting. Consensus is defined as everyone involved agreeing either to a course of action, or to being a 'loyal minority' who, while disagreeing with a decision, agree to support its enactment.

We clarified these decision-making procedures only recently. Years ago, authority began moving out from Peter, first to a group of departmental heads or 'focalisers', then to management groups. In 1983, the decision to buy the Caravan Park, at a time of financial crisis when the purchase price of £380,000 was the same size as our debt, was taken by consensus. Since then, many people assumed that we operate by consensus, but this wasn't clearly defined, nor was it clear what we did if action was needed yet consensus couldn't be reached. With new members, problems arose when everyone had an equal voice while they didn't have an equal understanding or responsibility. Conflicting needs for efficient management and community participation posed a dilemma. The new procedures, while yet to prove themselves, seek to address this.

Legally, the Trustees control the charitable trust and the 'membership' have no formal say in running the Foundation. In practice, however, the Foundation is largely self-governing, and Trustees are unlikely to make a decision that the majority of members oppose. Trustees tend to approve initiatives originating within the body of the Community or to encourage directions which have been around for a while.

*   *   *

©FINDHORN FOUNDATION VISUALS DEPARTMENT

Community Centre with recent extension

Personally, I'm not sure where I now belong. For years I've been intimately involved with the Foundation, at different times editing our quarterly magazine *One Earth*, leading courses and workshops, working in our Personnel Department, and moving in and out of the management and core groups. In 1981, I became a Trustee. I've nurtured and encouraged a more inclusive participation in Community affairs and decision-making, and helped create space for personal and therapeutic work to support people in the changes they go through. And I've personally received a great deal of fulfilment through my involvement here.

But now, at age 50, I'm feeling there are aspects of myself and my life that I've neglected or overlooked. For years I've worked well over — often double — our current guideline of a 30-hour working week. It's difficult for me to say no to perceived needs which I know I could meet, or to invitations to share perspectives and skills which my longevity here gives me. I feel I *should* be available, that I won't really be accepted if I'm not — a dysfunctional attitude that isn't helped when people *do* get upset if I don't meet their expectations or requests! In fact, I'm not accepting parts of myself. Too often, I inappropriately override my personal needs and wants, and neglect my body and health.

It has also affected my intimate relationships. For years, although I had deep and satisfying friendships, my primary relationship was with the Community; whenever the possibility arose of a relationship with a 'significant other', the other lost out. Five years ago I began a relationship with a man with whom I now live. It's meant a re-ordering of my involvements and priorities; it rightly needs quality time and attention. Currently the relationship is shaky and I don't know whether it will continue. One of the contributing factors is that we both have workaholic patterns that are difficult for us to interrupt, despite our intentions to change. The Foundation also finds it difficult to interrupt, rather than support, patterns of over-work which, after all, help keep the place going!

Since 1987 my main work has been administering and running Transformation Game programmes both here and throughout the world. The Game is a playful yet

Mary (second from right) facilitating a Transformation Game

substantial approach to self-assessment and transformation, created by former member Joy Drake as a way of distilling the essence of the educational process that happens here as we begin to view life as a learning arena. I love this work, and theoretically it means I'm less Foundation-focused, particularly as I travel more. But in practice, I find myself constantly pulled into Community matters. Despite my best resolutions to disengage, I can't seem to hold to them, and my involvements creep up past the overload position again. Sometimes I wonder if I can actually manage to achieve more balance in my life without leaving the Community.

I'm also tired of some aspects of Foundation life, particularly the recycling of issues and structures. Each time a previous structure re-emerges it's heralded as 'new'; those creating the changes are enthusiastic and engaged, feeling they're contributing to our evolution. I know different forms are needed at different times to meet different needs; I see learning and growth happen for those involved, and whatever the structure, we keep going. Perhaps this recycling is part of the nature of the place, one of the 'class-rooms' in a flow-through, spiritual school? But I'd like to step out of some of it and leave it to others. Can I step out and still be here?

I'm also concerned that we may be verging on supplanting the spiritual with the pop-psychological. The excesses of the human potential movement haven't left us untouched. It's important to ask questions like 'What makes your heart sing?' or 'Does this serve me and my development?', but it's not always the appropriate or the critical question. The search for personal fulfilment can be a substitute or barrier to a deeper level of engagement with spirit. As one of the people who spoke up for the inclusion of personal work, I view with alarm how process has become primary in some of our educational offerings, and indeed in aspects of our lives. I won't ask some people, 'How are you?' when I meet them on the path; I don't want to listen to a catalogue of their recent (and not so recent!) emotional states. We need to provide space for personal and therapeutic work, but also need to define the boundaries.

I would like to see us step into a new cycle, rather than just recycle the old. For years we've had a vision of education being offered here which would serve the emergence of a new culture that sees all life on our planet as community. Together with the living education we already provide, it could combine a strong cognitive element, exploring the characteristics of cultural transformation. To some of us who've been here longer, both inside and outside the Foundation, this seems an obvious and inspiring next step, something the Foundation could coordinate, but which would draw on the whole Community as a teaching tool. But the Foundation hasn't yet really embraced the idea, while the wider Community can't do it alone. In order for it to happen, it will need to be a co-creative venture, and will require a willingness in the Foundation to let go of maintaining 'community' and 'education' in the ways we're used to.

Will I spend the rest of my life here? I don't know. When I began this chapter, it was springtime; as I revise it, it's autumn, and instead of yellow poppies in the garden there are thousands of fallen leaves, brown and soggy in November rain. I'm reminded of the seasonal cycles, that each autumn much dies, each winter preserves the essential structures, and each spring brings forth new life. I feel that parts of both myself and the Community are in a dying process.

Findhorn Foundation was not formed as an intentional community, but resulted from attunement to spirit, and obedience to what came from that attunement. Community was an outgrowth of this. Our forms have changed over the years, but hopefully they have led us into a deeper relationship with spirit and awakened us to an experience of community not dependent on place, but which reminds us of our connectedness with all life. As long as we provide an environment where we can explore and practise living this interconnectedness, I'll be involved, one way or another. What form that involvement will take... I'll wait to see what spring brings.

Cluny Hill College in the snow

Introduction: The Emissaries and Anne Blaney

©ANNE BLANEY

Anne Blaney

The Emissaries is near the town of 100 Mile House, north east of Vancouver in central British Columbia, Canada. Established in 1948, it is the third oldest communal group in this book. Since the death of its second charismatic leader, Martin Exeter, a British lord, The Emissaries has been undergoing some dramatic changes. As you will read, it is becoming less a commune and more a community, while still adhering to many of its original principles. The development of accountability is a key theme. There are several other Emissary communities in North America, but this story is mainly about 100 Mile Community.

Anne Blaney grew up in eastern Canada and trained as a social worker. She lived for several years in a classic 'hippie-commune' before joining The Emissaries in 1974. There, she has worked in numerous positions and is currently General Manager at 100 Mile Community.

It is possible to visit The Emissaries but only after making prior arrangements. They may be contacted at P.O. Box 9, 100 Mile House, British Columbia, VOK 2EO, Canada (fax: +1-604-3952143; or e-mail: ebclodge@netshop.net).

CHAPTER 12

The Emissaries: Hard Fall to Accountability

by Anne Blaney

Why do some people want to live communally — and why do other people think we're absolutely nuts? There's one certainty for us who choose to live in community: we're going to have to explain it for the rest of our lives!

After 23 years of explaining, here are some conclusions. In my life I have chosen *home* as a high priority. However, for me, home extends far past my immediate family. As others experience their nuclear family, I experience a larger network as nurturing, and a place where I nurture others. In other words, I like home, and home for me is *big*!

My Adolescent Communalism

I was part of the kick-off of the baby boom, born in 1946 in the aftermath of World War II. At that time there was blind optimism that the suffering was over. Unfortunately for the dream, not all of my generation believed that it *was* necessarily a better world.

The sudden death of my father, when I was five, was a catalyst for me to experience extended family. My own family simply wasn't enough, so I adopted other mothers and fathers and their animals, houses and children to fill my needs. My childhood neighborhood was a vital place. I began to doubt that what was missing in my family could ever be filled by a traditional nuclear family.

In 1955 I went with my widowed mother and younger brother to a family camp run by the YMCA in Ontario, Canada, where I grew up. Not long after our arrival, my mother, anticipating some quality time with her children, noticed that I was missing. I had plunged into the organized activities: I took swimming lessons, I loved the large noisy dining room, and I performed in a skit before the entire camp. I had my first communal experience and I loved it.

By my 20s I was hot on the trail of a different way of living, and my interest in spiritual matters was growing. When I graduated with a BA in Sociology, the work ethic was being questioned, and conformity was looking very unattractive, so a few of us took steps away from mainstream society. Miraculously, we were not struck dead! In fact, experimenting with the creation of what was to become a subculture or counter-culture was empowering.

As I couldn't see how to bring this counter-culture into my life, I worked two years for market and psychological research companies. My work included jetting from eastern Canadian cities to the remote regions of northern Manitoba, a province with many North American Indians. There, the planes were much smaller, often with pontoons in order to reach communities accessible only by barge or air. It was here, supervising a survey for the Federal Government, that I tasted small town life, met the individualistic men and women of Canada's north, and touched the unique spirituality of Indian culture. These were influences that impressed me deeply and offered pieces of the picture I was envisioning.

My Coming-of-Age Communalism

For the next two years I worked on a Master's Degree in social work at university in Vancouver. It wasn't only in school where I was learning, but in the school of life! It was 1970. By day I was a psychiatric social worker, by night I was a 'hippie', living in a condemned house, eating food stolen by enterprising residents, and discussing the upcoming sex-change operation of a transsexual neighbor. One evening my boyfriend and I returned from a rare dinner out, and walked into the aftermath of a drug arrest of a resident couple who ran a 'head shop'. The police had forced the couple to lead them to our house, whose population had decided to drop LSD that night. When the police broke into the house they *startled* 20 people tripping madly. One woman managed to eat a dozen 'hits' of acid, thereby destroying the evidence before her boyfriend was escorted to jail. I spent the rest of that night talking her (and others) down, while arranging bail for her boyfriend, in cooperation with The Black Panthers, a militant black group. It was a good night to have gone out for dinner!

Next year, I quit graduate school and returned to Toronto, to a relationship with someone else who wanted to change the world. I was with him because he had asked me a critical question, 'Why are you becoming a social worker?' I couldn't answer to *my* satisfaction let alone to his! It dawned on me that instead of assisting those who were having difficulties, I would try building a different type of society, and be a part of the solution rather than the problem. A new need had surfaced for me; the need to achieve a collective purpose with like-minded individuals. I was excited!

In Ontario in 1972, with my partner and me as leaders, we formed a commune called Granny's, named after the granola (breakfast cereal) we sold. We shared all material goods, supported ourselves by our business, and aspired to acts of charity for the larger community; goals we never quite achieved! We did manage, however, to make granola, ingest illegal substances, experiment sexually, make music and celebrate our separation from anything 'straight'. I adjusted to being out of step. The counter-culture was growing. It was clear that revolutionary changes in attitude were required! The top-heavy, materialistic monster of mainstream society was doomed and I was *out*! Just as I had quit graduate school, I was now quitting society. It was a scary yet irresistible path.

In Granny's Commune, I continued to explore the edges of my freedom. I learned from those I met, although life wasn't quite so dramatic as my double identity in Vancouver had been. Granny's was home to many, and as one of its originators and coupled to its leader, I felt a responsibility to the mostly younger members. My exploration was largely internal, revolving around relationships. I was challenged by my partner and by my own ideals to prove that relationship did not mean ownership. Intellectually I believed this, but emotionally it was difficult. As we experimented with multiple partners, I agonized over jealousy. I deliberately broke through layers of my own conventions by venturing into other sexual liaisons. In the end, I achieved a comfortable peace with my demons, deciding that I preferred quality to quantity! It was another invaluable lesson, to listen to my inner voice instead of to those around me. I also explored inner landscapes by means of psychedelic drugs, and by working with Primal Scream–Gestalt methodologies.

The 1970s' spiritual paths were part of our subculture. Psychedelics, eastern philosophy and ritual were everywhere, and many groups were actively recruiting. Although our leader's influence on the commune was more political than spiritual, some members were drawn in a spiritual direction. Granny's became notorious throughout Ontario by us selling granola and being colorful. We were interviewed by the media and had a steady stream of visitors. Granny's averaged a population of 22, and lasted two years. One of our more colourful residents was self-named 'Vince, the Prince, King of All Living Wombats in Captivity', an older man who had 'done time' (in prison), and was trying to wean himself from alcohol by switching to 'grass'. While Vince's happiness no longer came out of a bottle, his hair color did, and he provided us with some very 'off the wall' entertainment. One trick involved appearing in a trench coat, apparently wearing nothing underneath. He would ceremoniously 'flash', revealing that he was actually fully clothed, pant-legs rolled up. Laughter would go round the room, only to escalate when everyone noticed that although clothed, his fly was down, and ... !

In this communal setting, I chose to meet another challenge — motherhood — a profound experience which shaped my future choices. Unfortunately, my partnership did not survive the perils of freedom or the interpersonal conflicts in our group. As a mother, I now needed a stable social environment, with purpose and philosophy, where I could raise my child.

My Mature(?) Communalism

A member of Granny's Commune had joined a spiritual program called Emissaries of Divine Light, or EDL, which included communal living as part of its operation. EDL's mission was to 'carry forward a work of spiritual regeneration of mankind'. A worldwide organization, EDL had rural communes in various countries, plus numerous smaller, city communes where members lived this philosophy. The forms varied from a church in the USA to a non-profit society in Canada. EDL was a lifestyle and a subculture, some would say a cult. Although it was optional, most members shared in a collective economic base, receiving a monthly stipend with most money going to the organization both locally and internationally. The program presented a rearticulation of Christianity by its founder, Lloyd Meeker (known as Uranda), who first spoke his revelations in 1932, in Tennessee. Uranda claimed that Christ had not died on the cross, but instead, while alive, had gone through a transmutation, thereby setting a precedent of hope for all humans. Uranda taught that transmutation was possible for mankind while on earth.

Two major communes, Sunrise Ranch in Colorado, USA and 100 Mile Community in British Columbia, Canada, took shape under Uranda's charismatic leadership, before he died in 1954. Martin Exeter, a British Lord, succeeded Uranda and continued as spiritual leader until his death in 1988. Martin's style was more authoritative and attractive, with his spiritual practicality, so the Emissary ranks grew during his leadership. Hundreds of people came from other alternative lifestyles to join the Emissaries. These recruits included my daughter and me, and four members of the Granny's Commune. Five of us are still members.

I loved the spiritual strength of this well-established network, the rich teachings of Uranda, and the continuing discourses by Martin, in whom I found a kindred spirit. There was also a close-knit community for my daughter and me. After I joined in 1974, I lived for seven years in an Emissary commune in Toronto, where I worked as 'home staff', with other members working 'outside', while we pooled income. We offered our philosophy and way of life through public gatherings, spending time with people, and by sharing a healing service called 'attunements'.

With the Emissaries, I began as a neophyte. Emissary people were basically middle class, drawn to the inspirational philosophy, and many lived communally but not out of preference. For me, living in the Ontario group required considerable adjustment. One friend said that whenever he lost hope, he thought of me as proof that 'spirit' could accomplish anything! Naturally, we all came with various 'immaturities', but unfortunately, instead of these being 'mentored' through an educational process, personal issues were lesser parts of the more important cosmic viewpoint. In spite of the lifestyle compromises I was forced to make, it was worthwhile so that I could pursue a spiritual direction within a safe setting for my daughter. Ex-Granny's members, now Emissaries, would encourage each other through this cultural shock, agreeing that the beliefs rang true. EDL leaders astutely nudged us Granny's types into leadership, and I think we were a breath of fresh air. I eventually became the female leader for Emissaries in Toronto, teamed with a male Granny's associate! My communal experience helped in this full-time leadership job which included representing Emissary spirituality.

An intimate home setting was a high priority for Emissary communes, both for the spiritual well-being of residents and for those we attracted. Home facilitated healing and spiritual growth. We crossed a line into an experience of family where, as in a family, we weren't always friends but were undeniably and intimately connected. Martin Exeter, through twice-weekly addresses, was our patriarch, self-contained, stern but benevolent. Born an aristocrat, Martin was a quiet person who earned my respect by his intelligent, unswerving attention to spirituality. His laughter could fill a room. I was very fond of him.

One of Martin's themes was personal responsibility, but I could see a gap between theory and practice. EDL's organizational structure detracted from responsibility because it was patriarchal, top-down, with obedience expected. Because obedience fits into spiritual discipline, EDL ran smoothly. A healthy subculture of individuality and friendship flourished, although hindered by the structure. I strongly believed that individuals could know power through their spiritual awareness, organizational structure being secondary to one's personal power. Perhaps I was naive? As is often the case in collectives, it took real strength of character to maintain one's individuality. I accepted that challenge.

In 1981 my daughter and I moved to the larger commune at 100 Mile House, British Columbia, the home of our leader, Martin Exeter. There I found members similar to me, young and interested in spirituality.

PHOTO BY ANNE BLANEY

Martin Exeter Hall,
The Emissaries,
100 Mile Community

Perched on the edge of the town of 100 Mile House, of which Martin was the main pioneer and landowner, our commune was a small village of individual homes with about 125 people of all ages, with some founding members still resident. There was a large, organic vegetable garden, barns with poultry, beef and dairy cows, and goats. The large communal kitchen, dining room and chapel were the hub of activity. As in Ontario, residents either worked at home or were employed in Emissary and other businesses. Members received a stipend unless they chose to keep their finances private. The social life was promising if you were in your 30's and single, and even though I was a mother, I qualified.

Our hierarchical governance stemmed from our spiritual hierarchy. Martin was unquestionably at the top, followed by men who were his spiritual assistants. Leadership followed bloodlines through his son, Michael, and included Martin's stepchildren and their spouses. Such obvious nepotism was tolerated and rationalized by non-family.

Such a power structure wasn't appealing after my earlier leadership stint, so I chose positions such as caring for the children so that I could focus on being a mother. I made child care my career, with many children passing through my care. I remain passionate about child rearing, and we worked magic with our children, living out the adage that it is the community which raises the child. I also entered into relationships and was thriving personally, but wondered if I was 'copping out'. I was content with my life although aware of discrepancies.

In Emissary leadership culture, women played important roles, but always as supportive to male 'points of focus', and Martin was always flanked by two powerful women, his wife and his secretary. These women provided leadership to women, but this always deferred to the males' position. Unrecognized as equals, women leaders tended to covertly dominate where they could. Two tendencies prevailed: to deny one's negative reactions as being one's own spiritual immaturity, and to ignore behaviour considered inappropriate. Personal issues were suppressed outwardly but tension swirled beneath the surface.

Male leaders were also domineering, but it was futile to challenge the power structure because that meant challenging Martin, and that would have been like challenging God! Martin was accountable only to God, not to fellow human beings, and that created a problem. Martin did not assume full responsibility for the hierarchy beneath him which he had created. There was no personal accountability because theoretically, each individual was responsible to God.

Meanwhile, everyday life was full. Three daily meals were prepared for the community, dishes washed, rooms cleaned, cows milked, repairs and renovations done, and children cared for. As well, there were Martin's talks to be transcribed, classes offered to visitors from all over the world, choir and orchestral practices and, when I could fit it in, my own social life. Within our highly structured life, we still had room to move. We initiated study groups, aerobic classes and skiing, and involvement in the adjacent village was possible, if we wanted. The village had an Emissary mayor for decades, while we focused the local arts for years. We were liked by most villagers but to some we were highly suspect. Our sex lives were fuel for hot gossip!

Sexuality, being called 'the highest form of worship', was intrinsic to spirituality in Emissary philosophy. Compared to larger society, we had liberal attitudes: some open marriages, a modest open-mindedness towards homosexuality, and open communication about sex. Our overall pattern, however, was serial monogamy, traditional marriages and heterosexuality. Ideally, sexual relationships were undertaken in consultation with someone in leadership, although this didn't always happen and advice wasn't always followed. There were occasions when the cloudiness around power transgressed into sexual misconduct, without accountability. Some were wounded by such occurrences, while many were unaware they occurred. After initially receiving 'advice' from leaders, I chose to incorporate the spiritual component into my sexuality, but to proceed at my own discretion. As a group, we Emissaries were scrutinized by onlookers so we took care to be discreet. So, while unmarried couples would sleep together, there was a lot of 'night travel'. Eventually, singles objected to this secrecy and began living together openly.

There were about 20 children in the group. Raising a child in a commune is both a blessing and a perilous journey. I insisted on my daughter and I having our own personal circle of friends where we could talk freely, where there was the space to name inconsistencies, react and develop coping strategies. Martin's theme of personal responsibility inspired me in my role as a mother. Significant men entered my life and acted as father figures to my daughter, while other children became her siblings. I was at home in this active, communal world. Spiritually, I had found my place. I had chosen to participate in a unique social experiment, and I was delighted to continually grow as a result.

My Mid-Life-Crisis Communalism

Martin Exeter died in 1988. His death was handled in our typical way because death and grieving were not yet in our vocabulary. Like youngsters with illusions of immortality, essentially we denied anything had changed. Personally, I suspected that everything had changed, and was encouraged that there would be a new, albeit rough, cycle ahead. But outwardly it was business as usual with Michael, Martin's son, taking his father's place.

The changes began subtly. Our services lacked something, and interest waned. Attempts were made to articulate these lacks, but such articulation had no place. In the past, Martin would not brook contention. This refusal to respond to change was a life-threatening blow to the heart of our organization. Still, it was a shock when people began to tire of communality, and began to think of their financial futures. In our commune, those working off the property wanted to keep their salaries while those at home wanted their contributions to be equally respected. I supported the 'user-pays' system, believing that such a change was inevitable, given the real demands for autonomy. Even though this change could undermine our communal spirit, it was a gamble which we could not avoid. Perhaps losing Martin had led to a loss of confidence in our collective project, or maybe times were just a-changing?

This change in priorities was viewed with suspicion instead of being incorporated into a new value system. Now the spell was broken. People moved away, with awkwardness on both sides; 20-year friendships ended in grief. There was no overview that we were so used to hearing from Martin. *We had to make it make sense, ourselves!* Many members felt abandoned but couldn't admit it. It was like a number of marriages dissolving all at once. With the fuzziness of accountability, it was difficult to know whom to blame, and it was painful to face one's own compliance with a system now revealing its flaws.

Martin had once described a 'dark' part of his life: 'then, fortunately, adversity struck'. Responding to our 'darkness' some members sought help by reading, and exploring psychological tools. Individually and in groups, we at last began the arduous process of resolving buried issues and dealing with our present grief. Not everyone was interested, and understandably, many chose to leave and to salvage their personal lives. A new vocabulary was born within the Emissaries, including the word 'anger'. Our leadership remained scattered as there had been no preparation for this. But, as we gradually and painfully brought our truths into the picture, leadership began to look *very* different, being no longer one person, but many persons.

I, along with others who stepped forward, played an increasing role in this process. I was on the Provincial Board of Directors where we wrestled with emergency measures. Ironically, our 'great organization' lacked exactly that — organization! We were challenged to rebuild with true accountability and with leadership based on more than spiritual discernment. At times, our community meetings were filled with anger and confusion, so we employed instructors to teach us consensus decision-making. As the income for our self-sustaining economy disappeared, we scrambled for solutions, and the user-pays paradigm was the only resort. We hired a General Manager who bravely introduced a plan which essentially laid off most of our volunteer, stipend-paid staff. Those leaving were given a period of grace to find jobs, facing re-entry to the employment market, often after decades of working within The Emissaries. They showed resourcefulness, often borrowing from relatives so they could move on. Each month brought a new wave of departures, while our elected governing body was repeatedly demoralized by further loss. There was a high burn-out rate. I was running our communal kitchen and doing my part to sustain morale in what was still my home. It was a rocky time!

One of my hardest choices was to assume authority to do something about the downward spin which was enveloping us. Did I even want to? It was difficult to *not* judge what others were deciding for their lives, but to do what I needed to do, and *to understand what had happened* (perhaps because I had studied sociology and political science). Perhaps because what was at stake was my daughter's and my home, or because I deplore a victim's stance and didn't want to throw away 20 years of my life, or because I still wanted to accomplish something with a group of people, and here they were, or what was left of them, I decided to stay and see it through.

*   *   *

Today The Emissaries are drastically different from 1988, with all communities being much smaller. Most who left the 100 Mile House Community remain disconnected from our organization, but maintain friendships with individual members. This schism remains uncomfortably unresolved to me.

Our 100 Mile Community now operates on a market system with residents having jobs and paying for services received, rather than working to support EDL and our community. Some residents are EDL employees, while others work in town. EDL relies on donations and profits generated from business endeavours, but these are still insufficient, so cutbacks continue. EDL province-wide has shrunk by two-thirds, while our 100 Mile Community has shrunk by half to 60 people. Those remaining in our community rent their houses from EDL. Food is no longer prepared by volunteer members, but by members who are hired. Mostly it is our seniors who use this food service, most residents choosing to eat in their homes — something new for people who have eaten communally

PHOTO BY JUDITH SMOOKLER

Canning peaches (Anne is upper left)

for 20 years. I eat a combination of meals at home and meals with the group. Monthly 'pot-lucks' are gaining popularity. The jury is still out on whether it is necessary to eat together to remain a community.

Our governance becomes more grass-roots as members become involved with Emissary's governing bodies. Our Provincial EDL Board has transformed itself with members now being elected rather than appointed. The Board has hired staff, like me, now the Manager at 100 Mile Community. An Executive Director has recently been hired to manage and expand Emissary's sizeable assets province-wide. We are rewriting our constitution and by-laws, while Board policy is implemented by our management. We have redefined membership with a more eclectic description of spiritual interest, compared to our former (unwritten) 'dogma'. In order to live in one of the three Emissary communities in British Columbia one has to either be an EDL member or become one within a specified time. We are starting a retreat business using our facilities as spiritual gathering places. Our Board is reworking its relationship with the International EDL, changing a hierarchy into a partnership.

My Wisdom As a Communal Elder

As General Manager, I am acting on a vision which honors what was valid, such as our spiritual base, while creating what we now want. This is extremely challenging, requiring personal growth and professionalism as we rebuild EDL both from the bottom up and from the top down. I am far removed from the 'communal laborer' I once was. Because I appreciate challenges, I like my new job, even though there is an imbalance between politics and simplicity.

Today, we resemble a neighborhood more than a spiritual community, although our previous communal bonding remains latent. Our three communities in British Columbia exist because of their links to EDL. The Board's priority has been to reactivate EDL's purpose and then to focus on revitalizing the communities. In 100 Mile Community, a Residents' Committee has been elected and, through consensus, it forms community-related policy for residents. They screen people wishing to become residents, now being welcomed with a fragile new confidence. New residents undertake an interview process to determine their 'resonance' with our community. Residents are also examining their commitment to living in community — a healthy step!

Our flower gardens are less tidy, we sold our last milk cow, there's a small flock of chickens tended by volunteer labor, and the vegetable garden is a business owned by one member. Our spiritual services are run by a team using monthly teleconferencing with other Emissaries from around the world. We seldom use Martin's talks, although excerpts are published in our monthly newsletter published at Sunrise Ranch, our American sister community. Our spiritual material is eclectic, spoken by many rather than just by one spiritual leader.

Here in our community the spiritual forms have broadened. Some of us have become involved with North American 'Earth-Spirituality', through native teachers who visit our community, and we regularly attend native sweat lodges and celebrations carried out in 'the old ways'. Many of our men have taken the 'New Warrior' training, and participate in weekly men's groups. Some members explore their spirituality in smaller groups rather than using large gatherings as in the past.

PHOTO BY DAVID BALIAEN

Retreat staff in front of 100 Mile Lodge (Anne is center front)

I have gone through a spiritual metamorphosis. Painfully, I publicly extricated myself from the spiritual articulation coming through Michael, in order to sense and experience for myself. This was difficult, because Michael is a long-standing friend who was sincere in continuing his father's legacy, something I respect. I believe, however, that something entirely new is seeking expression. This has largely been resolved with

Michael stepping back, and his encouragement of his fellow international Trustees.

Here in the community I participate in two women's groups, and I attend 'sweats', ceremonies and 'talking circles' with a group of like-minded residents and friends. I have become increasingly involved in astrology, which I find assists my understanding of life and people. In other words, my spirituality is less organized by EDL and more personal.

I am proud of the choices I have made, although there have been times when I have experienced deep doubts about continuing in a form which might be seeking to die. I respond by saying that the old form *did* die, but that instead of dissolving the marriage, we can make new vows.

New members and old friends returning challenge our sense of community. Potluck dinners, regular residents' meetings, and celebrations like a special naming ceremony for a newborn baby help bring our community back together. At a recent gathering of leaders from Emissary groups worldwide, two techniques were introduced and effectively used by a South African colleague, 'heart-space' and 'truth-telling'. These, I hope, will increase our ability to cover emotional realities and to deal with conflict. In a way we are at square one. Did our past teach us anything? This, we shall discover.

*   *   *

PHOTO BY JUDITH SMOOKLER

*Anne, with friends,
working in the
control room
of Martin Exeter Hall*

We are not an isolated commune, but a community that is still economically, legally and philosophically linked to a larger organization, an organization which is weathering a major transformation. Our experience continues to be a social experiment in process. That process, as untidy and as painful as it has been, exemplifies the development of the communal wisdom of people involved in the dynamics of social change. This is a story about making spirituality accountable. This is also the story of my life, my communal family and my home. My story and my communal wisdom are part of the much larger communal story and wisdom that continues to unfold for all who are interested.

The best may be yet to come!

Anne with two friends in the kitchen

©THE EMISSARIES

Introduction: Los Horcones and Juan Robinson

PHOTO BY MIREYA BUSTAMENTE

Juan Robinson

Los Horcones was established in 1973 near Hermosillo in north western Mexico. Its professionally qualified founders were imbued with a passion for radical behaviorism. They sought to create an ideal society as posited by the famous American psychologist and utopian writer B.F. Skinner in 1948, in Walden Two, his best-known book and a utopian classic. Out of all the communal groups in this book, Los Horcones probably had the clearest, best developed blueprint when founded. It is one of the smaller groups in this book, but is also one of the most interesting. Los Horcones' members seek to combine humanism with 'the science of behavior' to create their ideal society.

Juan Robinson trained and worked as a psychologist before co-founding Los Horcones where he has lived ever since. While many of the communards in this book sound unsure about how to make communal living 'work' better, Juan is very clear and confident. The famous American intentional community, Twin Oaks, was also started as a 'Walden Two' community but its members have moved away from the clear ideals to which Juan Robinson and other Los Horcones members still adhere. Juan's passion and clarity present a fascinating story of communalism.

Visitors are welcomed, provided they have made arrangements in advance. Los Horcones may be contacted at: Apartado Postal # 372, Hermosillo, Sonora 83000, Mexico (fax: +52-62-147219; or e-mail walden@imparcial.com.mx).

CHAPTER 13

Comunidad Los Horcones: Radical Behaviorism in Mexico

by Juan Robinson

Seen from above, Los Horcones looks like a green oasis in the middle of the semi-arid Mexican countryside. Seen from the inside, there is a similar contrast regarding lifestyles between the cooperative and friendly relationships among the people of all ages who live in our intentional community, and the prevailing competitive and aggressive relationships found in mainstream society. There is also the same 'oasis-in-the-desert' feeling about the tranquil yet active social life in Los Horcones compared to the hurried and tense life in the city.

The cooperative social life of Los Horcones does not just accidentally result from our surroundings and circumstances, but rather results from the way in which we have carefully designed this community to foster cooperation, peace, equality and sharing. Los Horcones is a carefully, scientifically planned intentional community. Every day, we members plan and arrange things in order to have a better social and physical environment. By 'environment', we behaviorists refer to the social and physical structure in which each person lives. One's environment can be defined as everything that affects one's behavior, whether it originates inside or outside oneself. Our biological, chemical, physical and behavioral stimuli constitute our environment.

To plan and design the social environment is not easy, because in order to do so, it is necessary to change our behavior. Therefore, although Los Horcones is a planned environment it is not perfect. When compared to other places and lifestyles it may seem like a paradise, but compared to an ideal society, or utopia, Los Horcones still has a very long way to go. We have not sufficiently changed either ourselves or our environment. Our main motivation in continuing our utopian quest is that we want to build a better society here and now. Our constant challenge is to develop an effective educational technology which facilitates and encourages people to better learn cooperative behavior.

To a normal visitor, Los Horcones appears to be a regular, well-kept farming community with animals, gardens, houses and schools, and with people working and playing together. The careful observer, however, notices many differences between life in a regular farming community and communal life at Los Horcones. The differences range from the conspicuous, such as realizing that we members share all property when they see us selecting our clothes from a communal closet ('first come — best dressed'), to subtle differences, such as our governance, when they see that all women, children and men are heard and considered equally in our decision-making process. Some visitors are amazed to find that along the wall of our Personal-Relations office we have individual charts of data regarding the behavioral self-management programs which each member conducts to learn about and improve his/her communitarian behavior.

Los Horcones, however, is not just what people see when they visit. To visitors, our everyday reality can be either very pleasant or very unpleasant, depending upon from which perspective they look at us. Their appreciation depends on the attitude they take when visiting or living here. Usually, people see their social world from their own personal and emotional perspective rather than from an objective one. One's perspective

PHOTO BY MIREYA BUSTAMENTE

Fruit trees and kiosk, with pond in background. This is the center of Los Horcones

changes according to one's personal circumstances, day by day or even moment by moment. This makes observers either overlook or enhance the intrinsic value of Los Horcones as a long-term social experiment in alternative, sustainable living. It is sad to see people rejecting or embracing communal living on such a fragile basis.

Los Horcones is not merely what it has become up to this moment, because this community and we members are in constant change. We are an experimental intentional community, not a dogmatic one. We are in the process of becoming a 'Walden Two community', and that takes time. *Walden Two* is a novel written by B. F. Skinner in 1948, in which he proposed the use of behavioral psychology to design a better society, or a utopia. Los Horcones is a Walden Two community because we apply the science of behavior to the design of all of our cultural practices such as education, economy, governance and family life. A Walden Two community is where all human, social matters are approached from a radical behaviorist perspective.

When we established Los Horcones in 1973, I thought that it would only take us ten to twenty years to see it functioning like a complete Walden Two utopian commune. I believed then that more of those people who were dissatisfied with their lives would be interested in participating in this project as soon as they learned about it. But I was wrong. It has not turned out to be so easy. It will take us many more years to build a true Walden Two community, unless we find ways to increase our financial and human resources.

My Background

I was born in 1947 in Hermosillo, the capital city of the State of Sonora, in north west Mexico. One of my ancestors came from Scotland and his son married a Pima Indian, a native from central Sonora. The fifth of six children, I was raised mainly by my two aunts and my grandfather. I attended a private Catholic school, kept pets, and played and spent time at my father's farm near Hermosillo.

In 1964, when I was I7, I moved to southern Mexico to join a Franciscan seminary where I lived and studied for two years. Afterwards, I moved to Mexico City to study psychology at the Universidad Nacional Autónoma de México. In 1970, I married my home-town sweetheart, Mireya, who came back with me to Mexico City where we both attended university and completed our studies.

In 1971, we returned to Sonora to establish a school for developmentally retarded children who had a variety of behavioral problems, but mainly autism. With help from Dr sidney Bijour, we designed a learning environment to promote the behavior which these children needed to learn.

A year later, I was working as a behavioral psychologist, with my wife, Mireya helping me at the school, and our first son, Juanito, was born. I was also teaching psychology at the University of Sonora, and some of my students were interested in behavioral psychology as applied to special education. I gave them lectures and allowed these students to practice these techniques with the retarded children at my school. As soon as these students completed their training they joined Mireya and me in teaching these children. The application of principles derived from behavioral psychology had remarkably successful results, with all of the children progressing significantly.

Besides working at this school and teaching psychology, I also offered adult education courses about managing child behavior and improving marital relationships. After some time, however, Mireya and I realized that I was not applying within my own family life all that I was teaching other parents and couples to do. When I discussed this with my close friends, they also felt that they were in a similar position, finding too many obstacles to living their lives as they knew they should. We all felt trapped in a society that promoted competition, aggression, discrimination and an individualism which was oriented more toward materialistic than humanistic goals. We were all dissatisfied with the direction that our lives were taking, and we knew that we had to change. It was clear to us that our social environment was neither supportive of, nor conducive to, humanitarian actions such as mutual help, cooperation, sharing, non-violence and egalitarianism. We concluded that we needed to live in a society that would promote such humanitarian behavior. From our studies, we were confident that what we psychologists called 'the science of behavior' could dramatically contribute to the design of such an ideal, humane society. Of course, B.F. Skinner, along with a dozen of his fellow behaviorists, had already been writing about cultural and social design for years.

The Formation of Los Horcones

In the summer of 1973, Ramon, an old friend who was studying Ranch Administration, plus his wife Linda and brother Fernando, and Alejandro my former student who all taught at our school, along with Mireya and I, decided to dramatically change our way of life, and to start living communally, in order to really experience and live that ideal life about which we had for so long only talked and dreamed. From our academic studies and research, we believed that a 'science of behavior' could significantly contribute to the design of the ideal society and community we sought. A couple of months later, we started living together as a community, right where the school was located, on 45 acres (20 hectares) of land on the outskirts of Hermosillo, Sonora, Mexico. We named our community Los Horcones which is Spanish for 'The Pillars' (of a new society).

Our first activity at Los Horcones was to elaborate a behavioral code for ourselves, which we based on an experimental approach as suggested by the science of behavior.

We also started building, first a communal dining room and then a children's house where our children would live together and be reared by the group.

We legally established Los Horcones as a non-profit cooperative. We built additional communal facilities as our population grew and our children were born. Our conservative families didn't like us living communally, so they never supported our efforts, but that did not stop us. In the 1970s, intentional communities or communes were thought of in Mexico as part of a hippie movement that avoided responsibilities and promoted the use of recreational drugs and sexual orgies. This sort of hippie behavior was never characteristic of our communal life, and in fact Los Horcones was rejected by many early visitors who came here looking for just those things, but were discouraged not to find them.

Because we are hard-working, serious people, we have always lived on good terms with our neighbours, and we have established friendly, mutually supportive relationships with many people in the surrounding area. We at Los Horcones have always been open to visitors, and as people in the area got to know us better we became more socially accepted. Now, many 'mainstream society' people visit us on the weekends, and many schools and universities bring students to study our social experiment. However, we are still often seen by some of our visitors as 'rather strange!' people.

Radical Behaviorism

Radical behaviorism is the philosophy of a natural (as opposed to a merely theoretical) science of behavior. One of the most important statements made by this philosophy is that human behavior is a predictable natural phenomenon which follows scientific laws. Radical behaviorism defines behavior as not just the actions of an organism which can be observed by others, but also as the actions which are observable by the organism itself. These include thinking, feeling and imagining. Another behaviorist statement is that all human behavior is shaped by our interactions with our environment. Environment is defined as including all the physical, chemical, biological and social events which affect our behavior.

Behaviorists also believe that since our social behavior is learned we can therefore learn to behave differently. If we learned to compete, we can also learn to cooperate. If we learned to treat each other in a discriminating manner, we can also learn to treat each other in an egalitarian manner. If we learned to be aggressive, we can also learn to solve problems in non-violent ways. Because behavior is learned through the interactions of the organism with its environment, then in order to learn new behavior it is necessary to change that environment. Consequently, if we want cooperation we need to design an environment that promotes or reinforces cooperative rather than competitive behavior. A Walden Two community like Los Horcones is precisely about designing such an environment. Regardless of its type, however, no intentional community can exist unless communitarian behavior is encouraged and reinforced.

Some people wrongly believe that we behaviorists say that we are 'merely a product of our circumstances'. What we really say, however, is that we *interact* with our environment and, in this way, our behavior changes and thereby our environment also changes. We learn to behave as we do (for example, to cooperate or to compete) as a result of our interactions with the environment in which we live. We learn to speak the language we speak, to think the way we think, and to believe what we believe, simply because of our environment.

Communal living requires that members learn different social behavior, and in order to learn that, we need to design an environment which facilitates such learning. The consequences which our communitarian behavior has on our environment are what shapes and maintains it. If an intentional community is effectively designed to shape and maintain communitarian behavior, then it will endure. Despite this scientific 'law' of communal living, few intentional communities base their practices on this clear principle.

Psychology, when understood and practised as the natural science of behavior, can definitely contribute to the design of an intentional community which enables members to live satisfactory, creative and productive lives. Such designed communities help each individual member to develop as a complete, unique person.

Los Horcones Today

We established Los Horcones in 1973 because we were interested in applying the science of behavior to help solve global problems. Our main objective was to establish a cooperative, egalitarian, sharing, ecological and non-violent community. We knew that we could depend on nothing but our own hard work, sincerity and limited resources.

In 1981, we moved our community onto 250 acres (100 hectares) of semi-arid land, 40 miles (65 km) from Hermosillo, where we had first established. We moved further away from the city because we needed more space to live and to produce food for our growing population. We are now accessible by a paved road, and we have electricity, telephone and water.

Los Horcones' population is currently 30 adults and 15 children. It looks like a small town of whitewashed buildings with red tile porches sustained by rustic *Horcones* (pillars). We have comfortable but simple living quarters, including a separate children's house, a communal dining room, conference room, two schools and two libraries, plus various workshops and barns. Animals, flowers and fruit trees abound between our houses and other buildings.

PHOTO BY MIREYA BUSTAMENTE

Flowers along the front porch of the main communal building containing kitchen, dining room, living room, computer room, reading and TV rooms, and behavior office

The organizational structure of Los Horcones is participatory, non-hierarchical and non-monopolizing. This design fosters equality of both opportunities and responsibilities among members. Although we have common goals and collective means toward achieving them, each individual member is empowered with authority and decisive participation in our decision-making process and in all organizational matters. Our system of government, the result of more than ten years of research and analysis, we call 'Personocracy'.

For organizational purposes, Los Horcones is divided into 30 main areas, each having several sub-areas. One or more members coordinates each of these areas to ensure its proper functioning, maintenance and progress. Anyone can become a coordinator since the areas are not monopolized by experts or by long-standing members. Coordinators present a report of their achievements and future plans to all members at our bi-monthly assembly. Ordinary decisions are made by the coordinator(s) of the area. Important decisions are made by all community members who wish to, and are prepared to, participate in making that particular decision. All members who participate in such a decision-making process must reach agreement, or consensus, before a decision is final. Personocracy, unlike democracy, cares for each and every person and not just for the majority. This implies educating all members in governmental participation, an important aspect of our communal life.

Photo by Mireya Bustamente

Members socializing in the living room at Christmas time

We organize our labor under a time system whereby members who have similar physical capabilities are required to work the same number of hours. Children, disabled and elderly members participate in the productive life of our community according to their capabilities. Men and women have equal labor opportunities and duties. Child care and household chores have equal value with other, financially productive, work. We all work in a variety of activities ranging from the physical to the intellectual, including gardening, raising animals, building, maintenance, food processing, child rearing, teaching, organizing, conducting research, playing, studying, talking and singing. We can select most of our duties according to our personal preferences and skills, so we largely design our work schedules to our own satisfaction. When necessary, however, we must work in something other than what we choose (such as cleaning toilets).

All income from all members' work is placed in a common account. Most of Los Horcones' income derives from our health-food business and from the special school for autistic children which we operate, although we also run several other small industries and engage in some farming. Members have no private property, and use our shared property with respect. Nobody can tell me to take off the shirt I am wearing, or put down the book I am reading, because when I use something, it is mine. Some people might say that we are poor as individuals but rich as a community, but we do not think so. Since we see all communal property as being our own, we take care of it as we used to take care of our personal property before we lived in community. Each member is far richer than she/he could ever be if we did not share our property, and no less rich than she/he was when we did not share. Thanks to sharing all our property, we need fewer 'things', and we live a simpler, more ecological life without sacrificing comfort or technology. We have six cars, one satellite dish, one television and two computers for twelve families. We have a communal standard of living which is higher than what most of us could have had, if living without shared property.

We call our family practice 'open family'. The Los Horcones 'family' includes all members, adults and children, regardless of their biological or marital ties. The concept of 'open family' is based mainly on the behaviorist assumption that children are influenced not just by those in their immediate family, like father, mother and siblings, but also by other people with whom they frequently interact, and who thereby become relevant in their social environment. This can include friends, teachers, schoolmates, neighbors and even television characters. At Los Horcones, in relation to how we influence children, we all are the 'behavioral parents' of every child, while only two of us are a particular child's biological parents. The parenting functions which, in a nuclear family, are provided by the father and the mother, at Los Horcones are shared by all adult members. These functions include giving children love, education, health care and whatever they need for their development. In our open family, we share parental functions, but this does not mean that we also share our intimate marital relationships. Los Horcones encourages monogamous commitment that produces long and stable relationships.

At Los Horcones, our children are raised communally by men and women who are specially trained in child care and education. Communal child care is voluntary, not an obligation, for parents. However, because of the many advantages it offers to them, to their children and to the society as a whole, parents welcome it. Personally, being part of an open family has enhanced the enjoyable aspects of being a parent while reducing the responsibility and the onerous workload involved. I feel very satisfied with the results of having my three children raised as part of the first generation of communal children at Los Horcones. All of our grown-up children remain part of our community and want to continue to live here, although some of them are temporarily absent as they continue their higher education. They are happy, confident, good young adults who are certainly much better prepared for life than we were at their age. Today, it brings us great joy to be educating the second generation of Los Horcones' children.

Because we see and treat all of our communal children as being our own, we are careful in reaching agreements about what and how we want to teach them. We have a detailed list of behavioral objectives for each child. When all the adults respond to our children's appropriate and inappropriate behavior in similar ways, they learn much faster. We adults are aware of how our example influences their learning. If children see us doing what we preach, they also learn to do it. If they see us enjoying what we do, they also learn to enjoy it. It is very important to provide appropriate learning conditions. Our children's social education is oriented toward teaching them to enjoy cooperation, sharing, equality and being interested in and responsible for their surroundings. Children are always welcome to be with us, in whatever we do, and to ask whatever they want to know.

Juan working with Alejandra and Jesus, two Los Horcones children

We have always provided certified academic instruction to our children in Los Horcones. We have a school, which we call a 'study center', where our children study from pre-school through high school. Most of their courses are personalized, allowing each student to progress at her/his own pace by ensuring mastery of the previous material. In their academic education, we set a high priority on teaching our children to enjoy studying and learning.

Some visitors to Los Horcones have said things like, 'You cannot be a behaviorist and a humanist at once. I don't think that Los Horcones is a Walden Two community because it has humanistic objectives. You say that your educational system has the objective of teaching altruism, cooperation and equality, but this is contrary to what I understand behaviorism looks for, like control and manipulation.' We always feel sad about our community being misunderstood. We also feel sad to know that the science of behavior and its philosophy of radical behaviorism are so frequently misinterpreted.

Problems and Shortfalls at Los Horcones

To the casual observer, Los Horcones may sound like utopia but, to be honest, various problems have plagued our communal existence. Our different problems, however, all derive from one source: a lack of knowing ourselves. Knowing oneself is very important in order to live a satisfactory life — and it is essential for living in intentional community. We must know who we are, why we want to live here and what we need to change.

Mainstream Western culture does not teach us to know ourselves. It does not teach us to take into consideration the advances of a science of behavior which helps us to know ourselves better. What Western culture does teach us, unfortunately, is a concept of progress which is based on personal achievement, measured in material terms. It teaches us to think that we are progressing when we can afford to buy more things, or more sophisticated and expensive things, or when we have more personal prestige. Having learned this false 'wisdom', many of us devote our lives to pursuing material 'progress'. Then, often too late, we realize that our happiness, or unhappiness, was not related to material goods as we had thought. We realize that our happiness is mainly related to our personal relationships with other humans and with our own self. At Los Horcones, we progress as a person to the extent that we know ourselves better, and use that knowledge to learn communitarian behavior. Having a better understanding of oneself makes it possible to understand others and to help them to become better people.

A healthy community can only be formed by people who know themselves, and thus know why they are living as they do. When we formed Los Horcones, this fundamental truth was not as clear to me as it is today. Back then, I was so naive as to think that all those people who said that they wanted to cooperate would really do so, and that all those people who came and said that they wanted to live communally would really do it. I discovered, however, that the words we say and the feelings we have about communitarian life are not the same as really living communally.

I have observed at Los Horcones people who came from various parts of the world with diverse educational backgrounds and philosophies. Many of them believed themselves to be different and more communitarian than they really were. The reasons they gave for wanting to live in intentional community were very different from their real reasons. Most of them had not learned to know themselves although they had read hundreds of books, spent years in university studies, attended many conferences and participated in many philosophical, religious and even mystical experiences. Nevertheless, they still didn't know why they behaved as they did, or even why they wanted to live communally. They said that they wanted to cooperate for the common good, but cooperation was for them just another way of competing and reinforcing their individualism, their own egocentric objectives. For them, the common good did not go beyond their personal interests or benefits. They also said that they wanted to share, but they shared only what they did not really want or were not attached to. They talked about egalitarianism, but were discriminating in their actions, thoughts and feelings.

It is only through knowing ourselves that we can form authentic intentional communities, and intentional communities can only start and endure with authentic individuals. Learning to become a better person, and helping others to become better people, is the main objective of healthy communal life.

Why Radical Behaviorism is Critical at Los Horcones

I have lived in this intentional community for most of my adult life. During all this time, I have felt a great commitment to a communal lifestyle. I believe that communal living is the ideal environment in which an individual can become a better person, and thereby build a better society.

I am very committed to a science of behavior. I believe that only by applying this science can we design a better community. It is impossible to achieve a better world through implementing traditional political, philosophical and religious ideas. A science of behavior, or perhaps better stated as an *appropriate* application of this science, can enormously contribute to our shaping of an ideal society and solving global problems.

Although many people probably agree that in order to survive we need to live more communally, or at least more in community, very few of these people will agree that the science of behavior is an essential tool in achieving this solution. People who reject the science of behavior generally don't understand it because, unfortunately, most books and articles about it have been written by authors other than behavioral analysts, and they frequently misrepresent this science.

When I say that a great part of the solution to the world's problems lies in science, I am, of course, referring to the appropriate application of science. I strongly believe that the appropriate application of a science of behavior can help to build a better world for all humans. But it is necessary to realize that this science of behavior is not a cold and mechanistic science which serves to control or manipulate people, as some critics wrongly suggest.

A German academic observer recently wrote about us, 'the question should not be whether we want our behavior to be controlled by the environment (it is controlled no matter what we want), but what this environment should look like to bring out the best in people. Those who live at Los Horcones treat each other with such warmth, respect and love that it is simply ridiculous to think of them as the product of devious, cold-hearted controllers'.

Building an intentional community which endures requires effective, accurate knowledge about people and about human behavior. At Los Horcones, we encourage people to learn about human behavior, especially about their own behavior and the reasons for it. Self-knowledge is essential for an authentic communitarian life.

Summary and Conclusion

A true intentional community functions as a school in which all communal members are both students and teachers at the same time. As students, members learn to behave in a communitarian fashion, and as teachers, they learn to help others to learn and practise communitarian behavior. But the most effective communal teaching is not based simply on common sense, on being willing to teach, or in believing that good intentions, by themselves, produce results. In order to teach effectively, communal members need to know both what and how to teach, and the community must be an environment where teaching and learning are promoted. Members must also be enjoying their communal living, day-by-day. Radical behaviorism teaches us how to become more communitarian in our lives. We need to learn from this science of behavior and to teach these lessons — and to live and demonstrate the results.

No one comes to an intentional community knowing instinctively how to live communally. The communal group must teach itself. An intentional community will be successful only so far as it is capable of performing its educational functions. To find an effective communitarian educational technology, and to live the lessons from this radical behaviorism in our daily lives, has been our objective at Los Horcones during more than two decades.

Los Horcones should be examined and appreciated more for the possibilities of social change it represents, rather than for what we have achieved so far in terms of becoming an ideal society. We have not yet developed a perfect communal society at Los Horcones, but radical behaviorism helps us to find our way along that difficult and challenging road.

Introduction: Kibbutz Einat and Idit Paz

Kibbutz Einat is one of the almost 300 Israeli kibbutzim. The first kibbutz started in 1909, while Einat was founded in 1952 by combining members of two pre-existing communes. Israel is the only country where communal living has been more the norm than the exception, at least ideologically if not numerically. Kibbutzim have long caught the interest of social scientists as well as the general public because of how completely they adopted the ideals of communalism. Everything belonged to the collective, and even children were raised communally, living in a children's house rather than with their parents. Recently, kibbutzim have undergone dramatic changes away from communalism and toward privatisation. At the 1995 International Communal Studies Association Conference about half the papers addressed what is widely known as "The Crisis of the Kibbutz". Einat, with about 400 residents, is a fairly typical kibbutz, and its problems are similar to those of many other kibbutzim. Einat is not far from Tel Aviv.

PHOTO BY HELEN BEST

Idit Paz was born into a kibbutz in 1936, and has lived communally ever since, being one of the original members of Einat. She taught school for many years but now works as an editor and translator. She was raised within the communal system, as were her own children. I met Idit in 1988 when I spent two months of academic study leave at Yad Tabenkin Centre For Communal Studies, Tel Aviv, where she works part time. We have met several times at international conferences although I did not visit her at Kibbutz Einat until mid 1995.

Innumerable books have been written about the Israeli kibbutzim but the dramatic changes of recent years make much of that material out of date. The small journal, *Kibbutz Trends*, published by Yad Tabenkin, Ramat Efal 52960, Israel, and co-edited by Idit Paz, offers useful and up-to-date information (e-mail: YAD_TABEN@VAX.TRENDLINE.CO.IL). Visitors can live on a kibbutz and take part in the communal life while working as a volunteer. Details can be obtained from the Kibbutz Program Center, Hayarkon Street 124, P.O. Box 3167, Tel Aviv, Israel (phone: +972-3-5246156; or fax: +972-3-5239966).

CHAPTER 14

Kibbutz Einat: My Lifetime of Communal Living

by Idit Paz

I was born in 1936, on Kibbutz Givat HaShlosha (Hill of the Three), eleven years after it was founded. My parents were among the thousands of Jewish youths who, through Zionist youth movements in eastern Europe, immigrated to Eretz Israel (Palestine), where they went directly to a kibbutz. My father, like most of his friends, both men and women, saw in cultivating the land his ultimate personal fulfilment. He became a tractor operator and worked in the fields for about 20 years, and then worked as a designer and stitcher in our shoe factory, and finally as a gardener. My mother worked first in the cowshed and then as a *metapelet* for many years.

When I was born, kibbutz children lived and slept together in separate houses specially designed for them. As a child, these arrangements seemed only natural, and even now, as I look back at it, they still make sense. My parents, like all other kibbutz members, lived in a small, four-by-four metre (thirteen foot square) room, in a hut of five to six similar rooms, with a long, narrow porch connecting all of them and with two taps and sinks at either side. Bathrooms and toilets were in a small building serving several huts. We children, however, lived in substantial brick buildings, with inside baths and hot water on tap, in much better physical conditions than those of our parents.

We lived this way until the end of World War II, when better houses began to replace the old huts. By 1947, all 400 commune members lived in brick buildings, in private rooms with a tap and a sink on each small balcony. Around this time members were also allowed to have their own radios and facilities for making tea or coffee in their private room, a change which at the time aroused a lot of arguments about whether or not such 'rampant and indulgent individualism' would mean the end of the communal life of the kibbutz!

*   *   *

I remember my childhood as a happy one, with daily trips around the kibbutz, playing in our fields and orchards, as well as in the bare, uncultivated areas. We observed the abundant wildlife with fun and interest. There were lizards, turtles, skinks, ants and beetles, and birds such as finches, crows, warblers and wagtails, and lots of wild flowers in the landscape of my childhood.

During my 17 years in the communal children's houses, there were very few unpleasant episodes that I can recall. One such episode, however, concerns a *metapelet* — but I should first say something about what *metapelet* means. A *metapelet* took care of children; that was her job, sometimes her profession, sometimes her vocation. Since she was not hired by the parents, but was a kibbutz member like them, parents had no say in their children's everyday life. The *metapelet* usually knew, or thought she knew, better than the parents what was good for the children. So we children saw no point in telling our parents anything about the *metapelet*, even if we thought she wronged us, since it was almost certain that the parents would take her side. It is important to note that *metapelet* is a feminine form (the masculine would be *metapel*). Though people talked about gender equality, what they actually intended was that women take part in men's traditional work, but *not* vice versa. I know of very few men who worked as *metapel*. Two of the men who did, also served as General Secretary of the United Kibbutz Movement, and they may have wished to set an example.

Let me recount an episode that happened to me during communal child rearing, when I was four. We were supposed to sleep after lunch, but not all of us were tired enough. We were not allowed to speak during these 'rest-hours'. I remember the metapelet entering our room, coming to each of we four kids, and shouting, 'I know you aren't sleeping. You're only pretending!' then slapping each of our bottoms. I know that such episodes might happen also within a family, but that was the first time I questioned the reasoning and sense of justice of grown-ups in general, and of the metapelet in particular. I never spoke of it to my parents, nor have I ever mentioned it to this lady who is now over 85, and who still lives in a neighbouring kibbutz. The last time we met she *still* told me what a terrible eater I was as a little child...

There were also some practices in communal child-rearing that, in retrospect, may seem very cruel and inhuman. Children with diseases such as whooping cough or chicken pox would be moved to 'isolation', a house at the edge of the kibbutz, into which only the doctor and special *metaplot* (plural of *metapelet*) were allowed. The parents could only peep through the windows to see their kids. I still hear mothers talking about those times with horror. Yet what I mainly recall, as a child, is the feeling of unique importance that staying in isolation gave us.

At about four, I learned an important lesson in communalism, or at least in kibbutz ideology. It was during World War II, and Australian troops were passing through Palestine on their way to North Africa and Europe. Some of them visited our kibbutz. They represented 'the good ones' in the war that filled our parents' conversations. They looked warm and friendly. As a group of these soldiers entered our kindergarten, I, the youngest, being small and shy, found a niche between the wall and the closet, where I sat watching our guests. A tall, handsome Australian caught sight of me, crouched and gave me the biggest bar of chocolate I'd ever seen, wrapped in golden foil. I was tremendously excited, as a treasure had come my way! When the visit was over, however, the metapelet said, 'Now Idit, let's divide the chocolate among everybody'. It made sense, and I think I saw her point even then, but my strongest memory is of being robbed of my personal treasure.

Communal sleeping arrangements for children were not as bad as some people later described them. I remember more fun than fear or misery. I also remember, as a mother with my own children being reared communally, that we just took it for granted that some children have difficulty in saying good night to their parents. The second of my four children used to have me or her father sit for at least an hour in the room next to the children's bedroom, checking every ten minutes or so whether we were still there by calling 'Mommy?' or 'Daddy?' and we would answer, 'yes, I'm here'. This lasted for six or seven months, after which she seemed quite confident.

However, my father's diary reveals the doubts and worries of a young parent. His diary also describes a night when he became angry with me, as I had been naughty and so he left me without a goodnight kiss. He stood outside the room listening, and this is what he heard: 'Idit, if your Daddy won't love you, we will love you more'. I believe that what impressed him was the empathy and solidarity within the children's society. Ilana, the child who said this to me, is still a member of my kibbutz, as are two other women of my age-group. We women have come all this way together in the same commune, from babyhood until now when we are all grandmothers.

My school years were rewarding as I learned easily and enjoyably. My self-confidence increased and I became involved in the Cultural Committee, in the editorial board of our school's newspaper and so on.

We started kibbutz work for one hour a day at the age of 10, and for two hours daily from the age of 14. We worked in rotation in cleaning the children's house, taking care of the clean laundry, ironing and dividing it into the right compartments, cleaning the children's dining hall, washing dishes, etc. Best of all was the Children's Farm which was divided into vegetable and flower gardens, and animals. We had hens, ducks and geese, and an incubator in which we hatched our own chicks from eggs laid on our Children's Farm. One adult was in charge of all this, a woman named Rachel whom I've admired ever since. Those one-hour work periods with Rachel taught me more than did hundreds of hours spent in the classroom.

*   *   *

As children, we grasped major political events in our own way. I clearly remember the hatred we felt towards the British in 1946, when they would not allow Jewish immigrants to enter Palestine, and when they searched our kibbutz for underground facilities and weapons. Once, they surrounded our kibbutz for a whole day. We children were supposed to stay indoors, but after a few hours we lost our patience and then stood face-to-face with these hated British soldiers whom we mockingly called *Kalaniot* (anemones) because of their red caps. We had collected piles of stones to throw at them in case they tried to force their way in.

More than 20 years later, when we Israelis became the hated Occupation Army, I could not ignore those memories as they undoubtedly shaped my political viewpoint.

In November 1947, when the United Nations decided on the establishment of a Jewish State in part of Palestine, we were naive enough to believe that in one year's time peace would prevail. I remember our teacher giving us a topic for a composition: 'A Year from Now'. With the exception of one pupil who foresaw a hard war, all of us described a thriving state, with all the Jews coming to live in it, and with the Arabs accepting us as good neighbours. Our innocent dreams were soon disrupted! War broke out, and we lost two of our kibbutz youths. Death and bereavement were suddenly a reality to me. In 1956, we lost two other friends in Sinai, and between 1967 and 1970 a classmate of mine and two of my former pupils were killed. In 1973, a classmate of my son, a boy of only 19, was killed. I had watched them growing up together. To this day, Memorial Day has a very personal meaning for me, as it has, no doubt, for most Israelis.

*   *   *

We don't live at Kibbutz Givat HaShlosha any more. The town of Petah Tikva surrounded our settlement, while our cultivated lands were located near the Yarkon River, east of the town. In 1950, while celebrating our 25th anniversary, it was announced that

Idit Paz and Bill Metcalf in Kibbutz Einat's cemetery

we were going to move and build a new kibbutz on our agricultural land. We did not know yet of the split that would force us to build two kibbutzim instead of one.

In 1951 there was a serious, politically motivated split in our kibbutz, as well as within many other kibbutzim, and the consequences were unbelievable! After a bitter fight, when a split became inevitable, a solid wall was built along the middle of our dining hall and kitchen, and our school and all other institutions were divided. While the adults were preparing to build two new kibbutzim, we children felt neglected. I don't think we studied much during 1952–53. Each faction had too few children to form a class, and not enough teachers, therefore they hired teachers from the nearby town. We children felt that the adults were too busy to pay attention to us, so we just did whatever we liked.

The experience of building our new communal home, Kibbutz Einat, was exceptional. We came to a wasteland, with nothing on it but rocks and wild vegetation. On Tu B'shvat (Arbor Day) 1952 we planted our vineyard and the trees which were to surround our new settlement. We were so enthusiastic! Every day we followed the progress of our new buildings and of cultivating the fields. We teenagers were interested in getting to know the people who joined us from another kibbutz which had also suffered the Split. Academic research shows that kibbutz-born youths do not marry within their own kibbutz, at least not with close age groups. But here, while building Kibbutz Einat, we had young people from two different kibbutzim, and soon relationships formed.

Eitan, who would later become my husband, was from the other kibbutz. In the summer of 1953, when I was only 17, we became friends and, as he already had a room of his own, I moved in with him. My parents, like most kibbutz parents, had little to say in those matters. I remember my mother asking me, very much embarrassed, 'What will people say when they see you coming out of Eitan's room in the morning?' I just laughed.

My father asked me whether I was sure that this was the man, because he would not want to see me taking my belongings and moving again.

Since the summer of 1952 we students in the 10th, 11th and 12th grades had lived together with the young members who had already finished high school. Some of them still served in the army while others worked in our new agricultural areas. We all lived in temporary huts while more substantial houses were being built. This period might now seem too romantic and beautiful to be true, yet this is how I felt then. For the first time, we had neither parents nor metapelet to interfere in our lives. We prepared our own meals and had a campfire most nights. Youths from 16 to 30, in very humble conditions but with wide skies overhead, complete silence except for the train whistle on the Haifa–Jerusalem Railway, the rattle of the generator, and the jackals' howls — with lots of enthusiasm and plenty of romance! Many of us found our spouses then.

For the final year of school we were sent to another kibbutz, Ramat Rachel, near Jerusalem, to study with kids from other kibbutzim. This senior class was attached to the new Kibbutz Teachers College near the Hebrew University. With no adults to interfere, I studied only those subjects which interested me most: Literature, English and Hebrew. The rest of my time, I toured Jerusalem's streets and alleys, galleries and museums, and enjoyed the rehearsals of the symphonic orchestra. It was the first time I had pocket money, and that greatly increased my sense of freedom and independence. My teachers were great, much better than in our local school. According to kibbutz educational principles, we did not have to pass formal exams, so learning from those excellent teachers was a spiritual and intellectual experience for me.

To complete our education we moved to the Ruppin Institute to study agriculture as well as to gain some general knowledge of soils, irrigation, etc. I remember this time mainly for its never-ending fun. We also had an 'ideological seminar' from which we did not get much intellectual value, but we all enjoyed the atmosphere of a summer camp. We were then accepted 'en-bloc' by the General Meeting of our kibbutz as full members, our symbol of adulthood. No one had asked us whether we wished to be kibbutz members. We students did not have much deliberations about it either. Things have changed greatly since then — the world seemed to be simpler in the 1950s, and the future much clearer.

*   *   *

In 1954 I married Eitan Paz and we moved to a family room. Next year our first son, Arnon, was born. At first this was a new and exciting experience for me. I enjoyed being a wife and mother, although sometimes I felt incompetent and left Arnon in his grandmother's care. I sometimes felt as if I was just playing at being a grown-up, a role from which I could easily escape when I wished. My classmates joined the army while I started to work as a metapelet in the kindergarten.

Being the youngest and most inexperienced in the work crew, I was naturally bottom in the hierarchy, so I found little interest in my work. I felt trapped, and knew that unless I found work which I enjoyed, I would not be able to go on. In those days, the only professions open to kibbutz women were teaching and nursing. So, as an escape from boredom and frustration, I applied to study at a teachers college, but first I needed the approval of our kibbutz General Meeting. The decision, however, was to let me study for a teacher's certificate only after working one year in our communal kitchen. It was a hard blow for me. I remember crying a lot, declaring that I wanted to leave the kibbutz, that I would not have others dictating to me. However, my husband, my mother and mother-in-law all comforted me and said that this year would soon pass, that I was still young and would not miss anything by delaying my studies. My husband loved his work in the fields, growing clover and alfalfa for the cows, so he would not dream of leaving.

I was lucky to be accepted in the kitchen by very sensitive women who must have known how I felt, and each one of them tried to teach me what she knew. There were many hard days. We did many tasks such as cleaning raw fish and chicken, work that left me with the stench even after I showered and changed clothes. But, little by little, I began to enjoy cooking, I tried new recipes and by the end of the year I had acquired skills that I have used ever since. Cooking became almost my hobby.

My studies at the teachers college were fun. I made new friends, most of them from other kibbutzim. They were older than the average student. Here I did not skip classes; instead I discovered new interests, such as zoology, botany and interpretations of the Bible, all due to our exceptional teachers.

When I became a teacher, I began work in my own kibbutz as a fifth grade teacher, covering most subjects. I believe that I did a good job during the 22 years I taught school. I knew my subjects very well, and I was fair with the kids. Whatever I had enjoyed as a child in school, I passed on to my pupils. My favourite hour had been the last lesson of the week when our teacher read stories to us. Throughout my teaching years, I always carried a novel or short stories to read on special occasions and, of course, during the last lesson on Friday. 'You read *Jane Eyre* to us', my ex-pupils still gratefully remind me.

After eight years of teaching in our elementary school, I was entitled to take a year off for further studies. I chose to study English & American Literature, and Linguistics, at Tel Aviv University. I was already 31 years old, with four children, yet I found it quite natural to take advantage of being a kibbutz member and to study for my BA degree. I enjoyed my studies tremendously! Five of us married women between the ages of 31 and 40 formed a clique right from the beginning. Three of us were from Tel-Aviv, and two were kibbutzniks. We studied together, discussed our assignments, prepared for examinations, and got to know each other's families. These were years full of revelations. I remember telling my husband, 'You know, Shakespeare was a genius!' Such were my revelations: Shakespeare, Jane Austin, Henry James, Faulkner and Mark Twain, and the beauty of modern linguistic theory. I graduated with Distinction, then taught Literature and Language in our kibbutz high school, and later in our regional high school. During all this time I was also fully involved in the social and cultural life in Kibbutz Einat.

In the late 1970s I left teaching and joined the editorial board of the Kibbutz Movement Magazine, *Yahad* (Together) and worked as a journalist, with a part-time job at our kibbutz food store. While my work in our kibbutz enabled me to keep in touch with all members, my work on the magazine involved travelling and getting into new subjects. That's how I became interested in the global commune phenomenon. Since 1985, I've worked as an editor of various publications concerning kibbutz and communal ideas and practice. Currently, I edit the journal Kibbutz Trends and the *Bulletin of the International Communal Studies Association*. My other part-time job is translating, mainly novels, from English into Hebrew. Eitan has been managing the computer system of kibbutz Einat for the last ten years.

Both my and Eitan's parents, who came to Eretz Israel in 1930, went directly to their kibbutzim, then built Kibbutz Einat when they were in their 40s. They continued to work here to the end of their lives. They are all buried in our lovely cemetery. Our two daughters, Noa and Aya, live here in Kibbutz Einat. Our eldest son, Arnon, lives with his wife and two sons in kibbutz Nahsholim, on the Mediterranean coast, not far from Haifa. Our other son, Haggai, left the kibbutz and now lives with his wife and son in Tsoran, in the Sharon District. The distances between our places are not that great, since Israel is quite a small country. We enjoy visiting them and having them here at Einat for Shabbat and other holidays.

*   *   *

Currently, we are 220 members with about 100 children in Kibbutz Einat, plus 100 paying residents with their own children. Our communal income comes from two industrial plants — a bakery with a branch of long shelf-life products and a shoe factory — and from agriculture, mainly cotton, avocado and citrus groves, and from poultry. We also have several small businesses such as a ceramics workshop, a beauty parlour and my own Translations Office, the income from which all goes into our communal coffers. Also, about 30 people work outside Kibbutz Einat with their salaries going into our 'common purse'.

By the end of the 1980s the economic and demographic crisis in the Kibbutz

PHOTO BY HELEN BEST

Fields and houses of Kibbutz Einat

Movement was also being acutely felt here in Kibbutz Einat. It is beyond my ability to explain how this crisis situation developed, but the following facts probably contributed to it. We had changed sleeping arrangements, with the children now sleeping in their parents' homes rather than in the children's house. The cost of enlarging the apartments left us with enormous debts. We had also made business investments which proved to be unprofitable. Our serious economic problems were then worsened by a change in the

Israeli Government's economic policy toward kibbutzim.

In 1990, a group of our members looked into changes we could make to our communal life in order to overcome our economic crisis but, to my mind, this was not done properly. Their main slogan was simply 'privatisation' in order to facilitate and enforce more personal responsibility of members and less interference from the collective in the life of the individual. But this group, comprised mainly of managerial types, did not have sufficient patience and sensitivity to share their ideas with everyone. I do not know if they defined their goals even to themselves! I do not think they considered the far-reaching consequences of every specific change they glibly sought to implement. They were not attentive to the many concerns, doubts and fears of us communal members. The concept of achieving consensus was quite alien to them. Nevertheless, dramatic changes were instigated.

The changes implemented in Kibbutz Einat include privatisation of all consumption areas such as food and energy. As well, after finishing their army service, our young people can now work on this kibbutz or outside for salaries, and use their money for studies or for any other purpose. For five years, they can choose not to become members yet live here in our kibbutz apartments and pay only subsidised rent. Their medical insurance and other expenses are taken care of by the kibbutz for one year. Although the arrangement in itself is good, there is no indication that it helps overcome our demographic and economic crisis. I doubt whether our youth will suddenly find 'The New Kibbutz' more attractive.

Another fundamental change includes relating a member's personal budget to the number of hours worked, a change which threatens the weak and the old. There is also a great change in our kibbutz population because, since 1991, we have accepted paying residents in order to raise income through renting out available accommodation. The immediate result of this 'economically rational' policy is a growing number of unfamiliar faces within our communal home. We also accept children from the nearby town into our children's houses for the same economic reason, and because we do not have enough children of our own to justify maintaining our own education system. Our communal dining room now functions as a restaurant and catering business. Only lunch and holiday meals are still served to members, so many of us have stopped eating there altogether. There are now fewer opportunities for us communal members to casually meet each other. Our personal allowances have been increased to compensate for the lack of communal support — but somehow it is just not the same.

Our Work Coordinator is now hired from outside, and is called a 'Human Resources Coordinator' (that infamous Newspeak). Other key functions such as directors, accountants and consultants were all given to outsider 'professional experts' who are now more involved in decision-making than are most of we communal members. Most of our former committees do not exist any more. Our communal newspaper has ceased to appear. There is a Council of 25 elected members which nominates three committees: Economic Forum, Community Forum and Human Resources Forum, but these do not compensate for the genuine loss in members' autonomy and sense of common purpose. Our kibbutz management is now highly technocratic and centralised, with certain members serving in several public offices at the same time.

Kibbutz Einat's business and community financial accounts are now separated. Our community budget depends on the salaries and pensions from all members, plus

Einat members celebrating Pessach in the Dining Hall

income from paying residents. Each member receives a modest allowance to cover personal expenses, food and energy. Until recently, each member had complete medical coverage provided by the group. Part of our economic 'rationalisation', however, has been to make members pay 10% of the cost of psychological treatment, and now there is pressure to extend this 10% to apply to all medical treatment, medication and dentistry — ie. partial privatisation of our welfare budget. What worries me most about this is that having decided on 10% to be paid by the member, tomorrow they could make this 100%! That would mean that our entire welfare budget would be 'equally' distributed between all members — with each of us simply left to cope with our own troubles. This is certainly *not* healthy communalism as I understand it!

Some of these changes seem reasonable or even inevitable, yet I am concerned about the priorities they represent. The way they have been implemented, with utter disregard for proper procedures and for the feelings of the people involved, goes against our old sense of communal solidarity. As a result, while we still celebrate holidays together, I feel that the shell has been preserved while the soul has left, with fewer and fewer members even bothering to take part.

At the beginning of this change process I took an active part. I was elected to our Kibbutz Council and to the Community Forum which was supposed to fulfil the functions previously handled by our Kibbutz Secretariat. However, I soon became disillusioned. I discovered that most of the people who were involved in the public affairs of Kibbutz Einat did not share my convictions, especially concerning lawful, democratic procedures and equitable social policies. I found it hard to fight for my opinions while those with whom I worked seemed to play according to different rules, and even speak a different language. After two years of this struggle, I found that the price of being involved in our kibbutz politics was just too high. The endless arguments and quarrels made me literally sick, the emotional load was too heavy, so I resigned, abandoning the fray. I now concentrate on my own translating and editing work, on my family, and on the small joys which life still offers me.

*   *   *

I do not like the direction of changes in, nor the atmosphere brought about at, Kibbutz

PHOTO BY IDIT PAZ

Lovely gardens with dining hall on left

Einat, yet I have never seriously thought about leaving my communal life here. First of all, it should be remembered that Eitan and I are now 65 and 60, respectively, so it would be very hard for us to start anew, somewhere else. Besides, we have our family, children and grandchildren living here, and our parents and friends buried here. But that is not the main point. Whatever becomes of Kibbutz Einat in the future, it is my home! It has been home for all of my adult life, and I am certainly not going to give it up! I will do my best to live here according to my convictions, even within an organisational structure I dislike and with which I do not agree. I love my home, Kibbutz Einat, and many of my fellow communards. My husband and I enjoy our work. I feel that my roots are very deep in Kibbutz Einat, and that no ideological or political disagreement is worth severing these life-long ties.

Yet I cannot deny this deep feeling of loss.

Kibbutz Einat Dining Room

Introduction: Lothlorien and Sonia Christophe

PHOTO BY MIKLOS BURGER

Sonia Christophe

Lothlorien was established in 1982 in the state of Bahia, west of Salvador, in north eastern Brazil. It is the youngest as well as the smallest communal group in this book. During the process of this book being compiled, Lothlorien found itself in a serious crisis and it appeared at one time as if there might be no communal group left to write about! As you will read, however, Lothlorien is overcoming its problems and re-forming, hopefully as a stronger group. Lothlorien, like many communal groups around the world, was founded under inspiration from Findhorn Foundation. They sought to emulate Findhorn while adapting to Brazilian conditions. Lothlorien is in a beautiful location, a semi-tropical paradise.

Sonia Christophe trained as a school teacher, then worked at a number of jobs prior to helping found Lothlorien where she has lived ever since. Over the past year, while working on this project, I have shared their problems and joys, and have appreciated Sonia's fortitude and commitment. I wish Sonia and Lothlorien a long and happy future.

The latest I have heard (April 1996), Lothlorien members are overcoming the difficulties described in this chapter — but their survival is still far from assured.

Visitors are welcome at Lothlorien, provided that prior arrangements have been made. Their address is Lothlorien — Centro de Cura e Crescimento, Caeté-Açu (Capão) 46.940-000 Palmeiras, Bahia, Brazil (phone: +55-71-351 2008). "We normally charge around US$30 a day, per person, full board, with 3 excellent vegetarian meals. Low budget visitors may stay on a different basis, exchanging work for part of the costs."

CHAPTER 15

Lothlorien — A Brazilian Community in Crisis

by Sonia Maria Christophe

When I received Bill Metcalf's confirmation that Lothlorien and I were going to be the South American representatives of 'the communal elders' wisdom' — at that very moment our community entered what I consider as the most serious crisis in our existence. I then wondered, 'Will there be any intentional community left for me to write about?' As one of Lothlorien's founders, I've lived through several crises and many difficulties of different kinds, but this time it seemed like the sky had fallen upon our heads. The only thing I was sure about was that I wanted to remain in Lothlorien, working on this project, living in this intentional community, and in intimate contact with Mother Nature. I felt this urge strongly in my heart, in my veins, in my mind and in my soul.

Although we were six adult members, one teenager and five children, in the midst of the events that led us to this crisis, I knew deep inside me that there was only one other adult resident who felt the same as me, and who felt as passionately as I did that Lothlorien must survive. I didn't want to believe it, I refused to face that fact and accept it, and I'll tell you why. This resident is a woman called Mar, with whom I have had serious difficulties in getting along. There has always been love and hate, attraction and repulsion between us during the years we have been living together at Lothlorien. And now the Universe, the Great Spirit, God was putting me in this situation of having to work closely and almost solely with her.

What will come out of this?

* * *

I was born in 1948 in Brazil's largest city, São Paulo. I never dreamt that I would move to another city, let alone end up in a place like this. I graduated as a primary school teacher. Later on, I started university studies, but gave up after two months. I was then working all day long as a secretary, and at night, tired and sleepy, I just couldn't stand those boring university classes. I had studied and learned English from an old Englishman who didn't speak my native Portuguese, and for this reason I learned much more than I would have learned in a regular course. So I decided to follow up with my English studies, attending advanced courses, and then I started to study French as well. A typical, lower-middle-class girl, I was well on my way to getting married and raising children in the old-fashioned way, exactly as my mother, my aunts and my cousins had all done before me. Thank God! several strong blows changed my direction completely.

By 1977, disappointed and unsatisfied with the boring and predictable course of my life, and suffering a lot because of deep personal disappointments, I started to question the social values I had been taught, and the kind of life I was living. Shortly after then, I met Miklos, the man who was going to be my husband for more than 14 years, the father of my three beloved children, and my partner in an exciting new adventure. Both of us were frustrated with our lives in the big city and we were looking for something new. We wanted to change our lives, but didn't know exactly how. By a series of 'coincidences', we moved to Salvador, the capital of the state of Bahia, a medium-sized town by the sea in the north east of Brazil, near the Equator. That means hot weather, lots of beautiful beaches, sun, African influence — and Carnival.

Looking back, I realize that this was the moment when synchronicity started to happen more consistently in my life. We came to live in Salvador by a series of 'coincidences', and then 'by chance', we met Dr. Aureo Augusto. Miklos and I wanted to have a baby, and I didn't want a conventional delivery in a hospital. Aureo was a doctor who delivered babies at home. He also practised natural medicine, using natural healing procedures with water and earth, and the prescription of healthier eating habits. When Miklos and I came to consult with Aureo, I saw a long-haired, nice looking young man running towards our car as we arrived, and I thought to myself, 'It looks like this youngster thinks we came to see him, the poor boy, but we came to see the doctor!' Of course, the 'boy' was Aureo himself. Eventually we became friends. His first son was born only two months after ours. Aureo and Cecilia, his wife, became our son's godparents.

Eight months later, in 1982, we all went camping with our babies at Vale do Capão, a beautiful valley among magical mountains, at the very centre of the state of Bahia, 400 km (250 miles) west of Salvador. It enjoys completely different climatic conditions, although hot and sunny during summer. Vale do Capão is blessed with many rivers, streams, waterfalls and walking trails, all with lots of green vegetation. It provides a sensation of being in Mother Nature's lap. We found a very small village called Caeté-Açu, among banana and coffee plantations, richly endowed with huge mango and other fruit trees. We fell in love with the place and at once decided to buy a piece of land. Aureo and Cecilia quickly decided that they were going to live there. That seemed too much of a leap for me at that moment, but anyway we all were part of a joint project.

At that time, the four of us edited a small magazine on natural medicine, healthy food, alternative lifestyles, spirituality, etc. We agreed that Miklos and I were going to maintain this project while living in Salvador, and that Aureo and Cecilia were going to live on our communal land in Vale do Capão. We chose the name for our land and our project, 'Lothlorien', from J.R. Tolkien's book, *The Lord of the Rings*. It means 'Golden Dream'.

While Aureo and Cecilia were preparing to move to the country, we all attended a conference run by Sara Marriott who then lived at the Findhorn Foundation in Scotland. Sara has an angelic presence which impressed all of us. After that, Aureo and Cecilia decided that Lothlorien should become an intentional community just like Findhorn. The four of us had both private and group meetings with Sara, talking and learning about starting a new age community. As you can see, our links with Findhorn started very early.

Aureo and Cecilia moved to our land in Vale do Capão with all these new ideas in their mental luggage, while Miklos and I remained in Salvador. We spent all our holidays at Lothlorien until we were hooked by their enthusiasm, by this marvellous place and by the idea of living and working together on a communal project in which we deeply believed. Could we leave everything in the city and move to Lothlorien with our two little boys?

At that time we were studying and learning about Viking Runes, an ancient, occidental oracle. Obviously we decided to consult the Runes about our idea of also moving to Vale do Capão, to help develop Lothlorien Community. The Runes that came to us were very impressive. For the present moment we were given *Hagalaz*, which means disruption, elemental power, change, freedom, invention and liberation; and for the long-term outcome we received *Laguz* which means flow, water, fluidity, 'your desire to immerse yourself in the experience of living without having to evaluate or understand'. But what really impressed us about taking this Rune is that *Laguz* was the Rune we had previously chosen to represent Lothlorien Community, and as it appeared in the position representing the outcome, our future, we understood that it was a confirmation that our decision to live in Lothlorien was correct.

So two years after Aureo and Cecilia moved to Lothlorien, in Vale do Capão, Miklos and I, with our children, also moved there. During this two-year period they had received many people who stayed for different lengths of time and who enjoyed different kinds of experiences, but still they were the only permanent residents. For some reason, it looked like the Great Spirit wanted us to have similar experiences at the beginning of our time at Lothlorien, because a few weeks after our arrival, Aureo and Cecilia suddenly had to return to Salvador for urgent personal reasons. Lothlorien's two-year experience repeated itself, only the other way around, with Aureo and Cecilia as the connection in Salvador while Miklos and I lived in and tried to develop our intentional community.

When Aureo and Cecilia came back, two years later, we started a new phase in the communal life of Lothlorien, but still with our two families being the only permanent residents.

Since the beginning of Lothlorien, our clear goal was to start an intentional community, based mainly on the following ideas:

> *1) Working on our land, planting a garden and fruit trees. Our soil was very poor, so we had to spend a lot of time and money improving it, and we still have to do so. We also have had to face cyclical periods of drought, when sometimes we lose all our garden and have to start over again. Up to now, we have not been able to solve this problem once and for all — at least not yet.*

> *2) Practising natural medicine and healthy eating habits ourselves and with the people who come to visit us, and also with the local people. At this point, I feel it is important to say something more about what we mean by natural medicine, since it entails a completely new way of living, of facing life and death, nature, health and sickness. While we put a strong emphasis on changing eating habits — into using food which we think is healthier for us, we also must change our beliefs about health and sickness. We prefer to use the word 'crisis' instead of 'sickness' because we believe that crises are signs, given by our bodies, that something is wrong. So we do not want to suppress these symptoms, but to find out what they are trying to tell us and what it is that we are doing wrong to or with our body. We also believe that what heals us is our body's own vital energy (or* phisis *or* prana*) and that what we must do is make it possible and easier for our natural healing energy to work. It follows that we view nature and other living beings through different eyes. This has led us to the idea of* ahimsa *(harmlessness) which means that we do not kill or permit the killing of any animals at Lothlorien. For instance, nowadays I love frogs and there are always one or two of them living in my house. We do not kill snakes or spiders, as is so common among the native people here. Unfortunately, we are not yet so noble, pure and enlightened as to be able to extend our* ahimsa *philosophy to*

cockroaches and these damned mosquitos!

3) Trying to put into practice the idea of 'unconditional love', to promote residents' spiritual and emotional growth.

Soon after we arrived, we started our own elementary school because this was an urgent need. There was an old school building in a very precarious condition next to Lothlorien, where an illiterate woman gave classes to the local children. She was in no condition to teach anything to anybody. So we got permission from the mayor of the nearest town, to whom the village of Caeté-Açu is subject, to start our own elementary school in that old building, taking over the pre-existing local students and including our own children. It is important to mention that we did this in a tactful manner, being careful not to hurt the previous teacher's feelings, and we are now good friends. We really had to strive to get this school going! We had to teach all the classes ourselves — together with another couple who moved to the valley — while looking for teachers to take over this project. We had to function in that old and almost derelict building, built by the government many years before and since then completely ignored and forsaken. We had to organise several *mutirões* (community work days) with the children's parents, to repair the building. Although we asked for the mayor's support, we never received much more than promises. It was funny though, because when it next rained heavily, our school's roof of bare tiles proved that all our efforts to fix it had not been completely successful — it still leaked, damn it! But we celebrated anyhow because there was nothing else we could do since we could not go on with classes. Hence, we played in the rain — which is always a big pleasure. And we really did have a reason to celebrate: at least we had a reasonable school functioning all the other days when it didn't rain that strongly. That particular day has become a kind of school holiday at Lothlorien.

As for our Lothlorien community life, those were very hard times, with only four adults, one teenager and seven children, and so much work. For me personally, despite being happy because I was living in Mother Nature's lap, and trying a new way of life, communal living was not easy. Our dark sides emerged both too soon and too strongly. Emotional and personality issues had to be dealt with, and differences between our beliefs showed up very sharply. We tried to do our best, and we were always changing our rules and routines, all born from our dreams of how an intentional community *should* work, to fit in with the harsh reality of everyday life at Lothlorien. On top of that, I was resentful when Aureo and Cecilia decided to bring back to Lothlorien Cecilia's other three children, who had been living with their father, without having properly talked it through with the rest of us.

Then, fortunately, other people started to remain for longer periods at Lothlorien, and finally we had eleven permanent adult residents, plus eight youngsters, who all brought in new dreams and ideas. We had to keep on changing our routines as often as was necessary to cope with this dynamic growth and many membership changes. Flexibility and a willingness to change and to grow is one of the main characteristics of Lothlorien. I have learned a great deal, and am still learning more in this field, since I have a tendency to be of a more rigid character. This has been a great personal challenge to me and has helped me to grow personally.

Another of Lothlorien's main characteristics is that we always have children around, usually a lot of them, since our children's friends come often and seem to like to stay here. We have a small soccer field where they spend lots of time, and where Lothlorien's children and adults, boys and girls, men and women all play together. During all these years we have been learning how to raise our children within a new paradigm and with a new perspective, how to include them in our tasks, how to interact with them in different manners, and how to love and understand them better. And I love the results! Ignoring modesty, I can say that all of our children are delightful! They now have good schools to attend. Our early efforts led to the creation of the elementary school called *Brilho do Cristal* (Crystal's Glitter) — a name the children chose. Although the school was built on Lothlorien's ground, it is now run by other, better-prepared people. We still cooperate in many ways, including teaching classes in this school and with the other schools which were created later by our local public administrator.

We have an excellent relationship with the local people of Vale do Capão. After twelve years, we have a lot of friends amongst them, and a high level of interaction with most of them. They have learned to laugh at and yet still respect our 'eccentricities', such as not killing snakes, not eating meat, and bathing naked in the rivers. But also, we have always strived to understand and respect their beliefs, and not to offend them through our new age habits and beliefs. Many local residents rely on our free medical services every Tuesday morning, when we work with natural medicine and with other alternative practices. We also offer medical emergency services, assist them during pregnancy, and help with delivering babies. Helping children to arrive in this world in softer and more loving ways, I think, is one of our more beautiful and meaningful tasks. We also promote health agent's courses for other people who provide medical care for the poor, not only here but in several nearby towns. Local youngsters come frequently to Lothlorien's not-so-small library, from which we lend books to anyone who lives in this valley. We have many really good, useful and beautiful books, and we are very proud of our library and the services which we are able to offer through it.

All these services have helped us to be welcomed into this village of about 1500 inhabitants. We have never felt as strangers in this place. In fact, I have a deep feeling of belonging here — to these local people, to this village and valley, as well as to Lothlorien. Sometimes it seems as if my living in the big city belongs to a previous incarnation. I really love to live near Mother Nature, in intimate contact with Her elements. I draw strength, peace, joy and happiness from this contact. My deepest desire is to remain here at Lothlorien, in this valley, for the rest of my life.

Deriving from these feelings towards nature, we have developed another important activity here, bringing groups of people from Salvador and from other Brazilian cities for workshops during the main holidays. This is important for us, not only because it provides our main income, but also because we believe it is important to encourage people from the big cities to experience life in the country, to allow them to be closer to nature, eat healthier food, breathe pure air, go hiking and bathe in the crystalline waters of our rivers and waterfalls. People usually go back to town in a totally different mood, and are grateful for the experience. I think this is one of the moments when we at Lothlorien best put into practice our goal of manifesting unconditional love.

*   *   *

Everybody says that life is a school. In that case, I think that life in an intentional community is like taking intensive courses — all the time! It is not at all easy, but I find it profoundly worthwhile and rewarding, despite all the challenges — or maybe exactly because of the challenges.

Members and guests 'tuning in' during a workshop

For instance, I told you in the beginning about the crisis we are experiencing at Lothlorien. Four years ago, we two couples who had started Lothlorien community separated, almost at the same time. Cecilia left Lothlorien a few months later, while my ex-partner, Miklos, remains loosely connected, but spends only one week per month here. Then, a few months ago, Aureo decided to leave, as he felt the need for new experiences in his life.

At first I was shocked. Afterwards I was angry and resentful. After all, he was the last of my co-founding companions, yet here he was abandoning our golden dream! We were profoundly shaken, since Aureo was a very special person in our organisation, although we have always tried not to have a leader. Nevertheless, together with what remained of our group, we decided to continue at Lothlorien in the same way that we had been going up to then.

However, many dramatic and emotional events started to happen, compelling us to face the necessity of changing Lothlorien drastically. To start with, a wildfire swept across a third of our valley's mountains, destroyed the forest at the back of Lothlorien and threatened our houses. After that, several of our residents became seriously ill. Later on, while some residents decided to travel for awhile, two other members simply decided to abandon our community. This was truly a crisis for my dream of Lothlorien!

During recent years we, at Lothlorien, had drifted into more individualistic ways of living, and so the changes now being forced onto our communal life are taking us back into being more thoroughly an intentional community. We have now moved from a work pattern whereby individuals chose when to accomplish their own tasks, to working together as a group, in all areas, every morning. We all try to gather very early each morning to practice yoga and meditation. We encourage everybody to come, but those who can't manage to wake up won't be crucified. We then eat breakfast together in our communal dining room, and afterwards we work in the area or on the project on which we have previously agreed. Although it is still winter, we often have hot sun around noon, so we normally all go together to the nearby river to bathe and refresh ourselves before lunch. We usually have lunch together. Most afternoons are free for us to attend to personal matters.

On Tuesday afternoons we have our weekly meeting for administrative and practical matters, and we discuss all our projects, ideas and problems. We make decisions by consensus, which means that when there are different opinions we talk at length about the subject, each side explains its ideas and usually, eventually, we all reach agreement. When someone still does not agree with the group, he/she usually submits to the majority's decision and agrees to be a 'loyal minority'. I don't remember a single occasion when we could not arrive at an agreement. Maybe it is because we are always willing to change our decisions if they prove not to work when put into practice. We used to have weekly meetings for personal and emotional matters, where we shared our personal difficulties, joys and sorrows, and when we tried to solve any emotional and personal disagreements. These were often challenging meetings, as you can guess, when we strove to put into practice all the techniques we had learned and all the experience we had gathered about human relationships. At this transitional moment we are not holding special meetings for these personal and emotional matters but are trying to solve them during our administrative meetings, or whenever we feel the necessity.

Here are some practical details about Lothlorien. We have 16 hectares (40 acres) of land on which we have five communal buildings:

> *The Communal House with kitchen, dining room, library and bathroom.*

> *The House of Harmony with two rooms for medical assistance and massage, and another room where we keep our accounts, our modest but sweetest computer, files, etc. (For some people it is surprising to find a computer here, even though an almost outmoded one.)*

> *The Temple where we meditate, practise yoga, hold meetings and conduct therapeutic work.*

> *The Lodging House where guests stay while doing our workshops.*

> *The Nave where our newly arrived young men live.*

We have six separate family houses where we permanent residents live — or at least lived until very recently. At this moment, we have little idea what will become of those houses whose residents have left Lothlorien. The community owns the land, but the resident who builds a house owns it. This means that he/she can sell the house if he/she leaves Lothlorien, but the sale must be approved by the remaining community members.

For Lothlorien's income we offer workshops and structured holiday experiences, when we can receive up to 30 guests. We also welcome people just to visit Lothlorien, to spend some days in contact with nature, or to experience life in our intentional community, usually for periods of two to ten days.

We hold our money as individuals, but we share what we earn as a group among all residents, after having paid all expenses and put aside Lothlorien's share. Some of us, mainly the former adult residents and their children who can afford to, pay a small monthly 'tax', to help pay for the community's expenses. We pay for our own food, with all of us usually having our meals in Lothlorien's dining room.

*   *   *

PHOTO BY MIKLOS BURGER

Working together in the garden

Between the time since I started to write this chapter and the present moment, many things have been happening, and Lothlorien community has been changing a lot. Mar and I have been learning a great deal about each other, about ourselves and about new ways of relating to each other. We have been doing a lot of work on ourselves, since we know that it is essential to our intentional community's survival. Attraction and repulsion is still present in our interaction, but we are beginning to stay more in the loving than in the hating side. We both have lovely children, and we both really love each other's children. We are being required to make a lot of decisions and to take a lot of responsibilities.

Mar is a pretty, young woman, the mother of two little girls. She came to Lothlorien three years ago, when pregnant with her second daughter. She married Giancarlo, one of our members. Giancarlo got seriously ill and travelled to his home country (Italy) for three months. He has just returned and decided to stay in Lothlorien, but separated from Mar. After a period of adjustment, Mar became very active and involved with our community. We agree deeply on all fundamental matters, although our personalities often engage in disagreements and misunderstandings. It is still painful, but I really believe that we are making progress. I thank Mar for having brought the flowers to Lothlorien. We had been so busy, that we never found time for planting flowers, but now she has awakened in us the drive to grow beautiful flower gardens.

Fortunately, the Universe has sent Lothlorien two young men who are willing to work with us and to participate in reviving Lothlorien. One of them, the son of a previous resident, decided to remain when his mother left. Ajuricaba is only 18 and he is almost like one of our children who has developed into a nice young man. The other, Hugo, arrived only a couple of months ago, by another series of 'coincidences', and has immediately fitted into our group. They are working with Mar and me, sharing all these new ideas, bringing a youthful drive to our new directions, and pushing us, or at least me, to get on with the changes which we have to make. Their participation, together with Mar's, has been important in balancing my tendency to think and worry too long before moving, as well as to stick too long to established forms.

A couple of my friends outside Lothlorien have commented about me having to write about our community during this time of crisis, as offering me a very good opportunity for pondering on the meanings and lessons of our crisis. What went wrong? Did anything actually go wrong? The more I think about this, the more I become convinced that nothing went wrong. It was time for a big change at Lothlorien, we had to take another step forward, and in order to shake us out of our inertia, the Universe gave us a little(?) slap to wake us up and help us to re-engage with the Lothlorien Spirit's plan.

And at this point you may ask who, for God's sake, is this Lothlorien Spirit anyhow? Well, we believe that there is an angel or a spiritual being which we call Lothlorien, who has special qualities and purposes, and who needs to manifest them in this time and place. We have already figured out some of these qualities and purposes: joyful willingness to change; manifesting unconditional love; practising natural medicine; researching new ways of living; learning to heal ourselves; and sharing this knowledge. We see ourselves as channels or instruments through which this Lothlorien Spirit can manifest itself. We have our children with us, and this gives us strength and faith. We are re-structuring ourselves, re-evaluating all our rules and routines, and trying to figure out new ways to interact as an intentional community. Of course, we ask the Lothlorien Spirit for guidance and help, as we have always done. We understand that these are challenging, transforming times for all of us on planet Earth. We strive to maintain our courage and optimism, and we are full of energy, trust and faith.

*   *   *

PHOTO BY MIKLOS BURGER

Meeting in the Temple

I have experienced many painful times, fearing that Lothlorien wouldn't survive. I have felt insecure about my ability to take over so many responsibilities. I have been anxious about having to make all the critical decisions, together with Mar, about the feasibility of us getting along well and sharing all our fears and hopes at this challenging moment — and I admit that I still feel a little like this sometimes.

I don't know exactly why I believe that our intentional community will survive, but I feel it in the air, in the sunlight that bathes our mountains, in the blue of our sky, and in the butterflies that float around us. During the moments of meditation when I feel a strong link with this spiritual being we call Lothlorien Spirit, I know that we will make our Lothlorien community survive, grow and prosper.

Introduction: New Meadow Run Bruderhof and Justin Peters

PHOTO BY CHARIUS ZUMPE

Justin Peters

New Meadow Run is part of the Bruderhof Movement which started in Europe in 1920, and which is loosely part of the centuries-old communal Anabaptist movement. New Meadow Run Bruderhof was established in 1957 near Uniontown in southwest Pennsylvania, USA. It now has about 350 members, about average size for the groups in this book. The Bruderhof have often been compared favourably with the Israeli kibbutzim in terms of their scale, industriousness, degree of communality, and economic power. Given their commitment to non-violence and social justice, the Bruderhof may be considered to be counter-cultural, although their strong Christian commitment makes them different from most counter-cultural groups. There are six Bruderhofs in USA and two in England.

Justin Peters was four years old when his family joined the Bruderhof in 1954, and he has lived there ever since, first at Woodcrest, then in 1986 joining New Meadow Run. Justin, a graduate of Cornell University, works in their factory making wooden classroom furniture as well as equipment for disabled people.

I visited New Meadow Run Bruderhof in 1991 and was thoroughly impressed. Set in a lovely rural area, their clean and tidy buildings and attractive farm were in stark contrast to the somewhat depressed rural area in which they are located. Visiting members in their private quarters, at communal meals and while helping at work, I was struck by their camaraderie and obvious sense of joy.

Many books have been written about the Bruderhof. The best self-explanation of their ideology can be found in *Discipleship* by J.H. Arnold, and in *Why We Live in Community* by E. Arnold & T. Merton (both by Farmington: Plough Publishing). A more analytical account by the well-known communal scholar, Professor Yaacov Oved, will be published in mid 1996 as *The Witness of The Brothers* (New Brunswick: Transaction Press). Professor Yaacov Oved's *Distant Brothers* (Israel: Yad Tebenkin), also about the Bruderhof, is available through Plough Publishing. Finally, readers may learn more about the Bruderhof on http://www.esslink.com/-brud/bruderhof.html. Visitors are welcome but should always write first. New Meadow Run's address is P.O. Box 240, Route 40, Farmington PA 15437, USA (fax: +1-412-329-1270; or e-mail: brud@esslink.com).

CHAPTER 16

New Meadow Run: A Christian Witness for the 21st Century

by Justin Peters

It was the summer of 1942, and hundreds of thousands of Allied troops were massed in southern England. In Brighton, the College of Art opened its doors to the soldiers for free art lessons. One evening a 23-year-old private in the Canadian Artillery Survey Corps walked in and asked one of the teachers for a live subject to draw. Next day, the teacher brought in her daughter's pet rabbit. When he had drawn the rabbit, the soldier told the teacher that he actually wanted to draw a *real* person, and did she know of anyone who would be willing? The following day she brought her daughter, just turned seventeen, and he drew her.

That soldier, Don Peters, was my father, and the teacher's daughter, Anne, was my mother. Not knowing when Dad would be sent into battle, or whether he would return, they married six months later, in spite of Mum's age.

Soon after, Dad's unit was headed for Algiers, then Sicily, and then into a long artillery battle against German forces, as the Allies inched their way up Italy. One of the platoon leaders, a quiet man of high moral standards and an inner strength that was compelling and attractive, was a socialist. Before the war was over, Dad was a socialist too.

Meanwhile, Mum was studying at the College of Art, where she was greatly influenced by a teacher who was a communist.

Thus, when my parents finally got together again in March 1946, they were both ardent socialists. They worked at organizing cooperatives in the Chicago slums. Later, in Ottawa, Canada, they joined the left-wing Canadian Cooperative Federation political party.

In Ottawa they met Leonore Sommers, the sister of one of Mum's childhood friends. Then, in Seattle, Leonore went to a meeting of the Fellowship of Reconciliation, where she heard two men talk about an intentional Christian commune in the backwoods of Paraguay. Leonore thought, 'Don and Anne will want to hear about this', and wrote to them.

Soon my parents were corresponding with Primavera Bruderhof in Paraguay, and with Wheathill Bruderhof in England. They couldn't both afford to travel that far, and both Bruderhofs told them to wait until they could come together. Impasse. Finally, Woodcrest Bruderhof was founded in New York State in June 1954. In December 1954 our whole family came to Woodcrest: Dad and Mum, my older sisters, Rilla and Esther, and me, aged four.

*   *   *

Unwittingly, we had arrived at a crucial time. Eberhard Arnold, the visionary founder of the Bruderhof in 1920, had been dead for 19 years. Now the Bruderhof, at its branches in Europe and South America, was also dying under a burden of cold-heartedness, legalism, and power politics. An abstract belief in community had replaced the fresh, spontaneous, fiery love for Jesus and for each other.

One person who agonized over the decline was Eberhard's son Heinrich Arnold. Heinrich was hated and feared by the people in power. When the membership insisted on appointing him to the ministry, the leaders hoped to neutralize him by shipping him off to the nascent outpost of Woodcrest Bruderhof in North America. I remember the Arnolds' arrival in February 1955.

Woodcrest was born into a storm of radical ferment. Even as Senator Joseph McCarthy raged in Washington, multitudes on North America's left socialist fringe were looking for a society of real justice and peace. They came from the Quakers, the Church of the Brethren, and the Mennonites. They came from intentional communities and universities. And many of them came to Woodcrest Bruderhof. Heinrich had the wisdom to see that these new arrivals had no interest in tradition or 'correct' form; all they wanted was truthful, authentic, sleeves-rolled-up socialist and communal action.

People came from all over North America to stay in Woodcrest. Soon we numbered over 200 people. Houses shot up one after another, even if the lumber was green and there was no siding.

But more important than the exuberance of a young and rapidly growing Bruderhof was the sense of belonging to a great cause. Without ever consciously thinking about it, we children felt that we belonged to the civil rights movement, to the ban-the-bomb movement, and to any and every movement for real peace and justice. These were the matters about which the grown-ups cared, so we shared their passion.

Martin Luther King's *Stride Toward Freedom*, the story of the Montgomery bus boycott, was read at our communal mealtimes, and members of Macedonia Community, which joined Woodcrest soon after, were directly involved in that boycott. The Committee for Nonviolent Action made Woodcrest a regular stop on their nuclear peace marches. One Saturday evening, a Soviet delegation to the United Nations had communal supper with us, followed by a long and lively dialogue. *Ishi, Last of His Tribe*, the story of the last unconquered native American, was also read to us, and I was moved to a sense of deep solidarity with these oppressed people. We enjoyed a cultural richness, alive with hope for a new social reality.

Late in the winter of 1965 we gathered around the radio in our home. President Lyndon Johnson, the victorious 'peace' candidate, addressed the nation. We were incredulous — he was sending hundreds of thousands of Americans into war in Vietnam!

What could one teenager do? I joined the Political Science Club at Kingston High School. There we watched David Halberstam's documentary of life behind the North Vietnamese lines; the Vietnamese were remarkably like us! In the mid-sixties, however, the peace movement was only a radical fringe. I couldn't get any of my friends to see why the war was wrong. I read and soaked up vast amounts of anti-war comment, but what could I do?

1968 was an important year. In January, the Vietcong's Tet Offensive shocked America — the Communist forces seemed able to attack at will anywhere, and more Americans started to see that something was morally wrong with this war. Then Eugene McCarthy challenged President Johnson, promising to pull America out of the Vietnam War, and like millions of other young Americans, I hoped wildly that he would win.

Then everything went dark! On the evening of April 4, the radio announced that Martin Luther King had been shot and killed. 'Why?' I asked my mother. 'If anyone ever trusted God, it was he. Why didn't God protect him?' She was quiet for a little while. Then she said gently, 'Think of Jesus. Think how he trusted God. And what happened to him?'

Then Robert Kennedy was shot. Eugene McCarthy lost the nomination. Richard Nixon won the American presidential election. The Vietnam War thundered on. I was looking for a source of hope. Politics didn't seem to have it.

In the spring of 1969, one of my courses at Cornell University was on 'The History of Western Thought'. By April, we were up to Thomas Aquinas. This provided the introduction that helped us talk about Christianity. The central point, it seemed, was to be sure that you were 'saved'. I had never thought much about this, but it seemed to make sense. Jesus talked a lot about entering the kingdom of heaven.

But something in me passionately hated such a belief. What did my being saved have to do with the unravelling civil rights movement? With Detroit and Newark in flames from racial riots? With Vietnamese civilians being massacred?

At this point, my parents received a new translation of one of Christoph Blumhardt's sermons. Blumhardt had been expelled from the German Lutheran Church in the late 1800s, and had joined the Socialist Party. The atheistic Socialists, with their on-the-ground hope for earthly justice, were far more Christian, in his eyes, than the pious churchgoers who wouldn't risk anything to fight injustice. The main point of Christianity, said Blumhardt, was 'Thy Kingdom come, Thy Will be done on earth as it is in Heaven'. Dad read this to our family.

What a contrast! Two Christianities. Both looked biblical. Which one was true? If salvation was the main point, I was not going to be a Christian. I was never going to forsake everything I cared about for something so small as my own salvation. I talked it over with Mum and Dad, but they insisted I solve the problem myself. I decided that Blumhardt's view breathed the compassion, the justice, and the true greatness of the God in whom I was coming to believe. Heaven certainly existed, but I was going to live for the earth.

Spring 1970. I was studying food crop production at Cornell University, hoping in some small way to combat starvation in the world. Meanwhile, the war was spilling over into Cambodia. My roommate, a US Marine corporal less than a year home from Vietnam, was driving carloads of students to peace rallies.

Suddenly the peace movement was growing! We weren't just the crazy fringe anymore. The whole student body — and millions more across America — were going on strike! The university administration allowed any who wished to, to strike with impunity, and most did. I went to class. I couldn't see how staying away from school would help achieve peace, since I was going to school to learn to fight hunger.

I started to look for root causes. The Sixties Generation wanted to change the world, to end war, racism and poverty, and I am avidly part of that generation. But I was noticing that there were fundamental causes behind these evils.

That September, as Dad drove me back to school, we talked about 'the church' for the first time ever. It was far greater than the sum of its little human parts, he said. Dad and Mum never suggested that I should join Woodcrest Bruderhof, but also never let me doubt that they would stay there until they died. 'What is happening in Woodcrest is significant for the whole world.' I started to wonder if what was happening at Woodcrest might have something to do with those root causes. I heard Heinrich Arnold say, 'We cannot speak only about world suffering without being unjust to God. It is a matter of a great worldwide sin. If we merely talk about the suffering and fail to say that it is caused by sin, we let the blame fall on God.' For now, I had but a vague intimation of this. But I was increasingly sensing a gap, a blind spot in the peace movement. What caused war? What caused racism? Could it be that a movement, even if small, which saw and over-came the root causes, could be more effective — more relevant, as we loved to say? Was this what the Bruderhof was about?

*   *   *

Thus it was that when I walked out of my last class, college completed, in December 1971, I headed for Woodcrest Bruderhof. Now the real trouble started! It was far easier to protest a war 10,000 miles away than to deal with the bramble thicket of root causes within myself! Cornell University was a great place to grow a strong ego, but now my ego was getting banged and bruised within the Bruderhof.

For a long, unhappy year I lived at Woodcrest, root causes intact but their presence painfully obvious beneath the stubborn fog. But above the fog was a sun I hadn't planned on. Again I had landed in Woodcrest at a decisive time.

Eleven years before, the Bruderhof had been through a terrible but liberating crisis. Hundreds of people had left. Those who stayed wanted to return to the original vision. They had asked Heinrich to lead their decimated ranks back to it, and had retrenched from eleven communities to three: Woodcrest, (in New York State), Deer-spring (in Connecticut), and New Meadow Run (in Pennsylvania).

1972 was a wonderful time to be young in Woodcrest. Dozens of Bruderhof baby-boomers who had been scattered across the world were coming back. Woodcrest's pop-ulation of around 300 included a young singles group of over 100! We had a great time together as young people, doing folk dances, singing, playing games, and doing work projects. For every special occasion we decorated the communal dining room with bouquets of flowers, large murals we had painted, and on one memorable occasion we created the entire solar system out of illuminated fiberglass globes, hung from the high ceiling on ellipses of copper wire to represent each planet's orbit around the sun!

Hans Hermann Arnold, Heinrich's brother, was diagnosed with rapidly advancing cancer in August. Suddenly there was a great urgency to find that vision of the Bruder-hof's childhood again. Heinrich and Hans Hermann told us story after story about their parents, Eberhard and Emmy, and the Bruderhof's early years. At the center of their stories was Jesus. He was not the petty Jesus of my history class. He was a person and a spirit of vast joy who wanted to, and could, take on all the war, racism, greed and pride around; before Him they would vanish like ice cubes in summer. I was at last finding an answer — an infinite, all-embracing answer.

In 1981, we were a family of four in Woodcrest: Dad, Mum, my sister Rilla, and I. In November, Mum was diagnosed with cancer. She fought hard for life, and sometimes it seemed that she was recovering, but soon she was in bed all the time.

Mum was 56. I had never imagined that I would be living with someone going to meet death in full consciousness, clear in mind but already living in a vaster, broader universe. On the morning of April 6, Mum awoke radiant; 'I have been given a holy healing', she told us. Later that morning, she died.

Later that month I was walking over the hill behind Heinrich's house, when I happened to see Heinrich standing at his window. When he saw me look up, he waved warmly, not just with his hand, but with his whole arm. I waved back. Then I went on over the hill. That was our farewell.

On July 23, the whole Woodcrest community gathered to sing to Heinrich early in the morning. Our little family of three was there too. For about half an hour we sang hymns of faith. His children were inside with him, and all the rest of us were outside. Around 7 am, Heinrich died.

The next day, my sister Rilla went to see an eye doctor. She had been having severe headaches. The doctor knew almost immediately that it was severe cancer. More tests followed in the next days. Yes, it was cancer. No, there was no hope that any treatment would cure it.

Rilla was with us for ten more weeks. She was only 35. One might assume she would have been crushed by the thought of her imminent death, but nowhere else have I ever seen such deep joy as in her. The last months with my mother, and then with Heinrich, had prepared her for this last great moment as she faced her early death.

There was a strange and moving intensity to her last weeks. Rilla's hours were numbered, and she was not going to waste one of them. At every family mealtime, she had us invite someone. At every communal mealtime, when her strength allowed, she stayed afterward to talk to people. She wrote many letters, and sorted through her books, papers, clippings and belongings, deciding to whom to give each item. On October 1, 1982 Rilla asked the young people to come and visit her, and she asked them to sing Eleanor Farjeon's hymn: 'Joyfully foregather! / Sorrow now is done! / We have found a Father, / We have found a Son!'

Rilla died two days later.

*   *   *

One Saturday afternoon about three years later our singles' group was helping to clear a piece of land so that pine tree saplings could be planted there for future harvest as Christmas trees. I showed Linda how to pull out thorny barberry bushes without getting thorns in her hands. Although neither of us told the other this till later, that 'prickly' moment was the beginning of our interest in each other.

Young single members of the Bruderhof do not date. If a young man falls in love with a young woman, he first tells the Elder of the Bruderhof about it. If the Elder feels that this young man and this young woman will lead each other closer to a true discipleship of Jesus, through a relationship of love, he gives his permission for them to write letters to each other, not love letters, but letters about what is important to them spiritually. We believe that a marriage which is not built on firmly held and shared Christian convictions will not stay together long. First there must be communion of spirit, then of emotions, and only then of bodies.

Sexual activity outside of marriage is sin. The Bruderhof is ready to accept any repentant sinner into our midst, but we cannot accept a person continuing in a sinful relationship, whether heterosexual or homosexual. We have members who gave up their homosexual lifestyle and sexual promiscuity in order to follow Jesus fully in Christian community here at the Bruderhof.

When I asked our Elder for permission to get to know Linda better, to see if what I felt for her was true and lasting love, he gave us his permission to write letters to each other. This went on for several weeks. Then we were allowed to go on walks together and to talk about what was important to us spiritually, and to find out if we really felt united in soul and spirit. We did, and so we became engaged to each other in a prayer meeting attended by all the members of the Bruderhof. Two weeks later, on July 13, 1986, we were married.

After a week of honeymoon we moved to New Meadow Run Bruderhof in Pennsylvania. What a joyful surprise awaited me in marriage! This was what I had been needing — someone to share my life and heart with completely.

PHOTO BY CHARIUS ZUMPE

Main residence and schools with playing fields in foreground

Linda's parents had joined the Bruderhof in 1962 after searching for years for a life all of whose facets — school, work, recreation, family, and friends — would be part of a whole, instead of in their separate little boxes. Upon visiting New Meadow Run Bruderhof, Linda's parents felt that here was the place they had been looking for! In June of 1962 they arrived to stay, bringing with them their four children. Linda was seven years old. She grew up in the Bruderhof, went to public high school as all of our children do, and then went on to college for four years to become a teacher. Linda worked part-time while at college to help pay her expenses, as well as getting several scholarships. The Bruderhof can not afford to pay for the education of all our college-age young people, so we expect them to try to obtain scholarships, and to also work part-time to help pay for their education.

We live communally, like the first Christians in Jerusalem (see Acts 2:43–47 and 4:32–37 in the Bible), sharing everything except our spouses, and we do not have any private property. The Bruderhof provides for all our needs; everything from housing to clothing to toothpaste. No member has any money of her or his own, but if cash is needed for a trip to town to see a doctor, for instance, the brother who cares for our finances gives out as much cash as is needed, along with a key to one of our small fleet of communally owned vehicles. Upon returning from town, any unused cash is returned, along with the car key ('Please clean the car and fill the gas tank!') so that the vehicle is ready for the next person who needs it.

Now we are a family of three: Linda, our daughter Kendra, and me. Kendra has just begun first grade in our Bruderhof school, which is staffed by our members. Beginning school is a joyful communal event, attended by the entire Bruderhof, from babies to grandparents. Each child who is entering first grade comes up in front of the whole gathering and writes his or her name on a chalkboard. The children have been practising all summer to write their names in preparation for this big event. After writing their names, each new first grade child receives a large paper cone, beautifully decorated on the outside and clearly labelled with his or her name. But, best of all, inside the paper cone are all kinds of goodies: crayons, paper, coloring book, candy, and a large balloon. All the new first grade children and their teachers line up for photographs and then proceed to their new classroom, where they sit at their desks, look at their new books, and enjoy the contents of their paper cones. Soon, the entire Bruderhof comes to the school and tours through each classroom to see the children and teachers in their new setting. What a joyful communal experience, and a what a great way to set the tone for a new school year!

New Meadow Run's main building housing most members, offices, laundry, sewing room, clinic and archives

PHOTO BY CHARIUS ZUMPE

Linda taught in our Bruderhof school for several years, but now works here as a secretary. She has also worked in our communal laundry, kitchen and sewing room, at computer drafting in our factory, and on the cleaning crew. Every member of the Bruderhof, regardless of education levels, skills or expertise in any given field, promises to work wherever he or she is asked. One 'brother' and one 'sister' distribute the work, making sure it all gets done, and rotating jobs as needed. I work in our factory in which we make wooden classroom furniture, and equipment for disabled people. In recent years we have worked to change our factory so that women and men, young and old, will enjoy working there. Even those with no skill in woodworking or upholstery can find meaningful, productive work now. We have spent large amounts of time and energy to simplify and clarify our instructions and setups so that anyone can come and make parts, assemble products, and pack them for shipment. This has not meant a loss in production or quality, but rather the opposite — we get more work done, the quality is even better, plus everyone has a great time working together.

The elderly in our community work as long and as much as their strength permits. Grandmas operate computers, while others fold laundry or help set our communal dining tables.

Recently, our work assignments have changed drastically. Many women work in our factory and in other work departments which were largely staffed by men previously. Yet we feel that women's and men's intrinsic qualities are neither identical nor interchangeable but that they are equal in value. There are precious qualities which are only to be found in women, and precious qualities which are only to be found in men. Everyone is created in the image of God, and every person is a thought of God. We work to help that thought of God develop and grow in each individual, in every aspect of their lives.

PHOTO BY CHARIUS ZUMPE

Working in the large, modern factory

The day begins with breakfast in our family apartment. Then, after dishes are washed and beds made, we all head off at 7.30 to office, factory and school. Everything is within a few minutes' walk at New Meadow Run Bruderhof. The children are cared for by communal members during the day in their age groups, from six weeks of age on, year round. Kendra spends each morning learning to read, write, do arithmetic, and play cooperatively (we hope!).

After lunch in the communal dining room at 12.15, we head home to our family apartment for 'rest-time' until 2pm when all the men go back to work. Mothers and children stay home until 3pm. Then, Linda takes Kendra back to the school for the afternoon. Dancing, arts and crafts, games, choir, projects, vegetable gardening, swimming and free play are some of the varied activities which fill the afternoon for our school children. At 5.30 the mothers and children return to their family apartments, and at 6pm the men return from work. Then for an hour we are all together, getting Kendra ready for bed, reading, singing, and enjoying each other's company. During the evening's communal meal, the adults take turns babysitting the younger children in their family apartments. The young children eat supper around 5pm in their age groups, either in the Babyhouse, Kindergarten or School. Usually, after the evening meal, there is either a prayer meeting or a members' meeting where all decisions are made unanimously, or sometimes a social event such as a campfire to sing around.

There is rarely a routine day in the Bruderhof. Particularly when there is too much work to do and too few hands to do it, we find excuses for fun. A few days ago there was so much work to do in the factory that we closed it down and played softball for an hour. What a great way to pump new enthusiasm into our work! Another time the bell that rings to call us to meals suddenly began to ring in the middle of the morning. Everyone dropped what we were doing and rushed to the dining hall. A bus load of people had just arrived from one of our other Bruderhofs to surprise us. A joyful hubbub ensued as each person was welcomed and we found someone to invite home to our apartment.

About 350 people live at New Meadow Run. This includes many children, and many elderly. We care for our elderly and sick right here at the Bruderhof, since we have doctors and nurses among our members. If specialized medical care is needed, we use the local hospitals. We do not send our older members to homes for the aged, but care for them here in the Bruderhof until their death.

After their years of schooling, many of our young people spend time away from the Bruderhof. We encourage this. Being a member of the Bruderhof is a permanent commitment, for life, and every person, regardless of whether or not they grew up in the Bruderhof, must make a personal decision to join the Bruderhof or not. Many of our young people do return after a time away, and become lifetime members through 'Believer's Baptism'.

Every year, we send out dozens of missionaries. Our communal life depends on our staying in touch with the rest of the world. Our airline bill includes tickets to Russia, Nigeria, India, Palestine and Peru. We also reach out to people in prison. In the three American states where we have Bruderhof communities, popular sentiment for the death penalty is strong. People are once again being executed. We try to be friends with the bruised, oppressed, poor people — all sinners like us — whom we come to know in our local jails. Some of these, even children, face imminent death at the hands of the state.

Justin helping build a new communal dwelling

Part of our communal mission is publishing, sending our *Plough Magazine* to thousands of people around the globe, and printing books that reflect our understanding of Christianity and communal living. The publication of Heinrich Arnold's book, *Discipleship*, was especially meaningful to me in a very personal way. As Linda and I read it, we often remembered Heinrich speaking the very words we read, and recognize the wisdom that helped form our lives. So it is a special joy to us that this book has received wider and more enthusiastic acceptance than any other we've published.

Another book soon to be published by the Bruderhof is *A Plea for Purity* which deals with many topics relating to family, marriage, purity, sexuality, and the place of singles in Christian living. We have read the manuscript in our members' meetings, and again had to realize the wisdom that helped form our lives. We hope that this book will also be welcomed and read by many.

Our Bruderhofs today provide a communal home for over 2000 people, in six communities in the United States, and two in England.

*   *   *

You who read my story and the story of the Bruderhof — we want to be your friends, your sisters and brothers. Let's join together in living, working, praying, and even dying for a new, more communal time on this earth.

CHAPTER 17

Summary and Conclusion

By Bill Metcalf

How does one draw together the common threads and point out the obvious differences found within these 15 stories of communal living? Indeed, should we even attempt to do this sort of 'distilling-of-the-essence' exercise, or should these subjective, biographical accounts of communal living be allowed to stand as they are, as self-explanatory, without analysis?

As pointed out in my Introduction, a certain implicit analysis has, of course, already been applied to these communal stories because of the application of my method of 'biographical discourse'. This technique implies that the editor/discussant (myself) has some clear ideas about the key issues involved in communal living, and that from within that paradigm and understanding prompts, cajoles and 'harasses' the subjects into discussing whatever aspects have been pre-ordained to be important, while other aspects of the life story may, inadvertently and unfortunately, be played down or even ignored.

For readers who wish to leave their biographical accounts unsullied by analysis, who feel that from one or more of the previous accounts of communal living they have found their questions answered or their prejudices confirmed — for them I suggest reading no further.

Differences and Similarities Among Communal Groups

These 15 diverse communal groups from eleven countries on five continents are, of course, very different in many respects while remarkably similar in others. From my previous research I have identified several critical areas which are important to understanding communalism, and I now look at how these groups compare.

I must stress that these analytical observations are my own, based on the stories presented by these communards, as well as on my own observations when visiting the groups. In some cases I have been able to discuss my observations with members of the communal group, while in other cases I have not. I suspect that several of these communards might not agree with all my analysis, and that is their prerogative. Some of the readers may not agree with me either. That is healthy. Nevertheless it is my self-appointed task to offer generalisations, observations and prognostications — so here goes...

Personal Backgrounds. It is often alleged that communal living only appeals to those of middle-class origins. While several of these communards fit that mould, obviously people like Chris Palmer (Riverside), Reverend Chandy (Christavashram), Idit Paz (Kibbutz Einat) and Thérèse Parodi (l'Arche) do not. These 15 communards' family backgrounds range from the intensely religious and conservative to the almost non-existent, broken family. While higher education was critical in the development of communal ideas in Anne Blaney (The Emissaries), Bill Sullivan (Auroville), Sigrid Niemer (UFA-Fabrik), Mary Inglis (Findhorn Foundation) and Juan Robinson (Los Horcones), it was much less important with others such as Chris Palmer, Atsuyoshi Niijima (Yamagishi Toyosato) and Thérèse Parodi.

Leadership. Christavashram and Padanaram have strong, centralised, charismatic leadership. Findhorn Foundation, l'Arche, The Emissaries and The Farm moved from having strong charismatic leaders to a more diffuse form of governance. The other communal groups have always been more egalitarian, mildly anarchistic and loosely consensus-based, even when theocratic such as with the Bruderhof. UFA-Fabrik, Los Horcones and Community Alternatives have an avoidance of hierarchy as fundamental to their group consciousness, although they recognise the importance of members showing leadership.

Spiritual / Religious / Secular. Christavashram, New Meadow Run Bruderhof and perhaps Padanaram could be considered 'religious', while for Auroville, l'Arche, Findhorn Foundation and Lothlorien 'spiritual' is a more appropriate term, since they do not subscribe to any larger religious grouping, yet obviously have an 'other-than-here-and-now' orientation. Riverside, Yamagishi Toyosato, UFA-Fabrik, Kibbutz Einat, Community Alternatives, The Farm and Los Horcones could best be considered predominantly secular. There is little relationship between how these groups are classified along this dimension and anything else about them with the exception that strong, charismatic leadership is more likely to be found in a religious than in a secular group. It is also obvious how this spiritual/religious/secular classification, of which communal scholars are so fond, tends to be fairly open to change, with several of these communal groups shifting categories over time.

Boundary Maintenance. While all of these communal groups are very open to casual visitors, there is a marked difference in the entry requirements for new members. Community Alternatives and Auroville require very little commitment upon joining, while Findhorn Foundation, UFA-Fabrik, The Farm, Lothlorien, Riverside and now The Emissaries require somewhat more. To join Kibbutz Einat, Yamagishi Toyosato, l'Arche, Bruderhof, Christavashram, Padanaram and Los Horcones, however, requires far more commitment from the novice communard, sometimes implying lifetime vows and handing over all worldly goods. It appears that the groups which are the hardest to join have the lowest membership turnover, but contrary to what one might expect, this does not appear to translate into different long-term prospects.

Size. These groups vary from Lothlorien at the very small end of the scale, through to the other extreme with Yamagishi Toyosato having 1600 members and Auroville with over 1000. Smaller communal groups are certainly easier to govern, and it is easier for them to maintain consensus decision-making, but there appears to be a minimum size smaller than which groups are unable to continue. Arguably Riverside, Lothlorien and Los Horcones suffer from being too small. Findhorn Foundation is becoming ever smaller in terms of its core communal membership (having dropped from about 300 to 150 over the past 20 years) while expanding as the centre of a diffuse community. As pointed out by Mary Inglis, however, its governance has not been simplified as a result.

Accessibility. Findhorn Foundation and Lothlorien mainly support themselves through being open to guests who pay to come and stay in order to learn from their host's communal lifestyle. While all the others are more or less open to casual visitors, the facilities offered vary greatly. UFA-Fabrik recently closed its guest house, while at Auroville guest facilities are only provided by entrepreneurial individuals rather than by the group. Within communal groups, visitors can be regarded as anything from a source of income, to a nuisance, a necessary evil, or the very reason for the group's existence. In general, however, most communal groups have enough of a proselytising and humanistic dimension to ensure that visitors are welcomed with a remarkably open heart. None of the groups within this book have closed themselves to public scrutiny, a feature often indicative of groups developing cult-like qualities.

Relationship Between Individual and Group. Does the communal group exist to serve individual members, or do members exist to serve the group? In other words, is the communal group seen as being above and beyond the sum of the individual members. Findhorn Foundation, Los Horcones, The Farm, l'Arche, Auroville and Yamagishi Toyosato, for a host of reasons, have each developed a world-view in which the individual member is secondary to the group. The same applies at Padanaram, New Meadow Run Bruderhof and Christavashram because of their religious connection. All these groups would continue more or less as they are even if there was a complete turnover of members. The other groups, but particularly Los Horcones and Lothlorien, are more dependent on the presence of particular individuals.

Recruitment. In order to ensure their survival, all social groups must recruit new members merely to counteract natural attrition. Communal groups can either recruit through having and retaining children, or through attracting other adults. New Meadow Run Bruderhof, Kibbutz Einat, and Padanaram mainly depend on their communal children for new members, a pattern now developing at The Farm and Los Horcones. At Findhorn Foundation, UFA-Fabrik, L'Arche and Community Alternatives, retaining children as members has been of very little importance. Christavashram has followed a path similar to 19th century Shakers, of taking in homeless orphans and raising them communally. Lothlorien, Los Horcones, The Emissaries and Riverside all face problems with inadequate recruitment.

Communal Ritual. All on-going social groups develop rituals to help mark the boundaries between 'us' and 'them'. For communal groups, rituals are very important as they allow the group to reaffirm their 'group-ness' and reassert their interconnectedness. Such rituals vary widely from the simple communal meals and games of Riverside, UFA-Fabrik, Community Alternatives and Lothlorien, to group meditation and prayers such as at l'Arche, Findhorn Foundation and Christavashram. Working together serves as an important binding ritual at Auroville, Los Horcones, The Emissaries and Padanaram. But while these examples are most important, a wide range of other rituals are also employed in each communal group. Several groups talked about the need to be able to laugh at themselves through their own entertainment. This feature is vitally important at Findhorn Foundation, Community Alternatives and Padanaram. When a communal group loses the ability to laugh at itself — I start to worry.

Conflict and Conflict Resolution. All social groups face conflict, and communal groups are no exception. The real issue is how conflict is handled, whether suppressed or resolved, and in the latter event, how it is resolved. Conflict has been partially resolved simply through the departure of members from communal groups such as Riverside, Auroville, Lothlorien, The Emissaries, The Farm, Los Horcones, Kibbutz Einat and Findhorn Foundation. Community Alternatives, Riverside, Findhorn Foundation, Los Horcones and Lothlorien all offer counselling and conflict resolution services to try to avoid losing members — with varying results. Hierarchical and theocratic groups such as New Meadow Run Bruderhof, Christavashram, Padanaram and l'Arche can all depend on their scriptural base and their overarching philosophy to resolve many issues which might otherwise build up and then explode into conflict. It is very helpful to a communal group to have a set of clear rights and wrongs against which conflicting views can be compared, as referred to at Community Alternatives, Los Horcones and Padanaram. All communal groups must develop conflict resolution mechanisms if they are to endure.

Utopian Quest. The dream of creating a new social order which will spread beyond the group's confines is probably expressed most clearly at Los Horcones, Padanaram, Auroville, The Emissaries, Yamagishi Toyosato, The Farm, New Meadow Run Bruder-hof and Findhorn Foundation. All of these communal groups have as part of their *raison d'être* fairly clear notions of themselves being active change agents in the world, each believing themselves to be forerunners of a new culture. At Riverside, Community Alter-natives, l'Arche, UFA-Fabrik, Christavashram and Lothlorien more modest goals are held, with the utopian change seeming to apply more to just the immediate group.

Gender Roles. Padanaram and New Meadow Run Bruderhof both defend their adherence to differential gender roles as being non-sexist. At Riverside and The Emissaries, gender differences were referred to as having been conflict issues. The other groups have either resolved gender issues or do not mention them. There is no reason to assume that one group's treatment of this issue is better than another's. It is critical not to confuse different gender roles with sexual discrimination — a point well made by Rachel Summerton.

Long-Term Prospects. Will any of these 15 communal groups still exist in 100 years? What about in 10 years? I do not have a crystal ball, but I am willing to offer some professional hunches and best guesses. Several of these groups face serious problems which might lead to their demise. UFA-Fabrik, Kibbutz Einat, The Emissaries and River-side may have just sort of run out of steam. They have an aging and in some cases decreasing membership, and their original raison d'être seems to have evaporated to some extent. Unless this changes and they receive an influx of new members and communal enthusiasm, these groups could well cease to exist within the next decade or two. Christavashram and Padanaram both have a strong, charismatic leader who is getting old — raising the issue of the group's stability after that leader's death. Findhorn Foundation and l'Arche coped very well after their charismatic leaders' departures, while The Emissaries and Auroville floundered for a time but then re-formed. Charismatic leadership is very efficient within a communal society, but the trick is for that leader to pass along the mantle of power slowly and progressively, while still present. This process happened fairly smoothly at The Farm and is currently underway at Padanaram. Lothlo-rien is currently facing a crisis from which it might collapse, but my hunch is that it will emerge stronger than ever, although altered.

No matter how good a group is at solving all these problems, it will collapse unless enough new members, adhering to the appropriate philosophy, are recruited to at least replace those who die or defect. Poor recruitment poses a serious problem for The Emis-saries, Los Horcones, Lothlorien, l'Arche and Riverside. Although Findhorn Foundation is reducing in membership numbers, it is happening as part of a more or less conscious policy of privatisation whereby the community's growth is through independent supporters rather than dependent members. If this policy persists beyond a given point, however, there will no longer be any core for the new associates to relate to.

There are too many unknowns for me to accurately predict the future of any of these 15 groups. They have each demonstrated a remarkable ability to cope with conflict and to adapt to a changing world. Certainly the communal elders who are represented in this book demonstrate an ability to grow, survive and endure. Perhaps all these communal groups will successfully adapt to changing circumstances while adhering to their fundamental beliefs and communal lifestyles. Let us hope so!

The Importance of Communal Experimentation

In an article appropriately entitled 'Yesterday's Dream, Tomorrow's Necessity', A. Belford[1] very wisely argues for the crucial, central function of experimentation with utopian communal living to our global survival. Utopian communalism 'entails pressing beyond the constraints of the crises in which we live and moving into a new order of possibility. Visionary activity is not an extra in society any longer, if ever it was. It is the only thing that has any chance of carrying us from the world in which we presently live ... which is destroying itself at such a rate that life within it cannot long be a possibility ... to a world that is informed by new values and a new understanding of being. ... This transformation ... will be brought about by a revolution in our imagination's exercise; by the dreaming up of new utopias.'

In 1890 Oscar Wilde[2] expressed a similar notion when arguing for the critical role of utopian experimentation and for the importance of us being well aware of the potentials and limits thereof. He rhetorically asked of his quest for a different, more communal way of life, 'Is this utopian?' He then offered his oft-quoted reply, 'A map of the world that does not include Utopia is not worth glancing at, for it leaves out the one country at which Humanity is always landing. And when Humanity lands there, it looks out, and, seeing a better country, sets sail. Progress is the realisation of Utopias.'

The quest for developing more humane ways of living together, and with our natural world, is crucial to global survival. Biographical discourse facilitates the wisdom of these communal elders to be better analysed and communicated to a mass audience. As well, the method helps these people to clarify their ideas, to gain self-confidence and to feel (and be) acknowledged for their life work. They rightly take on the mantle of a wise elder within the communal movement.

Umberto Eco[3] argues that a true counter-culture, holding any hope for changing the dominant culture, must have four features. It must be self-sufficient, and not be self-destructive, parasitic or dependent. 'Counter-culture comes about when those who transform the culture in which they live become critically conscious of what they are doing and elaborate a theory of their deviation from the dominant model (culture), *offering a model that is capable of sustaining itself.*'

The communal groups represented within this book appear to meet Eco's criteria. Arguably, these communal groups offer a viable counter-culture, or an alternative model for our common human future. As Juan Robinson of Los Horcones wisely pointed out, 'A true intentional community functions as a school in which all communal members are both students and teachers at the same time. As students, members learn to behave in a communitarian fashion, and as teachers, they learn to help others to learn and practice communitarian behavior.'

Shall we collectively learn from these models of communal living?

And Finally ...

As Professor Yaacov Oved[4], a world authority on communal living remarks, 'In a never-ending chain of failures and a new beginning, the march towards utopia continues; on this journey, the vision of the commune is there before them, like the North Star, steady in the heavens and guiding, revealing from time to time its vitality and constancy despite the ravages of time and circumstance.'

For those readers who are interested in living communally, I hope that these 15 stories, along with my brief analysis, have been helpful. There is no guarantee of success in life — least of all in living communally. To try to live communally and to fail can be painful and costly. But if you only have a utopian dream and you never even try to realise that ideal, then you are a far greater failure, your life a real tragedy.

If readers are interested in adopting a new, more communal lifestyle they could do far worse than follow the wisdom of the 15 communal elders represented in this book. Remember Juan Robinson's words, 'It is only through knowing ourselves that we can form authentic intentional communities, and intentional communities can only start and endure with authentic individuals. Learning to become a better person, and helping others to become better people, is the main objective of healthy communal life.'

It is possible to drop out of the mainstream rat-race and to live a quieter, more sane existence — and it can be fun. In fact to quote Albert Bates of The Farm, *'it had better be fun or no-one will want to do it'*.

(1)   A. Belford, 'Yesterday's Dream, Tomorrow's Necessity', in *Utopias: The American Experience*, (eds) G. Moment and O. Kraushaar, Metuchen: The Scarecrow Press, 1980, pp. 244–5.
(2)   O. Wilde, 'The Soul of Man Under Socialism' in *Complete Works of Oscar Wilde*, ed. V. Holland, London: Collins, 1966, p. 1089.
(3)   U. Eco, 'Does Counter-culture Exist?', in *Apocalypse Postponed*, ed. R. Lumley, London: Flamingo, 1995, p. 168.
(4)   Y. Oved, *Two Hundred Years of American Communes*, New Brunswick: Transaction, 1988, p. 483.